D0090304

PRAISE FOR

SOMETHING GREATER

"Pain and brokenness cry out in all of our hearts for relief, for healing, for a reason why, and for a new day. SOMETHING GREATER tells a compelling story of a Southern girl from Mississippi who knows the pain and horror of abuse, loss, betrayal, and more. Most who walk this road break— they give in or give up. Paula looked up. She developed a tenderness toward God and a fear of the Lord. She truly believes God is there and that He cares deeply for us. And as a result, God has and is continuing to do a refining work in and through her that we get to learn about in SOMETHING GREATER—a vivid reminder of God's steadfast love, grace, forgiveness, and mercy."

—Tim Clinton, president of the
American Association of Christian Counselors

"Authentic and transparent... Paula White-Cain reveals her deepest hurts and highest victories in SOMETHING GREATER. We believe Paula's personal story can be a tool to encourage those who have been wounded to drop the mask and step into the destiny God has planned. We encourage you to get your copy of SOMETHING GREATER; you will not want to put it down."

—Marcus and Joni Lamb,
founders of Daystar Television Network

"One of the great joys of my life these last three years has been getting to know Paula White-Cain. I am so glad she has written this account of her remarkable life story in her new book SOMETHING GREATER. Anyone who questions whether they can ever overcome their past mistakes or present hardships will be encouraged by Paula's fresh reminder of God's remarkable power to redeem and transform lives."

—Dr. Robert Jeffress,
pastor of First Baptist Church in Dallas

"SOMETHING GREATER is a heartfelt, emotional roller coaster that takes you through a young girl's journey of heartbreak and perseverance, which eventually leads to her steadfast walk in faith where she finds her true Father. Even as her husband, I can say it was truly a read I could not put down. I believe her story serves as an inspiration to the world: how one can overcome tragedy and setbacks in life and turn it around to inspire and minister to others around the globe."

—Jonathan Cain, keyboardist for Journey
and member of the Rock & Roll Hall of Fame

SOMETHING GREATER

Finding Triumph over Trials

PAULA WHITE-CAIN

FaithWords

New York   Nashville

Scriptures noted (AMP) are taken from the Amplified® Bible. Copyright © 1954, 1962, 1965, 1987 by The Lockman Foundation. Used by permission.

Scripture quotations marked (KJV) are taken from the King James Version of the Bible. Public domain.

Scripture quotations marked (NIV) are taken from the Holy Bible, New International Version®, NIV®. Copyright © 1973, 1978, 1984, 2011 by Biblica, Inc.™ Used by permission of Zondervan. All rights reserved worldwide. www.zondervan.com. The "NIV" and "New International Version" are trademarks registered in the United States Patent and Trademark Office by Biblica, Inc.™

Scripture marked (MSG) is taken from The Message. Copyright © 1993, 1994, 1995, 1996, 2000, 2001, 2002. Used by permission of NavPress Publishing Group.

FaithWords
Hachette Book Group
1290 Avenue of the Americas, New York, NY 10104
faithwords.com
twitter.com/faithwords

First Edition: October 2019

FaithWords is a division of Hachette Book Group, Inc. The FaithWords name and logo are trademarks of Hachette Book Group, Inc.

The publisher is not responsible for websites (or their content) that are not owned by the publisher.

The Hachette Speakers Bureau provides a wide range of authors for speaking events. To find out more, go to www.hachettespeakersbureau.com or call (866) 376-6591.

Library of Congress Cataloging-in-Publication Data
Names: White, Paula (Paula Michelle), author.
Title: Something greater : finding triumph over tragedy / Paula White-Cain.

Description: first [edition]. | New York : Faith Words, 2019.
Identifiers: LCCN 2019018605 | ISBN 9781546033479 (hardcover) |
ISBN 9781549122545 (audio download) | ISBN 9781546035695 (ebook)
Subjects: LCSH: White, Paula (Paula Michelle) | Christian biography—United States.
Classification: LCC BR1725.W434 A3 2019 | DDC 277.3/083092 [B]—dc23
LC record available at https://lccn.loc.gov/2019018605

ISBNs: 978-1-5460-3347-9 (hardcover), 978-1-5460-3569-5 (e-book)

Printed in the United States of America

LSC-C

10 9 8 7 6 5 4 3 2 1

In Him I live and move and have my being. To the One who gives me life every day. You are my source, my love, my heartbeat, and the very essence of my being. I dedicate this book to You, God, my true Father.

He has made everything beautiful *and* appropriate in its time. He has also planted eternity [a sense of divine purpose] in the human heart [a mysterious longing which nothing under the sun can satisfy, except God]—yet man cannot find out (comprehend, grasp) what God has done (His overall plan) from the beginning to the end.

—Ecclesiastes 3:11 AMP

CONTENTS

Contents

PRELUDE

As a five-year-old on a hillside just beyond my backyard, I hold a music box, knowing it is the last birthday gift my father will ever give me. Staring up at the sky I feel a longing as I watch the ballerina inside the box twirl to the delicate notes of "Für Elise," gently played on a glockenspiel.

Questions about my father's death five days ago torment me.

Daddy, didn't you love me?

Did I do something wrong?

Why did you leave me?

In the middle of this humid Memphis morning in 1971, a new reality begins to seep inside me, one that goes far deeper than the kind of rejection a school-age child might have known. It is worse than being denied or disliked; I feel abandoned. A cycle is begun where time after time the actions of those I love the most will seem to tell me the same thing: *Something's fundamentally flawed with you. Therefore, I'm going to leave you.*

Another occurrence this day will have a rippling impact. God starts to tug at me, even though in this moment I don't yet know His name or who He is.

Standing on that hill, surrounded by an open field that swallows my tiny frame, I talk to the heavens, believing in my heart that somebody hears me.

Thirty-three years later, I have spent my entire adulthood proclaiming God's message of salvation. The world knows my name, which I share with a thriving ministry that impacts millions worldwide. People know my fiery sermons, my smile, my shoes, and my success. Yet they don't know the deep pain and confusion I am experiencing when my life starts reeling out of control and falling apart in 2004. I'm lying on the floor of my home office, staring at the familiar sunrise with heaving, desperate cries, wondering if my marriage, my family, and my ministry have all been an illusion. A dreadful question fills my soul: *If those things aren't real, then what else is not real?*

This office holds many precious memories of spending hours in the presence of the Lord—praying, and fasting, and studying the Word. Still, surrounded by all the books that have given me some knowledge, I'm lost for words and see no way out. Kneeling on the rug, I face the wall of windows and catch the morning light. In its warmth I feel the Holy Spirit beckoning. This voice is crystal clear—not audible, but undeniable—and I experience it in the way I've been wooed, romanced, and corrected by God in the past. It's a *knowing*. Since being saved, I'd always had clarity when God spoke to me, but in the desperate days leading up to this morning I'd been struggling, feeling as if someone was scrambling those frequencies. But now the voice is strong and direct, asking me to say the things I'm grateful for. There's not much inside of me that feels grateful at this time, yet that I am so certain of this command is reassuring.

In the background I hear my children laughing, and suddenly I know. Of course, I'm grateful for each and every one of them. As soon as I acknowledge this, God whispers to me: *"Faith cometh by hearing, and hearing by the Word of God."*

"What else are you thankful for?" the Holy Spirit asks me. A warm glow bursts over the bay, as I've seen it do hundreds of times before, but this time I feel renewed appreciation for witnessing its beauty. I feel thankful for the sun's rising.

Another scripture is whispered gently: *"Blessed are your eyes, for they see: and your ears, for they hear."*

God has given me another new day, another opportunity to begin again, and another chance to fight for myself. All I need to do is get up off the floor and believe that this season is going to change. Maybe not today, and maybe not tomorrow, but in time there will be something greater in my life.

One of the positive things about loss is it forces us to look elsewhere, even if we don't realize it at the time. God watches and waits for us to follow Him.

Many people know the story from my childhood—little Paula talking to the sky after the death of her father. Very few know the truth about Pastor Paula White-Cain pleading with God as her marriage and her life in general unraveled. It was by no means just my marriage—it was me. It's a story I've carried with me for the past dozen years—a story I haven't wanted to tell. I've never wanted to hurt anybody, nor have I ever desired to relive those moments. Even just a couple of years ago, I still hadn't landed on how exactly I felt about it. I now know where I stand, and I see the purpose in sharing this story. I believe it can help others. I know I have something to say that can inspire someone and help them find their true place—their *something greater*—in this life.

Back then when life held me hostage, like a thief coming to steal my joy and rob me of my purpose, I always hoped that the pain and the bad memories wouldn't overshadow the whole picture, because there were many wonderful things happening in my ministry—lives were being transformed and souls were being saved. The picture is a lot clearer now that so many of the shadows have drifted away. I have enough clarity about that time, and feel strong enough, to revisit the end of our marriage and my life as it once was in a purposeful way. The scars are still there—and, believe me, I will always carry them with me—but the grace of God is covering them.

In the midst of earth-shattering brokenness, we are often reminded there is more. I didn't know God as a child, didn't know anything about Him, but I knew that I "heard" His voice. I didn't know what He was doing when my life was spiraling downward in the mid 2000s, yet I always knew *I* was heard. My life story is about how that young Mississippi girl became that wounded woman, and it's about how those wounds helped her become a warrior. It's also about how God was there for everything, and how He still uses those experiences for more.

If you want to know the heartbeat of my story, laced within the details I'm finally sharing with you now, it's simply this: my life is an amazing love story between me and God. I promise to reveal all the *Paula* parts—the fragments of a broken childhood and the lunacy of becoming a commodity—but the heartbeat of my story is our Almighty God, from beginning to end.

Like a tide rules the sea, all of us have this pull to something greater in our lives. The greatest blessing in my life is that God loved me enough to allow me to be broken, and in that brokenness I found true joy, love, peace, and purpose.

SOMETHING GREATER

PART ONE

A GOOD GIRL

1.

LOVE

I feel the sway, the steady, soothing rhythm of motion married to words. She rocks me and prays aloud in a cadence that sounds like celebration. I am safe, loved, and completely known. The words spoken over me linger like soft, bright clouds and will forever cover my life despite what storms come into view. These prayers never die; throughout my life they will wait in silence and then startle me when they're heard.

Spiritually, no one comes from nowhere; there's always something in your bloodline. Someone's prayers are going to produce a promise. For me, those prayers come from my great-grandmother, Momma Annie. This woman, who receives much rejection and unfounded hatred from some family members and complete adoration from others, is given the role of my caretaker from my infancy. And she lifts me up to the Lord without my knowing it. Her words are not only heard and answered by God, but they also become the music that fuels my life's ministry. Although during my childhood my faith journey is not guided by anyone, there's no doubt in my mind now that Momma Annie planted the seeds.

Momma Annie is frail, one hundred pounds at most. For much of the first five years of my life she is my primary caretaker, living in our home and watching me during the day while my parents work. Despite her tiny frame and arthritic joints, she holds me all day long. And by the time my parents return in the evening, I smell more like Bengay than baby powder.

The rocking lounge chair moves back and forth while Momma Annie holds me and speaks over me for hours. I'm spoiled, kept on the bottle until I'm five years old with rotted-out teeth. For years I grow up thinking Momma Annie is simply mumbling and making noise while she gently rocks me to sleep, but as an adult I will learn more about what she was doing; she was speaking in the spirit. Momma Annie shapes me more than she might have predicted. But in her arms all I know is one thing: love.

Memories of Momma Annie are some of my first, and of a time when I felt unconditional and devoted love all around me.

Mom says I came tumbling out of the womb. As quickly as I learned to walk I also began to do cartwheels, and by the time I was two Mom put me in dance classes. I was born with this energy; my parents know I can be a handful. And I'm the sort that as a kid would clap my hands for others and encourage them to greatness.

"Come on, we can do this! We can change the world!" I proclaim.

"What are we changing it to?" they ask.

I laugh. "A better place. We can do this!"

For years I question where this sort of passion comes from, but when I learn it's from my father, I'm not surprised. His name is Donald Paul Furr III. He's nicknamed by his family Peckie, or Peckie Lee.

As a child I like to watch as my dad finishes a work of art on my breakfast plate and then pushes it back across the table so I can see it. I look at the smiley face of maple syrup on the pancake and let out a high-pitched laugh. I don't know what I like more: seeing my father's playful creations or sitting across from him during our regular morning breakfast.

Daddy makes me laugh. I look up at him and see a larger-than-life figure: strong and tall and handsome. I don't know what it's like not to feel loved, not to feel protected. And my love for him is fierce and boundless.

After breakfast, Daddy often takes me to the country club. I assume this is his office. I don't know that he just plays golf and rummy with his buddies here. Later he'll take me to one of the two toy stores my parents own. My mother runs them while my father sees them as a Christmas tree that's full all year long. I know Daddy also owns restaurants and a seafood business, but those things don't really matter. What matters is when he introduces me to his friends or business colleagues.

"This is my baby girl, Paula."

Life isn't a struggle. How can it be when my father only knows one word: "Yes!" For the first five years of my life, I know a father's love. The kind that makes me feel like a princess, that never abandons me. My father's extreme love and how he doted on me will never fade from my memories. Everything I want in my life, my dad gives to me; I know without a doubt I am the apple of my father's eye.

Considering what happened to my father, one might think my view of God the Father might become warped and bad, and while there are some issues I would need to address, the exact opposite is true. After accepting God into my life, I will also easily accept the unconditional love He has for me as His daughter.

My father is from the third generation of wealth in his family. His grandfather was an electrician by the time he was fourteen years old and went on to help pioneer electricity in Mississippi. In my childhood, Dad is pretty irresponsible while living off his family's wealth. I never question why Dad always has new cars and how he can afford to give me all sorts of new toys.

I know someone's always going to be there for me regardless of what happens.

The same sort of charm that makes me adore Daddy so much is the kind that wooed my mother. I can already tell Mom and Dad have their differences, but it's very apparent that Mom completely loves him.

"Did you know that your mother was Miss Mississippi Southern?" Daddy asks me. "And she won a bunch of other pageants."

"Miss Water Valley and Lady of the Lake," Mom quickly adds, "and I was runner-up for Miss Mississippi."

I'm not surprised by any of this. My mother is beautiful. Yet the first thing I notice about my mother isn't her outward appearance—it's her inner strength. She's a businesswoman, with a tenacious work ethic and drive. She was raised in an entrepreneurial family. My grandpa owned a construction business, so life was always feast or famine. One minute they would be out skiing on the lake with their new boat and the next they'd be going to my great-grandfather's grocery store for food.

"Your mother was also the head majorette at school," Daddy says with a big grin.

"Not only that, but I was also the *featured* twirler," Mom informs me. "There's a big difference. The head majorette only does the marching and heads up the band, but the featured twirler gets to take center stage and show off all their talents. That's what made him fall for me."

"That's right," Daddy says. "When I saw your mother on the field that evening, I said, 'I'm going to marry that girl in one week.' So ten days later, we married."

"Three days late," Mom jokes.

"She couldn't resist my charm."

I already see my father's charm in his warm and loving personality, and that he's the life of the party. But what I don't know until later in my life is how my half brother, Mark, whom my mom had with her high school sweetheart, played a key role in bringing my parents together. When my mom, Janelle, first met the young man everybody calls Peckie, she was wooed by his adoration of Mark. This was one way he wins the heart of my mother—that, along with his irresistible charisma, sweeps my mom off her feet.

The problem with charming dreamers is eventually their feet need to be planted back onto the ground. My mother learned that deep in his heart, my father was a good guy, yet he was misguided in the belief that he was exempt from playing by the world's rules. You can only be an undisciplined playboy for so long. Eventually, you have to grow up.

My father never lived long enough to do that.

But in the short time I have him Dad is there for me in memorable ways. One night I'm rushed to the hospital with a 103-degree fever. Daddy's gone, traveling for work throughout Mississippi. I start to feel dizzy and warm, and by the time Mom takes my temperature again, the fever has spiked so high that it breaks the mercury thermometer. Putting me in a cold bath doesn't help, so I have to be taken to the hospital. When I wake up sometime early the next morning, I see my father by my side. All I can think about is one thing.

"I want bacon!"

The nurse overhears my request and shakes her head. "We don't have bacon."

"I need bacon," my voice, weak but persistent, calls out.

"It's two-thirty in the morning," the nurse says to us. "We're not getting bacon right now."

Daddy doesn't hesitate for one second. "My baby wants bacon, she's getting bacon," he says as he takes off.

I'm just a sick little girl, wanting something for comfort and trusting Daddy will get it for me. And he does. It's such a simple thing—bacon— yet the fact that he provides it pours intense love into my growing and open heart.

I'm his princess. Daddy's going to take care of me.

The downside to this insane amount of love I feel from my father, combined with my age, is that I can't see the dysfunction in our family. My father is the caretaker while my mother is the worker and the disciplinarian. My father's job is always "new" while my mother's is always "steady." I have this frail and crippled great-grandmother praying over me, yet I also have a grandmother, Mary Ruth, my father's mother, who clearly doesn't care for me and who is jealous of the affection my father shows me. Her rejection of me from the very beginning only grows worse over time. But I also know love with no boundaries. Therefore, my early life breeds some confusion in me about love.

* * *

The story of our childhood is a budding flower that blooms throughout the rest of our life. The older we become, the more we understand as we see it revealed in all its glory. There will be many things about my father that I won't learn until much later in life. Like why we moved from one house to another so many times. At the time, I simply thought it was cool and something very normal. I didn't realize that not only did Dad's inability to hold down a job cause us to keep moving, but also after his trips to Vegas we're suddenly forced to move or sell off a car.

Just before I turn five, Mom decides she's put up with enough of my father's irresponsibility. Peckie is drinking heavily, and the final straw comes when he takes whatever little money my mother has saved for our family. The milk money is squandered away, money that my mother earned through hard work. She is too prideful to keep going back to my great-grandparents, the source of our family wealth, to ask them for help. This is Mom's wake-up call. Taking Mark and me to Memphis isn't a decision to get a divorce, but it's simply an attempt to try to break up the craziness surrounding our lives, from my father's recklessness to the controlling relationship he has with his mother, Mary Ruth.

None of us can imagine he will die four days after my birthday.

There are things that will always remind me of that night. Like the sound of a steady rainstorm outside in the pitch black. They'll bring me back to this place time and time again.

The sudden knock on our Memphis apartment door on April 23, 1971, sounds different. When my mom opens the door, I hear conversation and feel a brief surge of excitement.

Daddy's home!

The voice I run to sounds different, and when I reach the doorway to see his face, Daddy looks different, too. Maybe the dim light is playing tricks on me. Maybe the shadows are hiding his smile. He greets me with a hug that feels strange; it reminds me of the way I cling to my teddy bear when I'm carrying him outside and don't want him to get dirty.

My father looks disheveled and distant, but I don't quite understand why. He's not acting like himself, nor is he talking like the kindhearted man I know him to be.

"Paula's coming with me," he says to Mom.

Something dangerous lingers beneath his words, something I've never quite heard before.

My mother moves toward the door. "Get out of here. Go back home."

"You're being ludicrous!"

"And you're drunk."

I'm in the middle, lost and wanting simply to make peace. I'm fine as long as they're going to come together and talk things out. I can be here and do this if they need me to. I just want them to stop.

Mark stands and watches as their voices continue to get louder. Soon I'm being pulled by my arm, Daddy urging me to come closer.

"You can't keep her from me!"

His voice sounds like thunder erupting in the room. My mother reaches out and grabs my wrist and jerks me toward her.

"You can't have her. Now get out of here."

Mom's voice is ferocious, her eyes full of rage. My heart races while my arms are tugged in opposing directions like a Raggedy Ann doll. I want to tell them both to stop, but I can't utter a single word. I don't think I can breathe.

For a moment, I'm jerked back and forth. Then my mother starts to scream just before my father releases me and strikes her in the face. I see those big hands of my father's—those beautiful, loving hands that have held me and comforted me—shoving my mother's head and then pounding it into the wall. I've never seen violence like this. I've never even seen my father frustrated before, so this...

What's happened to him?

"Mark, call the police," Mom shouts.

I hear my brother's footsteps running to get the phone while I feel the big hands clutch my arms.

"Give me Paula or I'll kill myself," the desperate voice says above my head.

Time seems to stop for a moment. I'm no longer five years and three days old. This figure isn't my father. He's not the man who makes me laugh and makes smiley faces on pancakes and waits for me to pick out a favorite toy.

My mother remains on her feet, defiant and undaunted from my father's blows. She covers me, shielding me from him as she continues to argue and negotiate with this stranger until there's another pounding at our door. Two police officers arrive and instantly seem to know what's happening.

"We'll keep him overnight so he can sober up," one of the men tells my mom.

They allow him to say goodbye to me. Daddy's hug is fierce, enveloping me in a way that makes me believe this is just temporary, that he will be back soon. I notice the policemen on each side of my father, leading him out the door. Somehow, deep inside, I already know the truth. I see his head and back turned as he walks away. All I want to do is sprint and catch up to him and take his hand and not let him go. I want him to stay, because I know he's never coming back. I know he's leaving me forever.

I wish I wasn't right.

As the darkness turns to dawn that morning, there is a phone call, and then the moments and seconds become vivid snapshots I'll forever carry with me. I pick up the phone and hear the officer's voice asking for my mother, and I already know what he's going to tell her. I hand her the phone and watch her face. With the sound of the rainstorm continuing outside, Mom is white and speechless as she holds the receiver to her ear, not seeming to even realize tears are streaming down her cheeks.

The truth comes like a freight train. There's been an accident and Daddy's dead. They put him in a drunk tank but for some reason he was let go.

Peckie was driving back to Tupelo when his car veered off a sharp curve and crashed into a deep embankment.

He did exactly what he said he was going to do, the very thing he threat-ened earlier the night before when he demanded to take me with him.

Suddenly I know what a hole in my heart feels like.

"I want to see him!"

It doesn't matter that Daddy's dead. I want to be able to see him just like everybody else will at the funeral. After causing a commotion in the car, I climb out the door and rush into the tent to look at him, but the casket is closed. I'm quickly escorted away.

Trying to picture Daddy's funeral is like seeing through a thick morning fog. I believe my brain and my heart have probably blocked out much of that day; trauma can wash away memories just like it can warp them. I do know Mary Ruth tells someone to take me to the pond so I won't see the ceremony.

When the sea of black suits and dresses descend on the gravestones in the distance, I can only watch with a babysitter who is nearby to make sure I stay away. I see the casket being lowered into the ground and wipe the tears off my cheeks. It's unfair and wrong that I can't be up there watching with everybody else.

My eyes survey the pond next to me and spot a duckling moving between two ducks. It makes me picture that horrible scene one more time, with Mom on one side and Daddy on the other, both of them yanking me and yelling at each other. I want to shout at them and tell them to stop; every-thing inside me wants to help them settle down and settle this. But I never say anything. It's amazing how the girl stuck between her parents becomes a woman who remains in the middle.

For the first time in the midst of this tragedy, without my realizing it, something becomes deeply embedded inside me, something put there solely by a loving God. It will be part of my destiny and my purpose.

2.

HELPLESSNESS

I wait by a window, looking outside and watching for any approaching neighbors while I hear the ticking beat of my heart. I still believe that some of the kids I've told will show up to my birthday party. Mom is pacing the apartment behind me, trying to encourage me but sounding like she doesn't think anybody's going to show. Every girl and boy I gave a personal invitation to told me "yes" and "we'll be there," so surely some of those kids will show up. I know it's a new neighborhood, but I made it a point to go out and get to know everybody a day or two after we arrived.

If I want to be a part of other kids' lives, why can't some of them, even just a few, want to be part of mine?

We've already moved twice since my father died. I'm trying not to focus on the fact that he's not going to be around to celebrate me turning six. I recognize that there won't be the usual big celebration today. Daddy's not coming around bringing balloons and a yellow cake and a new jewelry box with a dancing ballerina inside it. Time for my birthday party passes, and the slow-mounting disappointment becomes a gut punch when I realize nobody's going to show up.

When the knock on the door comes, it definitely surprises Mom and me. It's a young girl named Anita who holds a pair of Hershey chocolate bars tied together with red knit ribbon typically used for hair.

"Happy birthday," she says with a smile revealing crooked teeth. I grab her hand and rush her inside to start playing pin the tail on the donkey. A burst of joy fills my soul as I happily dance around as if the whole world had shown up for my party. I am so thankful for Anita, and I don't think too much about all the others, at least not in the next few hours.

We proceed with our party even though it's quite a bit smaller than planned. Later that night, in the darkness of my bedroom, I'm troubled by a notion that's been swirling around me since my father died.

Something's wrong with me. Only one person came to my party.

Instead of having my father lifting me off my feet and stirring my heart, I now feel stuck in this silence. I carry around a belief that fundamentally tells me I'm flawed and not worth being celebrated. And there's nothing I can do about it.

If only Daddy could come back and tell me I'm wrong. Instead, the next few years will only reinforce this deep-rooted belief, time and time again. Yet deep down, underneath the hurt, my spirit seems to know something I can't sum up or speak out loud. It's something real, something I can almost reach down and touch, something that's been with me since birth. Yet my own mind is blocking it, hiding it away, keeping it buried somewhere deep. A treasure waiting to be found.

Spending time with Mom, I see how much she's lost since my father's death. How much all of us have lost. She's the reason the toy stores ran so well, the business and the brains behind everything. After moving to Memphis and walking away from the toy businesses, her own future begins to look bleak, and she begins working for a hospital. Her work ethic has always been strong, but now her work becomes her life. She has no choice, however; Mary Ruth completely cut my mom off.

Everything feels different about our lives now that my dad isn't alive. It didn't feel like this when we moved into the small apartment, but now I keep hearing Mom talking about money with a concerned tone in her voice. Daddy and Grandpa always had the coolest cars and the shiniest toys and even had planes, but now nothing is cool and shiny and new. When she's not working,

I see Mom drinking, sometimes so much that I start to have to be the grown-up in the house, helping to put her to bed and clean up after everybody.

There are times when we don't even know where a meal will come from. This doesn't stop Mark and me from still acting like a typical brother and sister. One day when I realize he won't play with me or give me the attention I want, I decide to stick my foot in his small plate of spaghetti. Living in a house without food to spare, this infuriates Mark and prompts him to write a letter to Mom stating, "Why I Hate Paula."

My brother is older and different than me in more ways than I know, yet all I want is his love and acceptance. It's all I want from everyone. There is a craving in my heart to be valued and validated. Whenever he has friends over, I want to interact with them. Even from such a young age, I begin to search for a male figure to acknowledge me and fill the void caused by the absence of my father.

One night I observe Mom giving my brother a back massage on the couch and wonder when she'll ever do the same thing for me. They watch one of Mark's shows on television while I stare at them as if I'm at the zoo watching a mother bear tending to her cub through a clear glass window.

"Why don't you rub my back?" I ask her.

She just shakes her head, rolls her eyes, and says something in the way she does after she's been drinking. Her eyes also give her away, as does her unpredictable demeanor.

"God, why did you give me such a beautiful boy and such an ugly little girl?" Mom says in the most casual and carefree way a person could.

I receive the blow silently. I would probably stutter if I did try to speak. In my mind, I can only see Mark's cute smile while I picture my discolored and rotting teeth from all those years of taking a bottle. My brother casts a bright glance over at me, seeing that my squinty little eyes are trying their best to hide the hurt behind their narrow blinds.

She's just tired from working so hard.

The men and women talking on the television make others, including Mark and my mom, laugh.

I finally muster a response. "I'm going to be in that box one day. Just like those people inside the TV."

They both chuckle, but I know this time it's not the show they find amusing, because they're looking at me. It doesn't matter. I hold on to this belief.

I want a happy family, and I try to create one on the playground at the KinderCare afterschool program where my mom leaves me while she works. All I want is for all the kids to play together and have fun. I want every kid to climb on the merry-go-round and don't want anybody to be left out. So one day I find the perfect way to celebrate all my new friends.

The five-dollar bill I've received from Mary Ruth is quite a rare thing and a small fortune for someone like me. My grandmother spends lots of money on her own daughter and my brother—because she misses doting on my dad—so much I can't even count it, but whenever I ask for anything, she tells me no.

I have my five dollars broken into change so I can give everybody on the playground an equal share. When I'm back around all the kids, I tell everybody to climb up on the merry-go-round. "Let's all do this!" my six-year-old self shouts out. Once they all start seeing the quarters I'm handing out, everybody climbs aboard.

Mom will say I grew up always wanting to help others, always wanting to be there for others. She says it's because of all the pain in my life, and because I don't want anybody else to feel the same way, hurting and helpless. It begins as my attempt to overcome.

There's another thing inside of me, too, and it's not something I've learned but rather something I believe I was born with: a desire to do the right thing.

I'm six years old and I have five cents to spend on three Tootsie Rolls at a convenience store. I no longer have Daddy around to buy me any sort of treat I can imagine. Those days feel long gone. A few pieces of candy is a big deal.

When I slide into the backseat of Mom's green Chevy Impala, hoping to eat my candy before my mother comes with the rest of the groceries, I open up my bag and find there are only two Tootsie Rolls inside.

The lady at the counter must've dropped one of them.

I rush back into the store and promptly take another Tootsie Roll. I paid for three of them, so there's nothing wrong with taking what's rightfully mine. The moment I start to walk back out of the store, I begin to feel awful. I've never stolen anything in my life. Even though I paid for three and only ended up with two pieces of candy, this still feels wrong.

I am overwhelmed with a sinking feeling.

What if I'm the one who dropped it?

When Mom gets into the car, I can't suppress the emotion anymore. I start to cry and she asks me what's wrong, but I can't wait any longer. I get back out of the car, go inside the store, and plop all three Tootsie Rolls back on the counter, then I run back outside before anybody can ask me what I'm doing.

It's not like I'm going to Sunday school and learning about the Ten Commandments—we're not a churchgoing family—but there's something inside of me that knows when something's wrong. I don't want to break the rules, nor do I want to even bend them just a little.

I'm going to obey the rules, and I'm going to be a giver—just like my father used to give. At least whenever I have the opportunity to do it. It will give me some power over pain.

But there is so much pain.

I wrap my arms around my legs to stop the shivering even though the house is sticky from the summer heat. It's noontime, but this closet is dark and locked, and I don't know when they're going to let me out. Anytime I begin to picture my babysitter and her boyfriend, I try to unplug the mental screen. The visceral pain is more bearable than reliving those moments of sexual abuse. I feel helpless, dirty, and hollow. The only way to survive is to leave, to let my mind take me somewhere else. I imagine myself in a field with flowers, or on a beach with crashing waves—anywhere but here in the brokenness of a bruised body and soul.

I don't know what will happen in five minutes or tomorrow or next week or next month, and I don't think of any of that. I just think of now and what I need to do to get through this moment. So I detach. Find another dwelling place to breathe in. Forget this prison and their violation.

It will happen again, and there's nothing my six-year-old self can do to fend off this couple. My body won't be able to escape, but my mind will. I will be tied up and locked up, abused and completely powerless. From the first time, I have the choice all children who have been beaten and molested have. I can become an abuser, or I can use that pain in my life for some purpose. It will take a while to recognize this and to take on the process of transformation from darkness to the light that comes from refusing to live as a victim or in brokenness after abuse.

This pain carries over into my school life. I wither in my seat after wetting my pants. I know there's nothing I can do to hide the stain from my other first-grade classmates and, more importantly, to keep Ms. Shealy from seeing it.

It's a sad irony, being punished for something all the adults around me fail to see as a sign of my abuse. If only they opened their eyes to this and other telltale signs of how I am silently suffering, then maybe they could stop the madness happening to me at the hands of my babysitter and her boyfriend.

Ms. Shealy seems to hate me for some reason. She doesn't like how I rush into the classroom and she doesn't like how often I talk. She's already told me never to wet myself again, so this time she makes me stand up in the corner of the classroom with my nose to the wall so she can spank me in front of everybody and then force me to sit back down in my soaked pants.

One day she will write my mother a letter: "Paula might be something one day if she ever learns to shut her mouth."

Despite all this, something inside wants to show Ms. Shealy—to prove her wrong, to turn up the volume, and to never, ever stop talking. I want my mouth to drown out the shame in her voice and to have the last say.

That same something makes me write my full name onto notebook paper and then hand it to a boy with my autograph.

"That's twenty-five cents," I tell him.

"Twenty-five cents? For what?"

"For my autograph."

"Why would I give you a quarter for that?"

"Because I'm going to be famous one day."

The redheaded, freckle-faced kid who is a year older than me just stares in confusion. It's not exactly as if I understand this myself. I don't want to be famous and I have no idea how it might happen, but this thing inside me just knows. This weird, matter-of-fact feeling really knows it's going to happen one day. But how, and when, and why... I have no clue.

How can I seriously think my life is headed in one direction and one direction only?

My father is gone. Momma Annie and others are gone. Our wealth and stability are gone. My mom goes off the deep end for a few years. Meanwhile, the abuse continues. I will end up moving fourteen different times between ages five and eighteen. Psychologists will call this displacement, caused by having no real rooting, no real grounding, no real security.

There's nothing in my life and nothing in me that says I'm destined for something good, much less something great. What I don't know yet is that this has nothing to do with me.

Still, the enemy tries to tattoo lies onto my heart:

You're not lovable, Paula. You're not even liked. You're not wanted, and you're not worth saving. You should remain silent and invisible. You need to know your place.

Although I fight against them, some of these lies linger for too long.

Some of these faulty beliefs follow me.

Some of the world is ugly for many years.

Yet God makes everything beautiful in its own time. He plants eternity in the human heart, but even so, we cannot see the whole scope of God's work from beginning to end.

We can, however, find deliverance. No body and no soul will ever be wounded beyond the hope for spiritual deliverance.

Nothing in my external life tells me this, but somehow, I know. Somehow, I remain firm in my unstated belief. Somehow, someway, life is going to get better. I am going to get better.

"I'm not surrendering," I start telling the world when I'm only six.

"Surrender to me," a voice will tell me twelve years later. *"Surrender to me, Paula, and I will place everything you need for your body to heal, and I will place forgiveness and love in your soul."*

3.

DISCIPLINE

Our home is silent, with my brother asleep in his bedroom and my mother passed out on the couch. I find a blanket in Mom's bedroom and drape it over her.

By now I'm used to this. Mom is sad, and this is her way of not being sad anymore. I can't say anything to her. What would I say anyway? All I can do is try to help out, especially on nights like this when she won't remember. I clean her up as well as I can and tuck the blanket in around her.

Before I go to sleep, I find a Marathon candy bar resting on my pillow. Mom brings me that candy bar every day, and I know it's a sacrifice for her and a love note to me. I can eat it now and not brush my teeth and get away with it, but I don't. I save it for tomorrow. I hope tomorrow will be a better day.

Summers and holidays Mom drives or flies Mark and me back to Tupelo to spend time with family. We go to the mall, where I'm surrounded by toys I can't touch. I look out across the food court where I see Mark and my aunt Susan finishing their slices of pizza. It's strange to call Susan my aunt, since she was born a year after me. I guess it's easier for me to understand why Mary Ruth spoils her own daughter, but why she does the same for my brother and not me, I do not know. Soon I see them starting to play on the pinball machine, so I decide to ask my grandmother again, knowing the answer she's going to give.

"No, you can't go get a Slurpee or pizza. You don't have money."

Mark and Susan indulge all the time, because they both have a running tab to charge food items. I guess store owners can do that in the mall. I don't have a tab, however, so I need to have my own money.

"You have to earn that money," Mary Ruth tells me.

So I decide to do exactly that. It doesn't matter that I'm only seven.

The idea comes on our visit at Christmastime when I'm walking through a Reeds department store and see how they're offering free giftwrap. I decide this is what I'm going to do and pitch the idea to my grandmother. She gives in, probably assuming I'm not going to make any money. Or maybe thinking I'll stop asking her for money to spend on pizza.

I set up shop in the big warehouse in the back of the toy store. We order a table where we can do the wrapping, and instead of asking customers by myself, I recruit a few teenagers to walk up and down the aisles asking customers if they want to have their gifts wrapped. It's a deal for only fifty cents. Of course, I will share the profits with my team.

I've become an entrepreneur in second grade.

A couple years later, I turn my brother's room into a casino. Not exactly the sort of proud story a future pastor might tell, but it's the truth. It's 1975, and we're living in an apartment complex in Maryland. Mom's a wild child with an eclectic taste that mingles antiques and family furniture with hippie style. We just moved from Alabama, where she transformed the regular back porch of our apartment into a funky bar area, lined with brownish beads. She decorates the space with plenty of lava lamps. The centerpiece is the porcelain claw-foot bathtub, which is painted orange. Half a side of the tub is cut out and replaced with a cushion, making it the first bathtub couch I've ever seen.

Following Mom's example, I get some of her beads and hang them from the top of my brother's doorway to add to the ambiance. I move my father's old craps table into Mark's room, then find some neighborhood girls to stand at the door and collect a quarter cover charge. Inside, customers are able to play blackjack and craps. No "real" money is made, just enough to give me pocket change when the ice cream truck comes around.

I have many of these junior entrepreneur stories growing up. It turns out that creating businesses generally comes easily for me. But I begin my love-hate relationship with money at an early age, before and after my father's death. I grow used to having creative ideas and running with them. I'll never be a reckless risk-taker, but rather the calculating kind—never afraid to try something new as long as it makes sense.

One moment my mother is "Proud Mary," rolling off to work every morning and holding our lives together, while the next she is "Rhiannon," this cool and calm gypsy who sweeps through our apartment like a cat in the dark. On those overcast days when Mom appears melancholy, she is "Angie," wondering when the clouds above will disappear. When they finally do, later at night, she's back to "How Can You Mend a Broken Heart?"

Eclectic, beautiful, dynamic, tough—that's my mother, embodying all kinds of songs, stories, and their characters, singing to me at all hours of the day. They tell me about the world outside our door and teach me about the culture that Mom has embraced and invited into our home. The songs seem as diverse as my mother can be at different moments of the day. I don't always understand her, yet I never cease to be surprised and entertained by her.

There are dual sides to my mom. There's the hard-working secretary who is exact and proper and always pursuing higher education and a better life. Then there's the woman walking around in a halter top and a blond wig at night. Though she never talks about it, sometimes I wonder what her childhood was like and if she ever had a chance to have fun the way she sometimes does now. She dances and sings in a home scented with burning incense. She buys my brother a guitar and accompanies him on her flute as they play "California Dreamin'." She takes me to rock shows and festivals, where I get to see The Who and Earth, Wind & Fire perform live in front of my eight- or nine-year-old eyes.

The ache Daddy left me with surely resides in my mom, but she refuses to let it define her. I never see indifference inside her, nor do I ever detect any part of her giving up. She's not waiting for happiness to come knocking. Instead, every day she heads out to go find it and bring it back to Mark and me.

Mom doesn't let my father's death stop her from living her life. Nor does it prevent her from making sure I'm going to be able to live mine, too.

Moving becomes a regular part of life. Although I was used to Daddy moving us around when I was younger, I'm becoming weary. My mother marries a man named Charles, who eventually becomes a two-star admiral in the navy, and more moving remains on our horizon. In fact, from second to fourth grades, I end up moving from Alabama to Maryland to Mississippi and then back to Maryland.

Always being uprooted, I'm forced to socially adapt simply to survive. Every time I move, I discover another part of myself. On any given day, I might exhibit a different part of my personality, usually to fit in and feel accepted. Running one moment, then reading the next. Talking steadily, then completely silent. Knocking on neighbors' doors, then locking mine to keep strangers out. There are always the two parts, the extraverted girl on the go and the isolated and private child. Life for me can never be too stable or secure. I become different people for different circumstances. It's part of how I've learned to cope in order to survive.

Then I discover something new, something that goes beyond athletics and sports. I finally find competition, and I love it.

"I want to do gymnastics class, Mom."

"You're going into fourth grade," she tells me. "It's a little too late to start now."

"I can do it."

Mom's the one who watched me doing cartwheels right after I learned to walk, and the one who put me into dance when I was only two. She always encourages my athletic side.

"It's going to be costly," Mom says.

When my abilities are first tested, I'm put in the advanced class immediately. My mom and coaches see something in me. We all realize I'm good at this, especially with anything that involves my leg strength. But in order to move to the next level and to start competing, I have to be able to perform all the basics, and there's one I need to master: the back handspring. I still can't land it the way I need to. Mom sees this and immediately gives me an ultimatum: "You have one week to learn it or I'm pulling you out. This is too expensive for me."

For the next week, I set my alarm for four o'clock in the morning and sneak out of the house with my Snoopy sleeping bag in my arms. In the darkness, I begin to practice back handsprings over and over again. With only the moon lighting my way, I try to land on my hands, but every time I fall on my head again. Each time, I stand back up and try one more time.

If there's any way I'm going to continue to advance in gymnastics, I have to be able to nail this movement. My arms go up and my knees bend as I propel off the tops of my toes, falling backward and gently planting my hands while the rest of my body moves over them. When I don't land on my head, my entire weight shifts onto my hands and causes me to crumble. I know Mom is serious, however. She's been that way with me my entire life.

I am determined and want this; it takes me less than a week to perfect the back handspring.

Something important happens, something others will have to show me later in my life. I haven't just learned a necessary technique in gymnastics. Mom's ultimatum has awakened my inner drive, one I don't even realize is there.

Soon I'm faced with another hurdle. When my first official competition arrives, I still can't land the aerial. Every time I do it, I always throw my hands down at the last minute. I know I have the leg strength, so it's just a bad habit. This time, however, I'm not just competing for myself but for the whole team. When my turn comes, the coach comes over to me and says,

"We have to have this score." I know what I have to do in order for us to walk away with medals.

As I line up to perform the routine, I see myself doing the aerial. I'm in the air flipping and turning without a single finger touching the ground, and then I'm back on my feet.

I've got this and I can land this, I tell myself. *I can do this.*

I soar through the aerial without a single flaw. My score is just under ten—almost perfect. I realize right then how strong the mind can be for overcoming any doubt or fear and how powerful it can be to believe that you can do something. Gymnastics develops a mental fortitude in me as well. Summers are usually spent at a camp in Canada or Florida training and perfecting my skills. I am building a life of discipline.

And I learn by watching Mom every day. Each of the fourteen times we move during my childhood, Mom is the one who packs the house. She not only thrives at her own job but also helps propel my stepfather's career. It's an era when women aren't rising and succeeding in the workplace, but Mom is a survivor, always seeming to break the rules set before her. She's an avid reader, too, and will eventually earn two master's degrees.

Mom is even more adaptable than I am as our life shifts. She plays the part of the officer's wife and the party host, while still keeping me in line when I need it. There is no room for nonsense with my mom. You respect your elders, period. I try to abide by this.

Mom teaches me lots of good things, such as how to be responsible and moral. Some of her lessons come unintentionally. Years of cleaning up after her and watching what alcohol can do to someone trains me to do the opposite of what she does. I don't want to be like her, not when it comes to drinking.

In a life with so much out of my control, from losing my father to abuse, if there's anything I can control, then I will. I have no desire to get drunk.

This comes in handy one night at a party in eighth grade. Many of the kids are drinking and acting stupid, and this one boy wants to try to take advantage of me. I stop him and don't let it happen. I'm sober, in control, and not interested. Unlike most of the kids I know, I don't go to many parties, but avoid the drama and instead prefer to hang out with a friend.

When I get back home from this party, I see the ashtray in the family room overflowing, so I empty it one more time. Smoking is a habit Mom keeps until she's in her sixties. She tries so hard to quit at times, but then reverts to acting like a high school rebel, smoking in the bathroom and trying to hide the scent from me. Sometimes I find Mom asleep on the couch with half a cigarette still burning and resting on the tray. My fear is always that ash will end up dropping onto the ground and burning a hole in the carpet. Or worse, setting our whole place ablaze.

Maybe I sound paranoid. Or maybe I just sound like the daughter of a man who killed himself. All I know is that my underlying fears always force me to be disciplined, to be the one who takes care of everybody.

In my bedroom I discover a Marathon candy bar waiting for me. This particular night I tear right in and devour it, knowing Mom's still taking care of me, too.

God sends people into our lives who will identify the greatness in us. We shouldn't take them for granted. Their gifts can impact the rest of our lives.

Mr. Sheridan is my seventh-grade math teacher, and his gift to me is patience. Every morning he allows my hyper and energetic self to stand up on my desk and belt out a song as the class sings along:

Up in the air, Junior Birdman
Up in the air, upside down
Up in the air, Junior Birdman
Keep your noses off the ground

As I lead everybody in the singing, I'm able to get out all my energy, and it satisfies a longing to be the center of attention.

By my eighth grade year in 1979, we've moved again, this time to Florida. Ms. Rickard knows I'm the new kid and blesses me by taking a real interest in me. During the year, I start to struggle in math and begin to feel defeated. It is a subject I have always done well in. For some reason, this tough teacher, who also coaches softball and knows I love sports, sees something in me. So she says that if I stay after school and do the extra work in math, she'll put me in the lineup on the softball team. "Deal," I tell her.

The belief and encouragement of a teacher has tremendous power. I begin to flourish in math, later acing calculus in tenth grade. I don't do this because I love math, but because I love this woman who took time out of her days to help me.

My mom also pours goodness into my future in her own way. She'll tell me my whole life, "I love you madly. You're my sweetheart." I never doubt this. Her unconditional love always covers me, even when she doesn't know how to be the ideal mom.

We humans look for love in any way we can find it, and when we're alone and don't know the love of a Heavenly Father, we cling to anything that fills our heart with the love we long for. To the best of her ability, Myra Janelle Loar is the best mother she can be to me at each stage of her life. She teaches me hard work and discipline, but also this thing called tough love.

Yes, there's the abuse and the neglect in my life, but there's also this overwhelming love. In so many ways, it is easier for me to forgive my mom than for her to forgive herself. The wonderful thing we will both discover is that there is someone who has already paid the price for our forgiveness and set us free from all condemnation.

4.

DISCOVERY

I'm "Jessie's Girl" and a kiss on his list. Bright pop and rock and roll mirror the Florida sun and set the mood for young romance and *The Breakfast Club* types of friendships. I find my first romance and best friend at the start of the eighties, yet now it's being taken away from me.

Sweet and sixteen, I hold Thad Michael Riley's hand, knowing I'll be leaving the only boy I've ever gone steady with. Sure, it's a puppy sort of love, the kind you make out to while listening to those mushy pop songs, but I still wonder what will happen with this feeling inside me when I have to leave him. Thad is the boy I marked the moment I saw him in eighth grade while jumping on the trampoline with my best friend, Candace.

"That's Thad Michael Riley…He's mine."

It's not that I suddenly picture myself as some unattainable beauty. In my mind and heart I'm still that awkward girl struggling with my self-esteem. But Thad makes me feel special, and I have an influence on him, too. I've known this ever since I convinced him to start playing football while I was a cheerleader. Yes, I feel guilty when he gets his first concussion, but I think maybe a sweet kiss will help nurse him to feel better.

Candace and I are inseparable for the three years I live in Florida. We share laughs, cries, secrets, and a lot of fun times together.

"I can't believe I'm moving all the way to California," I say. "I can't believe they're doing this."

Florida is the place I've lived the longest since my father's death. The thought of leaving right after my sophomore year feels like ripping a Band-Aid off a wound that still hasn't healed from previous moves. I finally have a best friend and a group I hang out with that feels comfortable. I'm involved with the swim team and cheerleading, and those things keep me connected and occupied. I'm tired and honestly a little burnt out with gymnastics, which I'm not going to heavily pursue anymore. It is consuming and demands thirty to forty hours of working out every week. To qualify as an elite in the Junior Olympics program is so competitive. I decide I will have fun with it and do school competition instead. Candace and I do sailing regattas, go to the beach, and have a blast. Having to leave Florida is yet another disappointment in a string of broken promises. It all feels so unfair.

My parents have already moved out to Danville, California, and have been flying back and forth while I finish this school year. When it's done, and the moving truck pulls away with my things, my parents wait as I say goodbye to Thad and Candace. I think I've already told them a dozen times.

I wipe away the tears. I'm not sure if I'll ever see them again. I understand how this goes. I know how much it hurts to say goodbye.

The melodies of the era follow me to California, becoming moody and more aggressive like my feelings. I'm at "The Edge of Seventeen," furious at my mom and stepdad for uprooting my life once again. They promised me we wouldn't move. I'd finally found stability on the warm shores of Florida and loved every moment of being there. All I'd ever known was the East Coast, so everything about this move feels foreign and far away. We're all the way on the opposite side of the country, and California is a sprawling state that seems to just go on and on. Even the Pacific seems wilder and rougher with its sharp, rocky shoreline.

Damon is a senior in high school when I first meet him. He is a gentleman and very mature for his age, and what I feel right away is his absolute care for me. We date and fall in love. This is different than the sweet, innocent relationship I had with Thad. This is deeper. He's good to my parents, and my mom and stepfather adore him.

Eleventh grade in Danville feels like I've gone from *Porky's* to *Fast Times at Ridgemont High*. I quickly find my groove, never having had a problem with adjusting socially. My job at Wendy's keeps me busy in the evenings; I sometimes work until two in the morning. Damon picks me up; these attentive gestures cause my heart to turn to him. He's a responsible and stable guy, someone with a car and a job.

Not only do I have to adjust to a new school and neighborhood, but a whole new culture. The first party I'm invited to is eye-opening. I walk into the mansion, and a surfer guy smiles at me with stoned eyes, barely open, and a valley girl passes without any sort of glance. The music is blasting electronic pop, and I wonder where the parents are until I find them in the kitchen laughing with kids holding beer. I see lines of cocaine on a coffee table in the living room; this isn't the home of drug-dealing hippies, but of successful businesspeople.

I've been to a few parties and seen kids getting drunk. I've made out with my boyfriend in his car and have heard about girls who've gone all the way. But now, there's a whole other level of people being okay with things. I go to some more parties where people are openly having sex and freely taking drugs. I'm not a Christian girl who grew up in the church, yet I'm still a virgin and have been raised to be morally responsible. The people I'm introduced to have a completely different mentality, finding what's always been forbidden in my mind to be totally acceptable.

For a while it's true culture shock. It's not like my parents are saints, but now most of the adults I'm seeing are living the liberal Bay Area lifestyle of the eighties. I can't believe all the things my friends are able to get away with. Yet always I observe from the sidelines and never participate. I've never had a sip of alcohol or taken a drug in my life. This is partly rebellion against my mom, and it's my way of trying to be everything she's not at this point in time. So that means I'm the responsible one, the designated driver, the one who makes sure everyone is "safe" in some crazy way.

Every day, I still carry my past and its baggage around with me. The abuse and trauma I've gone through have never been addressed and dealt with. They are secret companions that I hide. They also are reasons for me to not party like everybody else, to remain in control of everything. For someone who's been abused like me, that includes my body. Like everything the enemy plans, my way of dealing with my pain will only grow darker and more desperate.

There are many firsts that junior year in California. Damon is the first boy I ever declare my love for. He's my first introduction to college friends, and he's the first wrestler I've ever really gotten to know. I'm in love for the first time, and this means something. It's real. Being with Damon helps me move beyond the hurt of leaving everybody and everything behind in Florida. All I want is stability and acceptance, and I find that with this really fun Italian-Polish guy.

Losing my virginity isn't some simple and thoughtless thing I do one night. I've never thought I would sleep with someone before marriage, but the longer I'm with Damon, the more contemplative I am about it. At a certain point, I realize it's going to happen, but I still wait for it. We date for seven months before it does. We're already serious; we take skiing trips to Tahoe, and I've bought him skis. I can picture us together for a long time.

One of my greatest battles begins innocently, through my pure love of sports. I get to know some of the wrestlers and watch how they purge before matches. For them, it's a mechanism, but for me, it becomes a real snare. The enemy is setting me up, and soon I'll be trapped with something truly demonic. The pressure never comes from Damon or his friends; when he first meets me, I'm heavier, yet that doesn't stop him from falling for me.

Control: the thing I crave in an out-of-control life. I can go to parties, but I won't get drunk. I don't have sex with just anybody; I'm intentional about when and where that happens. And now as I learn another way to control my body, I begin to purge myself. Most everyone I know in California is bulimic, so I don't think much about it when I start, yet very quickly my life is completely out of control.

I'm in California for less than a year, and then my mom tells me we're moving. Again.

I'm in love and I finally feel adjusted. Now this? I put my foot down. I'm not leaving in the middle of a school year.

The enemy finds a big, gaping hole to enter, so he does. Deep down I realize I don't control anything, yet that doesn't keep me from trying.

Mom leaves and moves back to Maryland, taking on a prestigious position as administrator of medical records with Columbia Hospital for Women in Washington, D.C. I am finishing my junior year in California while my stepfather goes back and forth between California and Maryland. At the end of the school year, I know the inevitable is upon me.

After loading up my green Toyota Corolla, I drive to Florida for a fun summer with Candace. She and I drive to Biloxi, Mississippi, and make a bunch of beach stops in between. What in the world are two teenage girls doing so carefree with no money or accountability to anyone? We make memories, many lasting ones. I finally show up in Maryland just before school starts.

During my senior year, I fly to California to see Damon or have my parents pay to have him fly out, all the while believing we belong together, believing our love can remain against all odds. But what's love got to do with it?

My last year of high school doesn't start badly, especially since I'm making new friends, like Jenny, and reconnecting with kids I've known since second grade. But a gradual downward spiral begins and isn't seen at first by my mother and stepfather, who pour themselves into work more than ever before. At first I'm still the disciplined and hard-working Paula, waking up and going tanning in the morning and then working at The Limited in the mall after school. I'm an old soul, wearing a dress and high heels while carrying a briefcase instead of wearing cut-up jeans and sneakers to school. I'm not very social at this point and don't walk around with a desire to be accepted.

The person who judges Paula Furr the most is me. My eating disorder grows worse, and midway through my senior year, one day feels like a thousand to me. I discover Damon is cheating on me, confirming not that he's a bad guy but just the difficulty of long-distance relationships in high school. Soon the overachieving girl from middle school is gone, and so is the carefree soul with the sun-soaked hair from tenth grade. I no longer care about most things in my life. Every day I step onto a battlefield to fight all my body issues and my bouts with depression.

With college on the horizon, I decide against attending the University of California, Berkeley, where I had intended to go. With Damon out of the picture, I now have no desire to go to UC Berkeley. A lot of my friends are heading to the University of Maryland, while everybody in my family expects me to go to Ole Miss like they did, like my mother, brother, father, sister-in-law—everybody. Ultimately, I choose the University of Maryland. Honestly, at this point in my life, education isn't that big of a deal. Not anymore. I'll end up settling to start at their community college.

For the first time in my life, I decide to simply get by in school. My GPA has always been high, and I've always taken AP courses. I've always tried to make straight A's or compete to win, to prove my worth to others. By the time I'm attending yet another high school, I've given up. My GPA might have been a big deal at one point, but it no longer matters. I know what my mom and stepdad are expecting from me in a family where the importance of education is so emphasized. Obviously at the very minimum I'll be earning a master's degree. At least that's how it's supposed to go, and yet I no longer care. Everyone has a threshold, and perhaps I've found mine. For eighteen years I've battled to believe there will be a better day, but suddenly all I can see is the hopeless carnage of today.

One night after graduation, I decide to head to Ocean City with Andrea, one of my closer friends. I'm driving, of course, since everybody will be partying and I'll be taking care of all of them. Even though I've changed in many ways, that part of myself is still the same. Always the designated driver. Always the good girl.

Andrea happens to be dating a guy named David who is six years older than she is and plays in a band called the Knight Brothers. It turns out they're playing in Germantown, so he tells Andrea we should come to his gig. She convinces me to come with her, and when we arrive I instantly notice the lead singer of the band, who looks like Tom Cruise from *Risky Business*.

"That's Dean Knight," Andrea tells me. "He's David's brother."

As I watch Dean on stage, he's all flirty, pretty-boy looks, and charm while singing better than Huey Lewis himself. I can't help thinking something: *Here's my summer fling. I'm going to have some fun with this guy.*

There's something about music that draws me in more than movies and books. It's not make-believe. The melodies and chords and lyrics all speak to me, and when a handsome man is behind them, well…that can be a dangerous thing.

Dean and the Knight Brothers are one of the first bands to ever make their debut on the television show *Star Search*. When we meet he seems like all of the other party boys I've been around. He's fun, and all I want to do is have some fun, too. My breakup with Damon has devastated me, so in many ways I'm searching for an anesthetic to numb my pain.

So here's the former overachieving Paula Furr, who can't tell a joke if her life depends on it. The girl who takes care of others, including her family, the serious thinker and over-analyzer. And she decides to hook up with Dean, a fun guy who is the life of the party.

Dean is exactly what I think I want and need: fun. And we certainly have a lot of that. At this point in my life, there's no grand plan for Paula, or even much of a plan at all. Soon Dean and I are living together, going to his gigs, and while the partying is part of the lifestyle, I continue to hang out and look after those around us. I'm going to college while he's attending part-time, working, and playing in a band. Like all those great songs from the eighties, life is indeed "a dance."

I'm too young to have a clear plan, and I've lost sight of the notion that there's some big purpose for my life. But my soundtrack is about to change monumentally.

What happens next in my life will truly be a miracle.

5.

GRACE

On just another ordinary day in an eighteen-year-old's ordinary life, God answers the prayers of the extraordinary woman from my childhood I called Momma Annie. Though she died when I was six, her prayers lived on. It's surprising and swift, and at the same time, it is so simple how it happens. The enemy doesn't want me here, not at this time, not now, yet nothing can prevent this meeting from happening.

This November afternoon in 1984 Mount Airy is murky; the sun is hidden, the temperature feels colder than usual, and there's a strong wind. I follow Dean into the single-wide trailer on Woodville Road next to Marvin Chapel Church. We're visiting his mom's mom, Grandma Green. I'm only starting to get to know his grandmother, but I already realize she's the glue of his family and the cement holding all of them together.

I'm sitting on a faded couch in the small living room when Dean introduces me to his mom's brother, Uncle Butch, who's visiting from several states away. He's in his forties, and when I first greet him, he looks at me with this piercing glance as if he knows something I don't.

"I know what you're going through, Paula," he tells me. "I can see all your pain."

I'm perplexed as I try to figure out what to say to him.

No, you don't. Nobody knows what I'm going through.

I'm immediately defensive because I know he can't see any visible pain on me. I've been successfully hiding my hurt for years. Right now, Dean and I are living together and having a great time, so what pain is this man talking about? We're just two young people being wild and having fun. Sure, my parents aren't too happy with me living with Dean. They take issue not with me sleeping with him, but with me splitting living expenses with him, saying that's handwriting on the wall, that I need to be careful. But I'm not going through anything except enjoying life. Plus, his uncle just met me. He has no idea who I am and what my background happens to be.

Uncle Butch gives me a gentle smile. "I've got the answers to your questions. The solution to your pain and problems."

I'm not asking anything, and I don't need anything solved.

There's something about this man and his earnest tone that draws me in, making me curious and willing to talk. He's serious, yet I feel safe when he invites me to sit with him at the small, round kitchenette table. In just a few moments, he begins to talk about God and starts unpacking truths, concepts, and ideas I've never heard about in my entire life.

"Do you know who you are, Paula? You're more than just a mind and a body sitting in this kitchen. You're a child of God, a spiritual being. God has a plan for your life."

This is some far-out stuff, this idea of being a spirit. Yet the notion of being a child of anybody speaks to me and pulls me in. He takes a thick black book and opens it up, then reads something from its razor-thin, worn pages.

"'For all have sinned, and come short of the glory of God.' Do you know what this means?"

I shake my head. I've heard about God before, but the concept of sin is foreign to me. I don't even know anything about the book he's reading from, the Bible. Uncle Butch begins to explain the idea of sin, about how I've done things not against others but against God, who created me to love and serve Him.

"'For the wages of sin is death; but the gift of God is eternal life through Jesus Christ our Lord,'" Uncle Butch reads from another part of the Bible. "Do you know who Jesus Christ is?"

"Yeah, sure. The baby in the manger at Christmas."

"Jesus is the Son of God, who came down to earth as a human being to die on the cross for *our* sins."

There's that word again: sin. I'm being told I've done wrong things, bad things, that I've messed up, and I don't particularly like it. Especially coming from a stranger I just met. This doesn't stop Uncle Butch from continuing. I begin to soften to this, because at the mention of what seems like a harsh word—sin—I feel the pull of an overwhelming force, the call of unexplainable love and purity.

"The punishment for our sins is an eternal death, but believing in Christ, that God raised Him from the dead, confessing with your mouth Jesus is Lord, and asking for forgiveness gives us eternal life. Do you understand this?"

"No," I admit. "What do you mean by 'eternal'?"

"It means forever. That this life of ours is just a blink to God. That our whole lives are meant to give God glory for the gift He's given us in His son, Jesus."

The longer Uncle Butch talks, the more naked and vulnerable I feel in front of him. I wonder if Dean's talked about me and told him secrets of mine. Yet he speaks with a kindness that doesn't make me want to leave, but rather somehow makes me want to hear more.

"You've been hurt, Paula. You're searching and have been searching your whole life for something greater, for something else. It's a deep-seated desire God plants in us, that we're all born with."

Nobody knows about my hurt and pain and all the problems I've gone through and deal with daily. Nobody knows about the brokenness of my childhood I so desperately desire to be freed from.

Uncle Butch leans over to me. "These fears you carry inside, they can be released. Romans 10:9 says, 'If you declare with your mouth, "Jesus is Lord" and believe in your heart that God raised him from the dead, you will be saved.'"

This very notion of the junk inside of me being lifted and erased? It's a fantasy, it has to be, but, boy, does it sound like a good one to imagine.

"We celebrate Christmas to celebrate the birth of Jesus, and we celebrate Easter to celebrate Jesus's death and resurrection."

"His what?" I ask.

"His resurrection. When Christ dies and is raised from the dead. And all He asks is for us to believe. To believe this isn't some fairy tale, to believe He truly went to the cross for our transgressions. He took our sins and He paid the price in order to save us."

The story—if it indeed truly happened—is profound and outrageous and magical and confounding and absolutely beautiful. The words and the atmosphere around us and around this moment all seem very important. I'm mesmerized, especially the more Uncle Butch reads from the Bible, talks to me, explains things, and seems to know exactly who I am. I'm invited to close my eyes while Uncle Butch prays for me.

"Please, Lord, let Paula know she's not a victim of the things that have happened to her, that's she's not to blame. Help her see that it's only through You that any of us can find the peace that passes all understanding. Deliver her from the demonic torment of her past. Lord, fill her now. Wash her in Your precious Holy Spirit. Show her who You are."

I'm weeping as I begin to realize the lost person I am and how I've been trying to walk through this world carrying a backpack of pain over my shoulders. I want the weight to be lifted, and I want to be free. I don't want to be trekking up this dangerous trail anymore.

"I want you to just take a deep breath and pray," Uncle Butch tells me in an assured voice. "I'm going to lay my hands on you and God will take that pain, that fear, that hurt, that anger away from you now or in time as you confess Jesus Christ as your Lord and Savior."

What is happening to me? Who is this man? Is he some healer or something?

As I begin to talk—to pray, even though I don't know what that means—

tears fall down my cheeks. I know. I just know and I've somehow known all along. There's someone I should be talking to, and it's not my father and it's not anybody else except who I'm speaking to now.

"God…I don't understand much or any of this. Not really. But I…"

My voice trembles as I feel the hands on my shoulder remain firm. I swallow. My mouth feels so dry.

"I want it all to go away. Help me. Please, God, help me. I believe and receive Jesus as Lord, and that you raised Him from the dead for me."

I picture this man called Jesus on this awful thing called a cross, and my heart goes out. I can't imagine…why? Dying for people like me, who don't know Him or acknowledge and live for Him.

Yet Butch says I'm known, that I've always been known, that God knows and has numbered the hairs on my head. It's mind-boggling and so deep. How can anyone know that, and why would they want to be so intimately involved in my life? Who is this God?

What I've always wanted and needed and hoped for my entire life is to be known and loved. To be cared for and protected. To belong to someone.

Can this really be? Can You really be there?

There's this explosion inside of me, not of desperation but of love. I don't completely understand, but somehow still I know this is *true* and this is *real* and this is happening for *a reason.*

"God is a perfect God with an awesome plan." Then Uncle Butch encourages me to rebuke this and renounce this and repent, and again, I have no idea what he's talking about. What does "repent" mean? I'm a child again in my understanding, but also a child with a heart that's suddenly been opened after being closed for a very long time. I'm open to not only listening and learning, but to acting on what I'm being told to do.

"'Therefore being justified by faith, we have peace with God through our Lord Jesus Christ,'" Uncle Butch reads.

I don't know the technical term for this supernatural event that is happening right this moment. I can't fathom something like my own salvation or deliverance. I've never heard of being born again and don't comprehend what it means to have a spiritual awakening. All I know is that I believe what Uncle Butch is telling me. Somehow, someway, in such a quick manner, I believe. And I ask God to forgive me for all those sins I didn't know I had even committed. To wash me clean. To deliver me through His son, Jesus Christ.

So many heavy memories I've tried to erase feel like they are falling off me. Saying I feel lighter sums it up in such a clichéd way, but it's true. I feel like I am floating.

When I finally leave several hours later, I step outside into an entirely different world.

I see colors. Bright, clear, varied streaks of vibrant color.

Sure, the clouds have dissipated and the sun is setting in the west, but that's not the reason things look different. I realize I've lived my entire life seeing the outside world in black and white, and now I can see the green glowing in the grass and the blue blushing in the sky.

I've spent eighteen years as a blind person, yet now I can truly see.

This is the easiest and most simple way to explain what's happened to me. I didn't know my entire existence was covered by this secret and seductive veil, a veil that's suddenly been ripped off me.

I feel something more than anything else, something that I have always desired.

Love. Unconditional, unexplainable, unending love.

I think of what Uncle Butch tells me before I leave.

"Nothing's going to separate you from God's love. Not death or life or yesterday or today or tomorrow. No man or woman or event or circumstance. Nothing can prevent you from finding God's love through Jesus Christ our Lord."

6.

DELIVERANCE

God, I don't know who You are. I don't know who I am. But I want answers for my life.

On my own, I barricade myself in this little bedroom, reading the Bible as much as I can when I'm not heading off to my different jobs or school. By day I'm selling shoes for commission, and by evening I'm cleaning offices. This isn't work; it's survival. I'm not worried about school one bit. I study the Word, wanting to know more about God, yet I don't know how to begin. I'm not even sure how to pray.

Help me see who You are, God. When I read this book, reveal Yourself to me.

Even as I pray those words, I don't fully know what I'm asking for. In the midst of this solitary place full of hope about the future, I find myself in love with God and His Word, hungry to know more about Him.

It's a cold, clammy February morning when Dean and I meet up for coffee. He's in his usual happy, fun, flirty demeanor, and he proceeds to tell me his plans for his birthday.

"Come on out to the show tonight for my birthday. I really want you there," he persists.

Dean's smile is the sort that gets girls into trouble. He's handsome and fun and a genuinely good guy. Yet none of those things prevent me from moving out of the house we've been living in, a structure that looks haunted situated in the middle of nowhere in Mount Airy. I rent a room in a stranger's house while I figure out where I'll end up next. What matters most to me is this amazing God I've just discovered.

"I still don't know why you feel like you have to leave," Dean says.

When I tell him I can't live with him anymore, there's no specific reason why. There's no exact rationale I can point to; something inside pushes me to do this. We haven't technically broken up. Dean is still my boyfriend, at least as much as we can be as his band travels a lot on the East Coast, doing gigs in places like New York and Baltimore.

"I can just imagine what it's going to be like," I say, excited about the show and celebrating Dean's day.

"It's going to be a blast," Dean says.

It's always a blast when it comes to the Knight Brothers. I go to their gig, and once again I'm reminded of Dean's amazing talent. They play soulful pop and rock and entertain the lively crowd at the bar. Dean captures the voice and style of Elvis Costello so closely. The celebration extends into the after party, where Dean convinces me to stay with him that night. It's his birthday, he keeps reminding me, so after telling him we probably shouldn't, I give in. Something inside urges me not to, but it's just one night.

I've been saved for about two months, but I still don't know what that even means. I started going to a Nazarene church because it's the only place I saw that had some young people, but I still don't understand what's happened to me. I know my hardened heart melted and is strangely warmed to this God I so desperately desire to know. I have no real comprehension of sin at this point; I've been raised to believe you can have sex as long as you're sure you're in love. I don't consider myself a promiscuous girl, having lost my virginity in eleventh grade to someone I genuinely loved. But once I understand the gravity of my actions in light of my newfound faith, I realize there is no excuse I can ever make for them. Though conviction is weighing on me, in this embryonic stage of my conversion sin is still such a foreign concept. I simply cannot interpret how all this translates into everyday life and decisions yet.

Three weeks later, we're walking together in an indoor mall in Frederick when I smell pizza and tell Dean I'm starving. Life is back to normal, with me on my own and Dean still playing and partying with the band. We still see each other, but it's not like we have some definitive plan where we are looking down the road. We head into the pizza parlor, and I proceed to eat an entire Sicilian pizza all by myself. Dean doesn't seem to think this is such a big deal, but as we begin to leave the food court, I suddenly know.

I'm pregnant.

Yet there's absolutely no way I can actually be pregnant. I've been on the pill the last few months, but not only that, I did something unusual the night of Dean's birthday. I told him to wear a condom.

All the times we had unprotected sex and it never happened.

I think of all the other issues that assure me I'm not expecting, first and foremost the fact that I have endometriosis. I've been in and out of the hospital throughout my senior year to have cysts removed from my ovaries, a particularly brutal procedure where they basically hold you down and rupture the cyst in order to drain it. No doctor has ever told me I couldn't have a baby, but I've heard them say I might have a tough time trying to conceive. *There is just no way.*

In my life, I won't be able to explain the mystery and miracle of the birth of Brad. I understand that I don't understand. Maybe this is the Lord's way of teaching me that an exceptional God makes exceptions. I don't believe any human being is an accident or a mistake. What I do know is God is sovereign, and His ways are beyond our ability to find out.

"The secret things belong to me, Paula. Those things that are revealed belong to you and your children forever so that you may obey my law."

This is the only way I will come to look at this very unexpected pregnancy. There are certain things in life we don't know and will never know. There are questions that I will never have an answer for.

When I'm given the test and I learn the news I already know, the clinician at Planned Parenthood asks me what I want to do. There's no question and there's no choice. There is no other thing *to* do, not in my mind. I'm flooded with fears and concerns; I begin to make list after list of every kind of worry imaginable. The reality hits hard. I don't have insurance. I'm eighteen years old trying to figure out my life. I still struggle with body issues and bulimia. I've dropped out of full-time college, and my parents have distanced themselves from me after hearing about my new faith along with the decisions I have made. Despite all of these things, I know I'll never, ever have an abortion. I'm not some seasoned or mature Christian believer thinking this. There's just no way I'm *not* going to have my child. Life is a gift. I realized that early on with my father's death.

Dean is with me when I learn the news that I'm pregnant. He's ecstatic and suggests we should get married right away. Deep inside of me, there's a desire that is finally coming true, this longing to have a family and to create an entity I never had growing up. Yet there's another voice inside screaming out even as Dean is proposing to me.

What are you doing? You don't have to do this!

Marriage seems to be the reasonable and right thing to do, so we decide to marry very quickly, and do so on March 24, 1985. My parents attend our wedding, perhaps only to urge me one last time not to do it. My mom's drinking has grown worse, and my stepfather has told me I can't enter their home if I'm going to mention Jesus to them. Before I walk down the aisle on our wedding day, Mom pulls me aside, sits me down, and then begs me not to do this. It's not that she has something against Dean. She knows I am young, and in her mind I'm making a difficult path for my future.

My mom is not one to ever show her fears, but I can see them covering her while she pleads with me.

"You don't have to do this," she tells me in a way that seems as if she understands what I'm going through.

I'm young and pregnant, and this is what I have to do. Dean is a great guy, and I know he'll eventually grow up. Both of us will. We'll get things figured out.

Before I head into the church to take my vows, Mom gives me one last warning: "Paula. You can pretty much lie to everybody else, but you can't lie to yourself."

My body trembles as I sit on the hard floor of this tiny bathroom and hear the toilet next to me filling back up with water. I cry and shake my head and know this isn't right, that I can't keep doing this, that's it not just my own body I'm hurting but my baby's.

"God...please...I don't want to do this."

The purging has to stop. I know it. But I cannot make myself quit. Every day, even while I spend time in the Bible and praying, I always find myself here. Again. And again. I'm pregnant, without insurance, and struggling both internally and externally. As I read the Word every day, there are glimpses of hope and promises I begin to see are for me. They just feel so far away. I am starting to develop in my faith and believe that God can and will do what He says. I tell myself, "One day at a time. You will make it through this."

I manage to get myself together as best as I can. I stop purging (during my pregnancy), stay in the Word, and find myself with an insatiable appetite, usually only satisfied by loads of peanut butter and jelly mixed together and piled on top of an English muffin. Ah, pregnancy! Packing on almost one hundred pounds, doubling the size of my former tiny frame, I wait for my bundle of joy to make his way into this world.

Little do I know my newborn's arrival will be rough, the shore after a torrential storm, the still after a furious squall. My precipitous pregnancy crescendos with a traumatic delivery. Yet, God sends His angels to watch over and protect us.

My baby is late and is almost nine pounds. Dean and I are the only two in the delivery room. Like many moments in my life, my parents are not by my side. Nor is there much care or compassion. The anesthesiologist misses my epidural. Twice. The nurse misses my vein when starting an IV. Five times. I can see blood everywhere. My lifelong phobia of needles begins.

"Why are you shaking?" my nurse shouts midway through my twenty-hour ordeal.

"I've never done this," I tell her.

She's chastising me for being afraid, for not getting this done, for wasting her time, for not performing my duties. I'm trying my best, trying to be the good girl and get the good grade and land the jump. After hours of labor there is a sudden clamor as the baby's heart rate suddenly drops drastically and they rush me for an emergency C-section. I can feel them cutting me, urgently working to get my baby out of danger. Nothing I can do will help, and with everything I'm trying.

Through waves of pain I witness my son being born.

When they put that beautiful baby boy on me, and I see those two little brown eyes look up at me, my world changes. It's as simple as that.

Nineteen years old and I've been wondering where my life has gone—seeing my friends out having fun, and I'm pregnant, and I'm living in a small apartment, and I'm loving God. But now...

Brad brings unmistakable love into my life, and his birth helps me become even more laser-focused on my responsibility in life.

I'm God's daughter and I'm Brad's mother.

My song is love unknown, my Savior's love for me, and I will sing about it in my own way for the rest of my days, not through songs but through the spoken word.

We move from our apartment in Germantown to this trailer in Mount Airy on Bill Moxley Road. Dean is the one who urges us to buy it from his uncle Butch, saying we can get it for cheap. It's next to the house he grew up in. I've received some of my trust fund money, and it seems like it might be a good investment for us with all the land it has.

After the birth of Brad, facing a move two weeks later, and still ninety pounds heavier than I was when I first got pregnant, I start struggling with bulimia again. In the dim light of the bathroom, I plead with my Heavenly Father.

"Help me, God. Please help me."

Hope remains, and God never abandons me. Like my daddy bringing me bacon when I was a child in the hospital, I will find miraculous deliverance in an unlikely way.

The weight of the bill pulls me down, like all those nagging worries tend to do. We're a month behind on our mortgage payment. It's only $376 but we don't have anybody in our lives who will lend us this sort of money. I worry about our place being repossessed. I don't mention this to the friends we have over tonight as we play Bible trivia and board games. I keep thinking about all the testimonies I hear at church, about couples and families getting money in so many wonderful and unexpected ways, and I can't help wondering why this doesn't happen to us. Maybe someone will give me the good ole Pentecostal handshake, slipping me some cash, or I'll find some money in the mailbox, but nothing like that ever happens.

After we marry, Dean is born again in the little church we attend. What I discover is that my new husband is a closet backslid Christian who grew up in the Church of God. He and his brothers come from a long line of Christians and grew up singing gospel songs. After their oldest brother, Chuck, died tragically at seventeen years old, from falling off the back of a truck in a work accident, Dean and his brothers became disillusioned with God and stopped talking about Him. They even stopped playing music for a few years from the devastation that hit their family. And here I thought he was just this good-looking guy I fell for. His renewed relationship with Jesus helps our marriage, but it doesn't mean our struggles, immaturity, and irresponsibility about being a family are all fixed.

On this evening, as I slip on a jacket I just bought from Goodwill, I feel a slight bulge in the side pocket and reach into it. I know right away it's enough twenty-dollar bills to be $320.

Did someone here sneak this money into my jacket? Or did an angel come and put it there? I don't know. I just know the money wasn't there when I bought the jacket and last wore it.

I go to the bedroom and find myself shedding a few tears, this time out of pure thankfulness, overwhelmed by the goodness of God.

It doesn't matter where this money came from or who put it there. It's absolutely a supernatural experience, and it tells me God can hear my prayers and He answered this one, this very specific need, in a very specific way. I have no doubt.

I go back to our small family room and join our friends. We're not in a church—but a trailer with rusty pipes and faded paneling—still, that doesn't stop me from testifying about the goodness of God. We're playing games and eating nachos I can't afford and suddenly I'm worshipping God and praying.

"Psalm 23 says the God you serve is a God that restores your soul."

I hear my own words stirring inside my soul.

"He doesn't just leave you in the condition that causes pain in your life, Paula. He restores. He replenishes. He refreshes. He renews."

I go into the kitchen and continue to worship, and time dissolves as I praise God for His glory. My friends join me, and soon all of us are bowing and praising our Maker.

"Those old things that passed away will become new in Christ."

Hours pass—two, three, four, maybe—and I suddenly feel released, from my feet and through my body up to my hands. God does something miraculous, something I will rarely talk about. A Christian cannot be possessed by a demon but they can be oppressed, and I feel this oppressive spirit leaving me.

God's not going to just slap a Band-Aid over you. He's resetting some things because He's going to heal you in every place you hurt. He's going to deliver you from everything that drains.

This night, God delivers me from many things, including this scourge of hatred against my own self and my body. A darkness and heaviness is lifted off me, and the shadows I invited in that led to my own captivity are blinded in God's healing light.

There is never any trauma or trouble that you will be tried with that God doesn't say there's a set time and a set day for deliverance.

My time and day have come. I never purge again after this night.

7.

CHOSEN

Give me eyes to see and ears to hear, Lord. Help me to understand what I'm about to read. Speak to my soul and open up the words from this Bible."

I don't know how I know to pray this, but somehow I do. I want to know God and understand His Word. I find myself asking what the Apostle Paul says in Ephesians 1:17 and 18, "that the God of our Lord Jesus Christ, the Father of glory, may give unto you the spirit of wisdom and revelation in the knowledge of him: The eyes of your understanding being enlightened; that ye may know what is the hope of his calling, and what the riches of the glory of his inheritance in the saints..."

The thick King James Version Thompson Chain-Reference Bible rests on the table in front of me, and I open it up once again to find God, to not only hear what He has to say to me, but to spend time with Him. I long for this time now. These passages I read and try to comprehend in their old-fashioned language are truly living water rushing over my dry, parched soul.

As I study, I read Ephesians 3:20–21 (KJV), which will become a life message and a signature scripture to my existence: "Now unto him that is able to do exceeding abundantly above all that we ask or think, according to the power that worketh in us, Unto him be glory in the church by Christ Jesus throughout all ages, world without end. Amen."

I ask for this abundance to be poured into me, and I believe God will do more than I can ever crave, desire, or beg for from Him. I sense that what I perceive as greatness is small compared to the vastness He must have for me.

My family calls me a Jesus freak, but then again, so does pretty much everyone else I know at the time. Eventually most of them will come around, seeing that this is not some "phase" in my life but a true conversion. My mother and stepfather have cut me off financially, thinking they are helping me. I'm not exactly living the life they envisioned for me. But I know there is another life waiting for me with God. I don't feel alone or afraid as I had before. Something is changing in me.

Dean's mother is deeply spiritual, a woman who always seems to be praying or interrupting her own conversation with a sudden "Glory, glory, glory!" I don't quite understand this new language yet, but it feels beautiful. Sincere and authentic. Dean's brothers like to make fun of her passionate Pentecostal roots and convictions, how every single thing in life has the Lord in it somehow, how she never stops talking about the Lord, the Lord, always the Lord. I respect this and am drawn toward her commitment. I see in Dean's mother the roots of a woman with faith, and faith is something I didn't know about while I was growing up.

In the small Nazarene church I attend, I meet a girl around my age, Noel, who is full of joy and energy. Her zeal for God is contagious, yet she never attends Sunday evening service. So I ask her why.

"I go get my fix," she says.

"I want to get my fix, too," I say, thinking it's some sort of party.

She brings me to a Church of God that I immediately think is pretty wild. I will later find out that Dean grew up in this church. I'm a new believer with such fervor for God, yet I barely understand basic fundamentals of Christianity, and I certainly don't know anything about Jericho Marches and speaking in tongues. That night, some of the people in church are moved by the Spirit of God and begin to march around the pews of the church, shouting, shaking their tambourines, and singing praises to God. I grab the back of the pew, holding on for dear life, wondering if I'll get swept up by whatever power is causing this movement. My mind is struggling to reason and make logical sense out of it all, yet I feel something deep inside that is peaceful and wonderful tugging at my heart.

This is me.

I feel the same presence of God and His power in this church that I felt talking to Uncle Butch. Maybe these people are deeper than what I have experienced in my short time with God. They're genuine and loving. I like what I'm experiencing. I want more.

Ultimately this will be the church I will get planted in and that will bring me in contact with three older women who will have a profound impact on my life and ministry: Jeannie, Beverly, and Darlene, who mentor me, teaching me how to fast and pray, spiritually surrounding my life.

One day in our trailer, after someone in the church gives me a turkey, I have an epiphany. The turkey is far too big for just Dean and me, and a question keeps coming to mind.

What can I do with what's in my hand?

By this time in 1985, nearby Washington, D.C., is being devastated by a crack epidemic, with crime increasing each year and swarms of homeless people on the streets. By the start of the nineties, D.C. will have so many homicides that it will be nicknamed the murder capital of the U.S. So I decide we can eat half of this turkey and will take the rest to someone in the city in need.

From this moment on, I just start feeding others, loving every time I get to hug someone and share what Butch had shared with me, the good news of the gospel. I have a knack for talking to strangers on the streets and in shelters. I walk away feeling really high and fired up, thinking that I can actually make a difference. It doesn't matter that I'm living in a trailer and struggling from day to day. My problems seem insignificant compared to what I encounter in some of the worst areas of D.C.

There are supernatural things that will happen, events I will never understand and circumstances that to some will sound strange and fanatical. They are inexplicable and sometimes indescribable, but I know they are real and sent by God.

On a wintry day in 1986 while I'm resting on a couch near three-month-old Brad doing the same in his playpen, I have a divine visitation that will forever change my life. I fall asleep praying when suddenly I am "placed" on almost every continent. To call this a dream is too simplistic, while saying it's a vision or trance makes it sound sensational. I can see myself there in my trailer, yet I'm in faraway countries. I'm nineteen years old, and every time I open my mouth to speak before a sea of people that goes on for miles and miles, something supernatural happens. Millions of men, women, and children listen and look up to God and find the same sort of life I'm given. They're saved through the Word of God coming out of my mouth.

"Paula might be something one day if she ever learns to shut her mouth."

Echoes of Ms. Shealy's note sound faint, then are lost in the songs and praise of the multitudes all around me. The more I speak, the louder the joyful thanks becomes. All these individuals—they're finding deliverance, restoration, salvation, hope, and healing through my sharing of His Word through the Spirit of God. When I stop speaking, the crowd goes quiet, and the bright light of hope begins to dim. The figures around me begin to fall the longer I'm silent. With closed lips I glance to my right and to my left and see the people all around me start to become shadows and then sink into the darkness underneath.

I'm not supposed to keep my mouth shut, Ms. Shealy. I'm supposed to speak up, and speak out loud, and to speak with a bold and big purpose.

My heart is pounding; I am in the presence of God, a holy moment.

This picture is crystal clear to me.

God wants me to preach.

This might as well be a fantasy, some trailer for a movie that's never going to be released. I'm living in a double-wide trailer off a country road in Mount Airy, Maryland, a place that has fewer than ten thousand people. All these eyes I can see that are watching me, these ears that are listening, these hearts that are opening; how could something like this ever possibly happen?

Deep inside, I feel His urgency fill me.

I'm calling you to preach the gospel.

I don't understand this and don't know a thing about speaking to others about God, much less preaching to the masses. Yet I see it. It's real and it's happening and it's wonderful.

The same mysterious and marvelous thing that happened to me the first time I met Uncle Butch is happening here. God is speaking to me in some way, and just like all those strange and sometimes confusing stories in the Bible, I'm not going to try to understand it. I just know what I'm seeing, hearing, and experiencing. I know this is God telling me something in a very definitive way.

The next day I go to my pastor and tell him what's happened. If God does indeed have a plan for me—for a ministry with a message to share with the masses—then He will show me and give me a divine way to fulfill this purpose.

I explain my experience to my pastor, sharing what happened and the picture I saw of myself preaching to many. I'm beyond excited.

"Great! Our janitor just quit. Show up on Tuesday nights and you can clean our church." Part of me had expected him to say, "Thanks but no thanks," and to simply dismiss what I've seen. Yet he doesn't, and I can't help but be thrilled by his offer. I'm already adept at cleaning toilets and sweeping floors, and now God's entrusting me to do this in His church. I feel like the most blessed girl in the world! Seriously, to be able to do anything in the House of God is very humbling and honoring to me. I don't have much, but I have everything I need. I am loved, and I am God's beloved. And everything inside of me wants to simply give back in any way I can. I will climb that ladder and make sure I get every nook and cranny of that wood beam ceiling with my Murphy Oil Soap.

God's ways are not our ways, and when He calls us we shouldn't assume the how, when, and what that will accompany that call. God is taking me through seminary, just in a very different way. I'm in His Word daily, as much as possible, while serving with all my heart.

After six months of cleaning the church, the pastor approaches me with another opportunity.

"I've been watching you, Paula. You've been faithful. I want you to serve in our nursery."

I am overwhelmed with gratitude for this assignment. There are times I can barely even get to church since money is scarce. Sometimes I can't get a ride or sometimes we don't have the gas to get me there, and sometimes I am praying for God to multiply the gas in that tank. Money isn't just tight for our family. It is virtually nonexistent. If I find a quarter in a phone booth, I'll pick it up and praise God for His goodness.

Soon I'm watching over infants, blessed to be left to care for them and determined to send them back to the parents better than when they came to me. I gather them up and pray over them during nursery time. And once again, our pastor takes notice, and eventually one thing leads to another.

"Paula, I want you to teach two- to four-year-olds," the pastor tells me one day.

"For real?"

After graciously accepting my new role, I bury myself in God's Word once again, studying for something like eighty-nine hours so I can doctrinally break down the Bible in simple terms for these young children. I revere the Scriptures, and I'm terrified that I won't be accurate, that I'll mess something up. My greatest desire is for these kids to receive the Word of God in a way that they can comprehend.

Very quickly, I've gone from moving a broom back and forth to moving little hearts. A major evolution is taking place in my life, even though I don't fully see it or fathom it at the time. I'm simply going through the door God opens.

"Ninety-four percent of people will never win someone for the Lord," the pastor says in his sermon Sunday night.

The statement startles me. I'm woken up in the pew, as if someone's warning us that our town is going to be burned before morning. I stay at the church, remaining at the altar. They tell us to tarry at it, so this is my time to do that, to pray, plead, petition, and pour my heart out. The pastor's words burn in my being. I cannot bear all those souls living separated from God, both here on earth and for eternity.

Is it true, Lord? Is that number accurate or close?

I accept this reality and focus on the number. It feels like a chance to jump on the merry-go-round and invite many others to come join me, yet it also feels like a challenge of doing a back handspring and landing. As I pray, the whispers of doubt try to wage a war within my soul.

I'm messed up and wrecked and too wounded to ever be useful for You.

Desperation takes my father, and brokenness fills the girl who lost her innocence. What do I have to give?

God, I want people to know you as their Lord and Savior . . . I just want to be used.

But of course, I can't be. I'm a woman. I've gotten pregnant out of wedlock. I'm poor, I didn't grow up in church, and I still need to complete my education. What do I have to offer anybody anyway?

"My thoughts are not your thoughts, Paula. You can't figure My mind out because you see lack and limit, but I see potential and possibility."

My future words speaking to the past Paula. The message and their meaning are being stamped on my heart by God.

"I see greatness and My power coming upon your life. Something big is coming, Paula."

"I just want to make a difference." I pray on this night into the early morning. "If You can, use me, Lord. I am Yours. Please put Your heart in me. Please, God—will You give me Your heart?"

There are so many reasons that I can see and hear them tell me why I can't be used for His glory. I'm a woman who can't sing or play the piano—things that are almost a must for a churchwoman in the eighties. I don't "preach." I have a broken past. My résumé is a wreck; I'm not ministry material. I'm only nineteen, so what do I know? What do I *really* know?

"I know I can work very hard for you," I tell my Lord.

I know I can do this. I've been working hard from the first moment I can remember, watching and learning from my mother even when I'm not trying to. Her drive and determination to work hard still inspires me, even though Mom and I have had our differences. Her work ethic boils in my DNA.

"Give me every hard job people don't want," I pray.

I want to be used for something bigger, for something better, for something greater in this life. I want to somehow give back a portion of the gifts my Lord has given to me, to shout to the world about His grace, to sound out an alarm to the silent army just waiting to be summoned for His glory.

Sleep never comes. I remain at the altar as my soul pleads and asks and receives, while my heart beats and waits.

It waits to be filled, to be overflowed.

"Pour Your love into me, Lord. I'm Yours and will forever be Yours. Use me mightily in some way, not for my glory but for Yours. Let me minister and let the masses come to know You. Lord, take this mess in me and make it whole for men and women to see."

The next morning, I can see.

To say it in such simple words requires the same sort of faith as a child, so easy to be dismissed, so simply deemed as nonsense. As I sit in the booth at the small café and look up at the waitress standing by my table, I can see into her eyes, in her soul. I see her when she was a child going through abuse and hurt. Suddenly, I see her as an adult in a relationship with much tension and fighting. I begin to speak to her by the "pictures or vision" God is giving me. I tell her that the Holy Spirit is showing me a root of rejection that happened in her childhood and is impacting her relationship today. I share with her that God loves her and sent His son Jesus to give her eternal life. She starts weeping and receives Jesus as her Lord and Savior.

God gives me His eyes to see. This isn't simply being a caring and nurturing person who notices others; I've been that my entire life. Suddenly I have this sense that can be confirmed through what I'm seeing, and I know.

God's done this to me. He's put this inside of me.

What I'm feeling isn't merely compassion. It's something far stronger and greater.

God's given me a piece of His heart and the ability to see a person the way He sees them.

Like meeting Butch and receiving Jesus Christ, and like holding Brad and feeling this new life breathing against my heart, I know that everything has changed inside me. God has deposited His love inside my heart for a greater purpose.

I want to acknowledge every good thing you give me, Jesus.

The Bible verses I've been memorizing are starting to truly stay with me, like another favorite, Philemon 1:6 (KJV): "That the communication of thy faith may become effectual by the acknowledging of every good thing which is in you in Christ Jesus."

Something's been turned on inside of me. Something in my life has been activated. All for the call of God on my life. I am beginning to understand purpose. It's the reason for which something is done or created, or for which something exists. I begin to see the Scriptures showing me purpose as God's decisions, His will, His choice, all along.

This activation is not a once-in-a-while occurrence but rather a shift that changes my perspective and approach to everything in my life. For the first time, I no longer see people according to their circumstances or condition, but in relation to what God intends for them. This ignites a deeper passion within me to help people know and serve God fully. I know God has called me to be a conduit to Him.

Sitting in the rocker and holding Brad in my arms after awaking to hear his cries, I see him contently looking up at me with eyes that seem to study me and watch in wonder. I think about my own mother, then about Momma Annie. I also think of Dean's grandmother, Grandma Green, and how she has the same gift Momma Annie had: praying over all her children and grandchildren constantly. She grew up wanting this worldwide ministry, but God gave her the role to pray, intercede, and be loving and kind to her family.

I sway Brad in my arms as I begin to pray over him. All I want is for him to feel safe, loved, and completely known. For him to know and serve God by fulfilling His purpose on the earth, whatever that may be. I long for the soft words I speak over him to forever cover his life despite whatever storms might block their view. I know they'll never die, that they'll echo throughout his life.

Like Momma Annie's prayers, I ask God for mine to produce a mighty promise.

PART TWO

A GREAT CAUSE

8.

INNOCENCE

Every day, God writes something new in my life, as I wait in the stillness of our trailer, watching for the Lord to show me the way.

If only I could see into the future. I wonder what I would do and what different roads I would take. I wonder what life would look like if I knew how to discern between the proper seeds to plant and those to root out.

The truth is all of those seeds shape the person I am now. Even those that produced blemished and broken fruit. Some of these are the seeds of discontentment.

I have learned to live at the humdrum level of existence necessary to survive. Now I am being challenged to change. There has to be more, and that more has to be available to me. I've read God is no respecter of persons. I just haven't discovered how to get there. Keep going, keep pursuing.

I'm standing near the science store in the mall where Dean works, watching his actions behind the counter. Brad is making soft noises while playing with a toy in his stroller in front of me. His father doesn't know I'm here. Going through postpartum "baby blues," I had decided to get out of the trailer and pay Dean a surprise visit. If he knew I was nearby, he wouldn't be acting so lighthearted and loose while flirting with the cute, petite blonde working in the store across the mall from him. I know her from high school.

Watching the two of them smiling and laughing, I feel angry and confused. Much of me feels overwhelmed by all the life changes and sudden responsibilities I now have. Some days it's as if I'm doing life on my own, just Brad and me making our own merry way. To come here and see Dean acting like himself, that carefree young guy I fell for, suddenly strikes me the wrong way. I know he's at work, but he's enjoying himself. And even though he's not doing anything inappropriate besides leaning over the counter and flirting, my mind tells me it's something more. I am resentful that he's smiling and I'm not. The scene sears itself inside me.

We're both young. I know that. Dean is fun-loving and can be irresponsible at times. But I'm probably too rigid and serious, and, honestly, I feel like I'm on shaky ground. Not the best combination, come to think of it, and I think a lot about it. I assume the worst.

They must have something going.

Yet they don't. The thought is born of my insecurities.

Staring at the blonde, I see she's blossomed since I saw her last at school. On the other hand, I've ballooned out with one hundred extra pounds from pregnancy. I'm aware of my insecurity about how I see myself, and I'm grateful God has delivered me from purging and trying to control my body issues. But I can't help this from happening. I'm not even fully aware of how offended I actually become, at the wound I actually receive.

You're loved, Paula. You're known. You're saved. You're His.

I try to believe these things, and I choose to be content to live off God's love. But sometimes I feel trapped inside that small trailer.

I feel I'm living someone else's life, while the mirror always reminds me it's Paula staring back; enlightened but overweight Paula Knight.

* * *

There are seeds of devotion…

I like watching the flames crackling up toward the heavens amid a group of fervent believers. We take turns throwing demonic objects into the bonfire, cheering and celebrating each item set ablaze. All of us have brought our records and cassettes in order to burn them. Pop bands with their hedonistic songs of sexuality and recklessness. Rock and roll groups with their satanic messages hidden behind backmasking. The album covers with pornographic photos and occult imagery.

All those songs that signified my youth—gone. All those vinyl albums—burnt. All in the name of Christ. All out of this passionate and devout calling.

I've really fallen in love with Jesus Christ. As I start growing, I can spend ten to twelve hours a day with God, praying and reading the Scriptures. I love spending time with Him. There's a healing inside of me that is beginning to take shape.

My faith is new and raw, radical and deep. I am learning about God and the devil, light and darkness. I am beginning to gain insight into the spiritual realm. Just as angels are everywhere, so are demons. They can be in anyone and anything. One night at a youth service I end up jumping on what I was told was a demon-possessed woman and sending us both careening to the ground, then rolling around while I attempt to pray over her. The others around me share a true conviction just like I do. Their dedication and deeds are born out of a consecrated life, a place of holiness. I respect them, especially the three women mentoring me. I value their convictions and their authenticity, and how they don't force me to put my hair up into a bun but accept me *as is*. I seriously doubt they would get my makeup off anyway.

Dean and I both attend a revival, and as we walk toward the back of the church we're greeted by our pastor's son, who has come to help his father with this service. The man, in his late twenties, shakes hands with everybody as they exit, and as he greets us he gives me an admiring smile.

"You know," he says to me, "if you were single, and I were single, we'd both be single."

He makes the corny joke in front of Dean, and both of us smile and continue walking. All I can think is *that's really weird*. I don't know at the time that my husband knows this man, Randy White, from his childhood, and in fact once kicked him in the groin when they were only kids.

* * *

There are seeds of disrespect...

One day I find a light gray box next to our television. I pick up the controller attached to it and stare in disbelief. We're struggling to make mortgage payments and buy food for Brad, yet he decides to buy *this*? By the time Dean gets back home, my anger is boiling over inside of me.

"Is this how you spent the bonus check we've been waiting on?" I ask.

He smiles and tries to play it off like it's no big deal, like we can get bonus checks any day.

"I'm so done here," I tell him. "You spend one hundred dollars on a Nintendo when we can barely pay for groceries? What are you thinking?"

I don't need to remind him how I've started a business cleaning toilets just to help bring in extra money. But he does feel the need to remind me that they just released *The Legend of Zelda* and just how cool it happens to be. This only upsets me more, which in turn only makes Dean chuckle and try to tickle me.

"I'm being serious," I say to him.

"You're always serious," he says.

"One of us needs to be. One of us has to be the grown-up."

Later on I recall my mother's story about my dad taking her milk money, and I suddenly understand the gravity of her feelings a little more. All the money would go through Mary Ruth, so Mom wanted to have her own income and not have to rely on her mother-in-law. So my mother finally gave Peckie Lee an ultimatum, telling him she wasn't going to put up with his behavior anymore.

In a way this is what I did, too. Yet I know our collective irresponsibility costs us our marriage. And I will always take ownership for the things I did wrong. So many things seem to be going right in my life now. I've discovered God's love and witnessed Brad's life. We've moved into a little apartment, and then to the trailer. I have gained the very thing I've been longing for my entire life: a family, filled with siblings, grandparents, and cousins. I love being around Dean's family, with its laughter and music and fun. I love the simple life. And I dearly love his grandma Green. She teaches me things for the first time in my life, like how to bake and how to make wedding cakes. She shows me the art of canning. I treasure my time with her as a special gift.

Despite all of this, I don't know what my love for Dean looks like. I feel like he's meant to be a best friend in my life, yet suddenly I'm pregnant, which to me naturally meant we needed to get married. Brad is one of God's greatest blessings for both Dean and me. I'm happy and grateful for my amazing son and for the plan of God. Dean and I are simply two very young and different people.

Dean is nice, whimsical, and a true artist at his core. My frustration with him is that he's not doing enough with his abilities.

"If I had an ounce of your talent I'd conquer the world," I tell him. "I have to work a thousand times harder for everything."

I admire dreamers, yet I don't envy them when they don't land. It's one thing to want to be a gymnast, but it's another thing to finally land that jump. My drive and discipline will be both a blessing and a burden. It won't be the only time it will bring a rift in relationships.

When respect diminishes, and when love is questioned, it's hard to make a relationship work out. While Dean and I struggle to make it in our marriage, I will always admire the father he is to Brad. Especially his consistent love, care, and attentiveness to our son.

* * *

There are seeds of disdain...

Meanwhile I try to focus on balance between mothering Brad and my increasing responsibility at church. One minute I'm scrubbing the floor of the church bathroom, then suddenly I'm sitting with a group of two-, three-, and four-year-olds, reading to them from God's Word. This quickly turns into leading a youth group and watching them grow.

It's 1987 and our church has only about one hundred members, but soon our group of teenagers starts to expand. I begin my efforts to connect by going down to where all of them hang out, at a McDonald's, and simply build relationships that will help me lead them to the Lord. Abruptly a few dozen students turns into two hundred, then three hundred, then more.

God sends a warning to me that Satan sees it as well. I'm not very knowledgeable about the devices of the enemy or how he operates at this point. I simply know his agenda is to steal, kill, and destroy. I understand he attacks at vulnerable places.

For me, it's my own arrogance and pride, and it rears its ugly head one day when I'm mad at my youth leaders and I berate their efforts: "I don't know what you guys are doing. You must not be doing anything—you don't pray and you don't fast. I know what I'm doing and look how God is blessing me." How could I be so immersed in God and so full of myself? My self-righteousness is starting to turn me into a real jerk.

Wow, Paula. You've become religious very quickly.

I'm suddenly doing the Lord's work, and then just as suddenly I'm letting the enemy in through my own self-importance.

* * *

There are seeds of disrepair...

I'm alone in our trailer when I feel an urgency to pray, so I stop everything and begin to call out to God. Brad is with Dean today while I'm running errands and cleaning the house. Dean tells me he'll keep Brad with him until later this evening. It's only midday, but I feel the Spirit leading me to deep intercession; with groaning, utterances, and words I am crying out to God. Like a woman giving birth, I am travailing in the Spirit. Minutes turn into hours where time seems to disappear in the Presence of God.

It's dusk when I begin to wonder where Dean and Brad are. I begin to call around, growing nervous with each person I talk to who doesn't know their whereabouts. I'm not sure why I forget to call Aunt Rosie, who many times watches Brad during the day. Instead, I begin to panic, especially when I get a call from the hospital.

"Mrs. Knight?" the woman asks as I stand there in our kitchen, the long phone cord swooping back and forth like a rope on a playground.

"Dean's been in an accident. A very bad accident. He's in intensive care right now, and they need to operate on him—"

"Where's our baby? Our son—was there a boy in the car—what happened? Where were they?"

I'm partially in shock, full of questions they can't answer.

"I'm sorry, ma'am, but we can't release that information," she tells me.

Pleading and crying don't get me anywhere. For a while, the world grows blurry. I'm not sure how I end up getting to the hospital. When I arrive, Dean is semiconscious after surgery. His head injury is life threatening, and initially they aren't sure if he's even going to live. But all I can think is to ask what happened to our son. "Where is Brad?"

I learn Brad is safely being watched by Aunt Rosie.

Thank you, Lord, thank you. Praise Jesus, thank you.

Dean initially said he'd keep Brad, yet he was unexpectedly called into work and dropped him off at Aunt Rosie's. Not long after that, while driving the old, red AMC car he bought from my stepfather's dad, while heading down a hill on a country road, something drops in his car, and as he goes to pick it up, his vehicle swerves into the other lane and collides head-on with an incoming car.

I understand something very clearly this day: God saved Brad's life by allowing him to not be in that big, bulky car. He also miraculously saved Dean, too. What I fail to understand until many years later is just how damaging this accident turns out to be. Dean won't be the only one left with scars. The impact will eventually wreck our fragile relationship for good.

* * *

There are seeds of discernment...

Occasionally Randy White comes to Damascus Church of God, where his father is pastor, to speak and help out. Just like Dean's connection to Randy, there are many other details I will come to learn about this charismatic man who can command a room like no one else I'd seen. His history of faith is completely opposite to mine, as he is a fifth-generation preacher. Randy knows how to build a church like he knows the back of his hand. He understands the church and knows religion. He's been brought up in a very strict, Pentecostal home, understanding spiritual gifts like speaking in tongues and healing. Unlike me, he didn't attend his prom, nor could he dance or go to see movies. I will come to learn Randy's childhood years were full of confusion.

I'm now working regularly at Damascus and begin to see more of Randy, who is now working at his dad's church as well. After Dean's accident, we're down to only one car, and since I need to get to Damascus, Dean has asked Randy to give me rides. I don't think anything of these rides. Over time, while I get to know Randy, I begin working for him while I'm helping to build the children's, youth, and evangelism ministries at the church. Perhaps he admires the abilities I'm discovering in these roles.

I come to learn that Randy married when he was only seventeen, even younger than I was, and now in his late twenties he has three children, Kristen, Angie, and Brandon. He's been separated on and off from his wife and has been working on his marriage. Right away Randy starts paying a lot of attention to me.

Around this time, I have a vivid dream that startles me awake one night.

In it, I can feel my mouth becoming swollen and sore, and as I touch my cheeks I can feel it's become bloated. As I try to open it and say something, my teeth begin to fall out and scatter on the ground below me. I reach to pick them up, but then recoil when I see how rotten they are.

This is more than a dream; I realize this is something spiritual, yet I don't understand what it means. All I can do is go into prayer and ask the Lord why He showed me this image. God puts something on my heart and in my mind, a simple and straightforward warning.

Keep your mouth shut. Don't say anything.

I don't know why I'm supposed to keep it shut nor do I know what I'm not supposed to say, but I heed this admonition I sense inside of myself. Shortly after this, while I am attending my Bible study with Jeannie and Beverly, they begin to converse about the church like they always do. Like all fallen humans starting with me, my mentors have the tendency to enjoy routine rounds of gossip, and this evening they bring up a rumor about a man named Randy along with a woman at the church. I usually don't get involved with these discussions, and this time I completely disengage from the topic, remembering my recent dream.

A few days later, when I'm at the church for another event, I see Randy and decide to tell him the truth. I'm not confronting him, nor am I trying to create any sort of bond with this man. I'm simply genuinely trying to stay pure and innocent.

I'm being true to God's Word. I'm doing the right thing.

I've never had a problem opening my mouth and telling the truth. So I do exactly that.

"Sir, I just want you to know there's slander out there about your name. Things are being said about you."

I tell him what I've heard and leave things at that. I don't need to hear any sort of explanation or defense from him about any supposed improprieties. I simply let him know what I've been hearing.

Of all the seeds that I'm planting at this time, I believe this incident plants a seed of trust within Randy for me.

Meanwhile, Dean and I go back and forth and back and forth, wondering if there's anything salvageable in our marriage. Eventually, I tell him this isn't going to work and pack a bag of clothes, planning to leave with Brad in one arm. His brothers are there to confront me, telling me I'm making the biggest mistake of my life. Understandable, as family means so much to them all.

"Are you done?" I eventually ask them. "Please get out of my way."

I rent someone's room for a while, then live in my parents' basement. My mom and Brad develop a close bond that remains tight until the day she passes. Dean and I live separated according to Maryland law before getting our final divorce.

* * *

There are seeds of disintegration…

There is no single reason why, nor is there a simple explanation for exactly what happens next. Yet there is nothing I can justify. Sin is sin, and I simply have to take ownership of it. There's not the usual physical attraction to Randy that I've had with others, not like the sort I experienced when first seeing Dean playing on stage. Everybody has a certain "type" in their life, and from an outward appearance, Randy certainly doesn't fit mine. There is something more pulling me. Perhaps initially I'm drawn to his authority. He's the state evangelism director for the Church of God and has helped build one of the largest churches around with thousands of members. He built a ministry that provided one of the largest feeding stations in the country for needy people.

Randy's heart for the poor and the underdog and the way he genuinely cares for the homeless are traits I truly admire and find attractive. He's very charismatic, and he knows how to speak a woman's language. He's one of the earliest to graduate with an engineering degree. After trying to work on his faltering marriage to no avail, Randy steps away from ministry to work at the State Department helping to build a communications center in

Greenbelt, Maryland. He's very smart, and this along with his presence and responsibility are things that make me like him.

My fifty-year-old self can see a hundred fault lines in place when revisiting this story, but I'm young, and searching, and still trying to fix that broken little girl I was. There is a lot of good and God that has happened with this massive life upheaval since I found Jesus and gave birth to Brad. I will find out that transformation is a life process, not a one-night occurrence. It's surprising how easily the enemy lures me to slip into sin even when it begins innocently enough with just being friends with Randy.

Randy and I become closer. His natural personality is flirtatious with other women, so knowing this up front perhaps allows me to begin an emotional relationship with him, still not imagining anything physical would ever happen. Yet I know the moment a boundary is crossed, the exact minute when things explicitly change.

Randy is driving me back home at night after an event at church. As always, we're talking and everything is normal until his hand touches mine.

"I'm sorry," he says as he looks at me, an expression I haven't seen before on him but one that still feels familiar, a glance that almost looks questioning. All the while his hand still rests on mine.

"That's okay," I say, as the world seems to spin.

It's not meant to be like this.

I feel light and I feel weak and I feel so many ways I shouldn't.

It seems so childish. I understand the definition of sin by now.

A boundary's been crossed tonight.

I know it at this moment and always will.

Something begins in this car ride. There's nothing innocent or appropriate about it. It will be a year before we have physical intimacy, and even then I'll cry, knowing it's wrong.

Randy and I have a rocky start, both in the middle of divorces. We go our separate ways for a while, and eventually come back together and start dating. When we marry, there will be true repentance for both of us for our former actions. He will ask me to forgive him and I will do the same.

The mistakes I make during my youth along with the ones I make as an adult are ones I will have to personally work through for the rest of my life.

There are many lessons I've learned from my teens and twenties, from being a mother and working in ministry. When I look back, more than thirty years later, there are many moments I would handle differently.

I know the enemy can have access in any way and through any door. I will learn to take the Word of God and seal it off in order to allow God's finished work to be done. All those seeds planted inside me—those God sows into my soul and those born from my own selfishness and insecurities—won't be wasted. God will use everything the enemy means for bad and He will turn it around for good.

9.

SERVICE

Though my story seems overshadowed by pain and bad memories, I still see the blessings in my life. There is goodness about this time, moments that I will cherish. I believe Randy and I started our marriage and ministry together with a true desire to serve and honor God.

I also believe the devil is a liar. That's right. He's extremely patient, extremely strategic, and when he strikes, he can take everything from you: your peace, your love, your laughter, and even your life. He waits for an open door, an opportunity to carry out his plans. I also know God is greater, that our ultimate victory is eternal, and during times of trial, His grace will be sufficient when you turn to Him.

There is an incident I will recount many times in sermons and in teaching, a time when Randy and I are dating that we get into a drawn-out, dramatic argument over something trivial. It's not the fight but it's how we handle it that will be so impactful. In the middle of hurtful words and erratic behavior, I feel myself losing ground, so I do what has always worked. I cry crocodile tears and say, "But you don't know what it is like for your dad to kill himself." This will always stop a fight dead in its tracks. However, not this time. He turns to me and tells me he'll talk to me again when I'm ready to act like an adult. He walks out and leaves me to process in silence. Two weeks pass as I remain stubborn. Eventually I look at myself in the mirror and realize I might be part of the problem. Growing up, I learned to use my life's misfortunes as emotional manipulation when I felt vulnerable. Randy sees through this behavior and is one of the first to make me confront myself.

Whether or not his reasons and motivation for leaving me this time are noble, I do believe Romans 8:28. God really can take anything meant for bad and end up using it for good. I'm forced to look at my own self, so I do, and I see the ways I need to change. Eventually I call Randy and apologize. I end up doing that a lot in our marriage. I can only remember Randy apologizing to me a couple of times. It was something we often joked about, so I took on the role of being the one in "the wrong." After all, he is older, more mature, and therefore he must be wiser, I conclude.

I learn very quickly to control my emotions around Randy. I don't see him in any fearful way, not at this time. I'm finding healing in my life, and I'm opening up about things that I would normally feel rejection from. I perceive our relationship to be a place of love and unconditional acceptance.

Maybe I'm still too broken to only see certain things. And maybe Randy likes that brokenness.

When Randy asks me to marry him, I'm up front with my feelings.

"I'll marry you on one condition," I say. "I never want to be called a 'pastor's wife.'"

"Why not?" he asks.

"Because they all look miserable."

Even with the visible flaws and cracks I can already see in our relationship, I'm so determined to make our marriage work in this new opportunity to build the family I've always wanted.

"God spoke to me. We need to go to Florida."

Randy shows me an ad in the back of *Charisma* magazine that says "Youth Pastor Wanted." The church listed is Bayshore United Methodist Church in Tampa.

"Really? Are you sure you're hearing this from God?"

"Absolutely," he tells me.

"All right."

This is my value system that I will live and stick by. I submit to my husband. I pray he has heard from God, knowing we'll be leaving a good and secure life behind.

The more I've studied and buried myself in God's Word, the more I've learned about spiritual authority and how God works in our lives through this. God places people in our lives who have authority over us spiritually. When we submit to those individuals, it releases great blessings and the promises of God. This is God's system of protocol, and it only works when the person I put my trust in is putting their trust in Him. Sadly, I will come to discover not everyone in a position of authority is safe. I have often overlooked someone with a flawed character. The backdrop of my life has allowed me to have difficulty discerning between good and bad. It will only be in time and through much pain that I will learn to put safeguards around myself to account for my blind spots and weaknesses.

At the start of my faith journey, with my love affair with the Lord, I was very black-and-white when it comes to certain principles such as these. Over the years, I try to justify my principles to God. *I'm walking in honor, Lord. I'm honoring the authority over me.* I learn and teach on how the Kingdom of God is a dynasty, how honor is such an important virtue, and how we are to honor our parents and authorities. I'm a principle person, so these values I discover in the Bible are highly esteemed. Yet what I will discover, sometimes the hard way, is that principles are right until they're twisted. Authority is a principle of God, yes, but He doesn't want it to be corrupted and abused.

When I first meet Randy, I'm wary of trusting him or anybody else in my life, but I eventually come to believe and understand that Randy is "greatly used by God in my life to bring healing and restoration." I'm quoting myself from my first book, *He Loves Me, He Loves Me Not,* and everything in me believes this, just like I believe he hears God speaking to him when He says to move to Tampa. Randy is my spiritual authority, so I accept this and trust his decision.

It's certainly an act of faith we're embarking on. We're living in Gaithersburg, Maryland, where Randy is working for the State Department. He is also serving as the associate pastor of a large church, National Church of God, where I'm the evangelism director. We're doing well financially, quite a change from the days of not knowing if I could afford next month's mortgage payment. Yet since he has three kids to support, 50 percent of Randy's income is going to child support, so when he says God is also telling him to leave everything behind, my faith is really tested. We do exactly that, however, giving away or selling our belongings. When we go down to Tampa, we'll only have about $1,300 in savings.

When Randy feels God is telling him to leave, he goes to Dr. T. L. Lowery, our pastor and a prominent pastor in the Church of God denomination whom he's served with. Together they pray and fast. Dr. Lowery tells Randy not to do this, that in time he will have his own church to lead, yet this doesn't change the plan. We leave for Tampa in 1990 in a U-Haul with the few remaining possessions we have and truckloads of faith. The new position at Bayshore United will pay Randy maybe $12,000, and I'll eventually get a part-time job as a teacher for the church earning another $7,800 a year. Times will be tough for quite a while.

"Sacrifice with me now, and I'll give you a future," Randy tells me over and over again.

So I trust him.

On our way to Tampa, after stopping at a small gas station in North Carolina to get some lunch and fuel, I see a stray dog wander over by our car. His hair is matted and mangy as he looks up at us. The poor thing looks like it hasn't eaten in a month. I decide to go buy a loaf of bread for the dog, but before I do Randy calls out to me.

"You better hang on to that money," he says. "We might need it."

I look into the eyes of the desperate doggie, then turn back to Randy with my pouty lips and shrugging shoulders as if saying, "How could you not?" He caves in and says, "Okay." I'm smiling and happy as we drive away watching the animal wolf down his meal and wag his tail.

"Are you sure you heard from God?" I ask him with a smile, half joking and half serious.

Our first home in Tampa is in Westshore, which sounds glamorous except it's a motel we're staying at: Crosstown Motel on Gandy Boulevard for only nineteen dollars a night. From there we graduate to an efficiency apartment in Westshore until eventually moving into a house on San Pedro Street. The thousand-square-foot single-family home has two bedrooms and one bath, and it's perfect for us. I fall in love with this house and believe I can spend the rest of my life here. Randy will have bigger dreams.

Those early days in Tampa... To be honest, I still don't know how we survived. With only $1,300 in savings, and with half of everything Randy makes going to child support, we truly only make it by God's grace. I like to joke and say half of my fasts back then were forced fasts. One week, all I end up eating is Keebler cookies left over from an outreach distribution. In order to make things fun with Brad, I end up frying them and chopping them up and baking them. To this day he hates the cookies.

During those early days, I stay at home with Brad until he's six years old. Later, when I'm traveling the world, I will find myself missing these simple times. I will miss my special zoo time with Brad. I will miss a lot of time with him.

After a year and a half at Bayshore Church, the youth group is growing, but Randy ends up leaving the church. I never know the true facts behind this, but Randy explains to me the agreement he made with Pastor Frank is that as long as he is the pastor at Bayshore, Randy will stay there. After Pastor Frank ends up taking a new assignment in Jacksonville, a new pastor comes in who doesn't mesh well with Randy. I'm even told Frank blesses Randy's agreement to leave and start a new church, and I believe him until Frank calls me one afternoon at home.

"Listen, Paula. Things aren't as they appear. Randy's not the guy he seems to be."

Frank ends up explaining the situation, trying to tell me what's happened without coming right out and saying anything. He alludes to inappropriate behavior on Randy's part with a female. Frank is not specific about anything, however; instead, he seems to condemn me right along with my husband.

"I hope God opens your eyes before it's too late," he tells me.

There's no way anything this man is telling me about Randy is true, so I'm saying as much, telling Frank he's wrong. Eventually, I tell him to lose my number, along with perhaps a few other choice words. I reason to myself that Frank, or the new guy, is playing church politics.

Sometimes I can be protective and loyal to a fault.

Randy has a gift of faith, of being a visionary, and I admire when he sees something, an opportunity, and then quickly says, "Let's go!" Perhaps this is one thing we both have in common.

I receive a "let's go" shortly after we leave Bayshore to go into the racially tense sections of Tampa. It's right after a man has had gasoline thrown on him and is set on fire because of the color of his skin. Things get so bad, ambulances won't even go to certain parts in the inner city. This is where I feel God tells us to go, to go in and get the kids and minister to them the love of God. I know how to evangelize on the streets from my work in D.C. "Let's do this. Let's make a difference." After all, the need is the call. Next thing we know, we're being called pastors, and after Randy leaves Bayshore, it's only natural to begin a new church in July of 1991.

South Tampa Christian Center begins with five people and a storefront at a strip mall located in an industrial park area built in the seventies. Maybe fifty people can squeeze inside the shabby space, which contains one restroom. We end up getting the first year free; then the rent is $1,200 a month. We ask people for everything, including the wallpaper, and our church supernaturally starts to grow.

We purchase a twenty-four-foot Ford truck for around six hundred dollars, which will be used for our "rolling theater." Going into some of the roughest neighborhoods around us, we minister to people from our truck with the sides that come down, becoming a platform.

Shortly after we open South Tampa Christian Center, the front windows of our church are egged. Randy discovers it's actually board members of the church we've just left. I can't believe him and ask why they'd do such a thing.

"They're jealous," he says.

Even though there is some tension, it's not like we take members from Bayshore. Maybe two or three couples follow us to South Tampa Christian Center, but we've not split a church or anything.

Our mantra becomes: "We're the perfect church for the people who are not." We start reaching out to the community in every way possible, starting services on Wednesdays and Sundays. Since Randy and I don't take salaries for a couple of years, we're literally praying for our meals on a daily basis.

I can still see our old Oldsmobile rumbling down the road, with its hood dinged up and rusting away after having only half survived a hailstorm.

I can hear Brad's laughter while we're playing charades or while I'm reading to him. We don't own a TV until he's around eight or nine, so we end up finding lots of ways to entertain each other.

I can see people sitting outside of our storefront church waiting to get in and trying to hear us preach the Word of God.

Randy never has a problem leading, nor working from six in the morning to seven at night. He's very routine and very regimented, sometimes veering into becoming a drill sergeant. He gets the job done, though. He tells us over and over, "A little job done is better than a big job talked about" and "The only place to find success before work is in the dictionary." So work is what we do, and this suits me just fine, since work is something I can do well.

A lot of people are saved . . . A lot of great things are done . . .

God works in simple and straightforward ways. One day Randy is getting his hair cut and discovers the woman next to him has a truckload of hundreds of turkeys she needs to do something with. Randy takes them all, yet then we realize there's no way we can cook them all for our Table in the

Wilderness ministry to feed the homeless. So we get the idea to go to the local deli near South Tampa Christian Center where we often have lunch, a little place with one waitress.

"Hey, can you cook these for us?" we ask.

We have hundreds of turkeys, but they're happy to start cooking the ones our members can't get to. A week after they help us, we pull up to this diner in the industrial park and see the rows of cars parked outside. People are waiting in line to order their food. The cook sees us arrive and comes over with an amazed expression covering her face.

"See what you did? See what you did? You preachers! Ever since we cooked those turkeys, we've gotten all this business."

The couple at the deli end up getting saved. It makes me realize, *this* is how God does this. This is the sovereignty of God. A haircut, a truckload of turkeys, a little restaurant with the owners helping us out, and suddenly both of their souls are redeemed.

It's as simple as me meeting Uncle Butch and starting to talk with him.

South Tampa Christian grows to a thousand attendees in its first year. By year five, we're up to five thousand people attending. Do I think Randy and I have the ability within our own power to orchestrate this? No. But I do believe God blesses us, and I know we have good people who believe and work hard. Randy is in his thirties and knows how to build a church and do certain things. He also likes to call himself the Oz behind the curtain. The rest of us are in our twenties, so we're young and gung-ho and energetic.

We move from our initial storefront to meeting in the cafeteria of Plant High School, and then from there we move into an industrial warehouse. Soon we're forced to look for a new location when we're suddenly told the owners are selling the building. We have thirty days to get out.

Randy sends us out like spies in the land to scout out possible locations. I come upon a vacant administration building and feel God is telling me it's ours. It used to be the offices for an insurance company on North Grady

Avenue and was next to the warehouse for Canada Dry, which we later purchase. I explain this to Randy, so he calls them and offers $1.2 million for the property.

"You're crazy. Call us back when you decide to give us a proper offer."

While we're continuing to try to find other possible locations, I feel the Lord urging us to call them again. So Randy calls and learns the owners sold the building in a bulk auction. They give Randy the name and number of the man they sold it to, so Randy calls him up in Atlanta and says he wants the building.

"Interesting you call," the man says to Randy. "I have the deed right here on my desk. Make me an offer."

"Six hundred thousand," he says, offering half of his first offer.

"Sold. But you have to pay with all cash."

When Randy tells us the news, we all celebrate. Of course, we don't have $600,000 in the bank just waiting to be used; we are able to pay the $10,000 deposit right away, with the remaining money due in thirty days. I joke with one of our staff members that we're going to have to get a whole lot of chickens for all the chicken bakes we'll be having to raise money. We do those and a lot more, like car washes and bake sales. What's more important is we pray and have faith.

A couple of weeks before closing, the building's owner calls to ask for the money. It has to be in escrow. Randy simply tells him it will be there.

"My father's very rich," Randy says.

Shortly before our thirty days are up, a woman calls our office and talks to Randy. It turns out Lorena Jaeb and her husband started a chain of grocery stores and also owned hundreds of convenience stores operating in Florida and South Georgia. Their philanthropic efforts include helping to build the David A. Straz Jr. Center for the Performing Arts in Tampa. She's visited our church once so she knows we're in the process of relocating.

"I hear you're trying to get this building," she says. "How much do you need? One hundred thousand? Two? Three? Four? Five? Six?"

"Yes!" Randy finally answers.

Just like that, we have a donor. Yet we don't hear from her again or see any money until the day of the closing arrives. Randy's not sure what we should do.

"I've been praying nonstop. But we still don't have the money."

"Go to the closing," I tell him. "God has a miracle for us."

When he arrives, sure enough, Lorena Jaeb shows up with a cashier's check for $650,000. It truly is a miracle, one we tell often and never grow tired of remembering. The building has been vandalized and needs extensive work inside, but with the help of our members who continue to grow, we rehabilitate the building for offices and classrooms. Yet we will outgrow this space and have to figure out where to meet as a congregation, so we end up purchasing a circus tent, one that comes complete with seating, lighting, and sound, large enough to seat more than five thousand.

These are fun times, doing ministry and life together, raising our children while also growing a church that we rename Without Walls International Church in 1997. The name comes from our focus on evangelism, on our belief in going outside the walls to proclaim the gospel and minister. We break down walls that divide people. We become one of the first megachurches that's truly an integrated church with a diverse set of members: white, African American, Hispanic, rich, poor, homeless. And I will eventually become one of the few female pastors to lead a megachurch.

Those sorts of accomplishments matter at the time, but in time they won't.

When Randy tells me we're moving in 1995, I tell him he's crazy. This time God isn't telling him to sell off all our things and drive off into the sunset, nor are we trying to escape a run-down apartment to move into something more habitable. The five-thousand-square-foot house in Cheval, seventeen miles north of Tampa, is too big and too expensive and too much.

"The house is in foreclosure," he says. "It's a steal."

"It's half a million dollars. We can't live in some gated community like that."

"No—we're going to move."

He's right that the house is a good deal, yet I'll discover that enough never seems to be enough for Randy. A favorite pastime for him is driving up and down Bayshore Boulevard, one of the most prestigious addresses in Tampa.

"We're going to own a home there one day," he tells me.

"I'm not sure about that," I say, knowing he's serious but also having strong reservations even at the thought of that.

Tampa is a big city that feels like a small one. Even with all these millions of people, it's still a tight-knit place, with an interesting history of rampant organized crime. Bayshore Boulevard is traditional money, so you don't just get to show up and move in. It's not just the wealthy who live in these homes, it's old money. This is a different level of society, a prestigious kind, and a kind where new money doesn't get to go.

There is more than a drive in Randy, who goes to the office seven days a week and is relentless in his work at the church. He works as if he has something to prove, and this will become a huge fundamental difference in how we approach both life and our ministry. My drive is for acceptance and love; Randy's drive is to prove something to the world. He shows how well he can build teams and what a good strategist he can be.

What's that saying? The bigger they are, the harder they fall?

There will be a fall for both of us, but in those early days, we're still building, still moving upward, always working. Nonstop work. And Randy will be the first to truly push me toward the pulpit.

"You can preach," he tells me. "You're a good communicator."

In this way he's like my mother, pulling traits and abilities out of me that I don't see myself. Randy believes in me more than I believe in myself. He sees strengths I don't recognize and knows all the ways I'm growing. He pushes me to do different things. I always thought one of his biggest gifts was his ability to see a piece of black coal and to help polish it and make it into a diamond. He can see people's gifts and their abilities, then take those and make them believe in themselves.

This is why it's all the more shocking when he begins to try to tear those things in me down, the very things he's spent so many years building up. Ultimately, Randy publicly says, "I made Paula" and often tells me, "I own you." I believe God uses people to help form us, but no one owns you but God.

Love is complicated, and marriages are complex, so to detail the disintegration of those two things is impossible in the short space of the paragraphs on these pages. The individual telling his or her story does so through filters of their own eyes and memories. My goal here is to be revealing and transparent without being hurtful. I also don't want to relinquish the dignity I've walked in for the last decade.

I simply want to tell enough truth to allow others to see how God uses broken people for His purposes and glory.

The narrative that unfolded is predictable, cliché, and easy to write off. Couple builds mega-ministry, becomes known as Barbie and Ken, then has scandal and divorces. Rumors abound. Lots will be written, and all the while, I realize there are two stories: one that's perceived and another that is real and not understood.

This strong, successful woman who seems to have it all from a worldly perspective has gone through cycles and seasons of brokenness and healing.

Back when we're still living on San Pedro Street in our small home, after Randy and I get in a fight that began about one of our employees but escalated into another situation, our drama plays out. He's trying to leave and I'm fearful of letting him, so I stand at the doorway blocking it, with both hands poised at the edges.

"Get out of my way," Randy says.

I'm not a hitter, but I'm also not going to budge. Randy pushes me to get out of the house, then I grab him to try to make him stop. In that moment, I'm that wounded little girl again.

Don't leave, please don't leave me.

When tensions between us erupt and something sets Randy off, he'll eventually want to get away, triggering those abandonment issues. He knows exactly what to do by now.

As he swats me aside and gets in his car, I run after him and jump in the seat next to him, refusing to budge for a few minutes. I'm tenacious, but I'm also nervous. To be honest, I realize a part of me is afraid of Randy. Part of me will never feel truly safe around him. First he's speeding down the road, then he slams on the brakes and demands that I get out. So I do.

But I'm not done yet. Our fight is not over.

He's not leaving me behind.

So I jump on the hood of the car just before he starts driving again.

That's right. I'm literally on top of the hood of his car, holding on and banging at the windshield. I can just imagine what the scene must have looked like.

Oh, look out on the street! It's Pastor Paula riding on that car!

Pretty quickly Randy and I both realize how ridiculous this has become, especially when he turns on the wipers and starts cleaning the windshield of me. Eventually we pull into the parking lot at a Boston Market. I've come to my senses and feel embarrassed. Once again, my issues have come back to haunt me.

Always the same; patterns become predictable. The approval and acceptance issues, especially when it comes to my husband. They won't go away, however. Things will grow so dysfunctional that the only time I will feel like he approves of me is when I come to him like a small child handing him a check I've earned or some award I've been given.

I take responsibility for my issues. Things are not all one-sided. Except for the fact that I'll never eat at a Boston Market again.

Randy always works closely with a female; I grow to accept that he's emotionally involved with another woman at all times. I assume he needs someone like this in his life to give him confidence and to stroke his ego. It's just the way things are in our offices at Without Walls.

Going back to a time at South Tampa Christian Center, one day while I'm in my office, one of the women working with Randy barges in and comes at me, her face covered in fury. I stand to try to see what's happening, and she throws me against the wall in a way that makes it look like she's about to hit me. Randy rushes in behind her.

"You choose today!" she demands. "Me or her."

Randy pulls the woman off me, and I'm left aghast at the sudden explosive encounter.

"What's this all about?" I ask while the two of them argue in front of me.

"Just shut up," he tells me as he ushers the woman out of my office.

Later that evening at home I start asking questions and promptly get shut down. I'm not allowed to talk about this incident with Randy, not unless I am looking for a major fight. He tells me I have to go to her house and talk to her and ask her to come back on staff, since she promptly quit after this. I go, and she refuses to answer the door.

She will never return, and I will never be told what this is all about, though I have my suspicions.

I start to realize there is duality in our relationship and more than meets the eye. I begin to feel conflicted by the extremes between his "doting" on me and his isolating areas of his life from me.

Randy is doing God's work. He has this crazy ability to believe God and trust that impossible things will come to pass. I don't want the memories to be so tainted even if there's a lot of darkness to come. He not only has tremendous faith, but there's something deep inside of him that wants to help out those in need, the desire to take care of the poor and the ability to be a huge giver.

There are tender places in Randy. Without Walls isn't started by someone who doesn't have that compassion in him. The story of Brad's best friend illustrates that.

In sixth grade Brad's world centers around his dog. Fea is a shar-pei, the kind with all those lovable wrinkles and a rough, dark coat. Brad is such an advocate for animals, and Fea is not only his best friend but also like his child. One day Fea runs out of the house and is hit by a car. Brad, who is in Maryland at the time visiting his dad, Dean, is devastated. Randy takes Fea to the vet, where he will stay for hours. Fea is in such bad shape that the logical thing to do is to put the dog down. Still, Randy makes it clear that he's willing to pay anything in order to keep Fea alive.

Fea ends up in ICU where they have her hooked up to an IV and are giving her oxygen. Randy goes and spends the night with the dog. He never questions the costs, which ends up being more than $3,000 to keep the animal alive. At this point in our lives, this sort of expense isn't impossible, yet it's still not a minor cost for us in any way. Sure enough, Fea does live; in fact, she ends up living a long and happy life.

This extreme act of compassion by Randy helps his relationship with Brad, and it illustrates one side of his nature. He stands up for the underdogs and the broken.

Perhaps this is one reason things change between us. When I meet Randy, I'm still a baby Christian, still very broken. The more I study God's Word and spend time around healthy people, the more I begin to work out the issues in my life. Yet somehow, the more healed I become, the worse things get between Randy and me.

I believe healing is a lifelong process that is continually being worked out in you. Every day should be a pursuit of transformation to becoming a better you. A major part of that will happen one day when God takes me back to that little girl. It is a spiritual encounter that will transform me.

I'm in God's Word and prayerful and seeking, and something happens I can't explain. I can't talk about the science of it, about locating a place in my brain where I can address a specific memory. This is something very deep spiritually for me. As crazy as it sounds, I feel the Holy Spirit telling me something.

"Take me to that place, Paula."

Those terrible places, the ones of trauma. Starting with the last time I ever saw my father. Then to times of crawling in a fetal position and being locked in a closet and trying to forget what's just happened. Yet now, the Spirit is telling me to remember once again, and not only that, but to bring God with me.

This is a moment I don't talk a lot about, because how do I adequately explain it?

In the Spirit, I close my eyes and return to our small apartment in Memphis. The storm is always followed by that awful stillness. The shouting, damning voices suddenly become silent. The door opens and then slams shut, and the anger swirling inside turns to ashes that cover everything.

I want to follow my father into the dark night, but I can't.

He is forever gone.

Life seems to hold its breath in that moment, with a five-year-old girl watching that front door and waiting. Waiting.

So many years later, she still sometimes waits.

Sometimes she can see the smudges of the ash over her skin.

Yet she knows now to invite someone else into that room, the place where her heart was broken and her fairy-tale world was shattered.

He enters and walks toward her, waiting for her, opening up His arms and wanting her to come to Him.

The wound of my last few moments with my father is one that I have carried with me for a long time, yet I know with what God is doing in this moment I won't ever have to be alone with that piercing memory. In my mind's eye, Jesus is there with me, wanting me to embrace Him, so I do now. I run to Him and feel secure in His arms.

I know I'm loved. And that He will never leave me.

God will accompany me to my moments of abuse, too. In the Spirit, I feel God healing that broken girl. All I can explain from this is that spiritually, there's no barrier and there's no time in God. He's as much present as He is past and future. I'm in prayer, in a deep place with the Spirit.

The suffering deep in my soul is gone.

We all have stories nobody knows about, and entire chapters of our lives that we try to figure out. The more our ministry thrives and the more whole I become, the more I want to know about those first eigh-teen years of my life, to go back over those pages to try to understand them. I'm almost thirty when I go visit my mom, wanting and needing some answers from her. I can't hear from my father, so I want to hear from her. I know this will be difficult, but in the end it will be good for both of us.

I desire to bring closure to my adolescence. So when I finally have my "come to Jesus" meeting with my mother, telling her I want to talk to her about the past, I discover much about my mom as well as myself.

After I talk for a while and try to understand where she was in the midst of my trauma, her defensiveness soon turns to a tearful despondency, yet this doesn't stop me from pressing her.

"Why didn't you fight for me?" I ask her.

I ask her about everything: the money Mary Ruth held from us, what really happened with my dad and her, why she left me alone so many times, even about some of the obvious signs of my abuse.

I get it all out and tell my mom everything. This will be a true break-through for Mom and me, a time of forgiveness and reconciliation.

"They sent me away when I had Mark," Mom starts to tell me, explaining in depth how my brother is in fact my half brother, how she got pregnant out of wedlock, and the huge shame there was to this back then. I begin to understand to a great extent how Mark and I can be so different and how her treatment of each of us was formed. In this moment, I grow more compassionate toward my mom.

"A Baptist minister tells me I'm going to Hell, that there's no redemption for me after getting pregnant. So I decide, well, if I'm going to Hell, I might as well live like Hell."

This is the moment she walks away from God and the church, the reason I grow up thinking Jesus Christ might as well be Santa or the Tooth Fairy. Thankfully, I discover at eighteen that Christ is real, and so does Mom years later. I will bring her to Florida and take her to a visiting church in Lake-land, where she walks to the altar after the sermon and surrenders her life to Christ. She tells me that she had confessed him before, but this time it "really took."

As we talk, I learn I'm a lot more like my mom than I ever could have imagined. My anger and resentment wilt away when I hear her tell me the stories from her past. It's almost too much for me . . . as I realize my own self-ishness and immaturity for pushing back on her for all these years. Now I'm feeling guilty for saying she never knew what I was going through when she knew all too well.

Mom reveals she lived through similar childhood abuse to what happened to me. In ways our lives absolutely mirror each other, and I'm stunned. Perhaps what she went through was even much worse. Mom grew up being a caretaker for her mother, and she reveals that when she gave birth to my brother, they shipped her to Arkansas out of shame.

On this day, I not only understand more about my mother, but I forgive her with every single fiber of my being. For so long, I've felt as if my mother has in some ways betrayed me, but I eventually come to learn and understand that she just didn't have it in her to try to fight anymore. She was already fighting hard enough for her survival, for our family's survival, for a new life for us all. And I learn Mom lives with a lot of guilt.

"Mom, don't . . . I've forgiven you. And God certainly has."

The mother I grow up with isn't the same mother I have now. Yet she's always been an amazing and awesome woman, the one who first gave me my strength, the one who initially awakened me. She teaches me how to use my brain, how to be independent and responsible, how to live life never being ashamed. She gives me my backbone and tenacity.

During my ministry, as I talk publicly about some of these stories, it can bother my mom, since people will say hurtful things to her about me. People can be vicious. It's not something you ever grow used to; however, she knows it's hard to tell one's own story without involving others.

"Mom . . . if you could do it all over again, what would you do differently?" I ask.

Before she answers, she begins to cry.

"Just about everything. Everything except you. You were the only thing planned. We wanted you. You were born out of love, and for the longest time you were the only thing I felt I did right."

As both of us sob, I feel the Holy Spirit bringing healing to an often fragile relationship between Mom and myself.

10.

GROWTH

Can one person make a difference?

This is the question I'll ask myself and others, many others—millions upon millions—time after time. It is a question they need to answer themselves, a question to figure out between them and God.

For me, it's a question that God answers in a monumental way.

My mouth is running a mile a minute, and even I realize I'm talking too much. Yet I can't help sharing everything that's happening at South Tampa Christian Center with Zonelle Thompson, the wife of the prominent evangelist Dwight Thompson. She has invited me to lunch, so I've been telling her about the growth of our church, the amazing stories of members of our staff who were once on welfare, about how we're reaching the inner city of Tampa. At a certain point she begins to tear up listening to me.

"Paula, I've been to China and passed out Bibles," Zonelle says. "I've been in Russia, Berlin, and all over the world. But what you guys are doing in Tampa—we desperately need this in L.A."

Dwight and Zonelle are living just outside of Los Angeles, a city that's been in turmoil since the riots last year in 1992. I heard someone on the news recently call L.A. a lost city, but I know every city and town in every state is lost. This one is just bigger and has been in the news for all the wrong reasons.

"You'll have to convince Randy," I tell Zonelle, knowing almost for certain that he will say no.

I'm surprised to get a call from Randy during our lunch. I've been trying to reach him for days since he's in Russia, dedicating a satellite with TBN, so the timing is providential. I put Zonelle on the line with Randy, and she tells him that I have to come out to L.A. to do what we're doing in Tampa. It's an amazing thing when Randy says yes, and it's a supernatural thing when I'm in Los Angeles the following Sunday night.

For the next nine months, I spend my week in California, flying there Monday mornings, and then flying back on a red-eye flight on Friday night.

This is the way my ministry unfolds my entire life. Most of the things I try to plan end up failing. Yet just like Ruth "happening" on the field to meet Boaz, which is not accidental but a divine orchestration, God orders my footsteps. I believe He does, and I pray every day for God to bind me to His will.

Can one person *really* make a difference?

If so, who is that person? Whose life is going to leave a legacy? Who will be a world changer? The one whose life alters the course of history?

I close my eyes.

There will be many divine moments that happen when I close my eyes. I do it not out of fear but to make sure I'm fully hearing and responding to God.

I'm standing in front of a large crowd doing our children's program, which I had developed in Tampa. Behind these small boys and girls, a group begins to gather. Many of them are young African American men, obvious gang members and quite intimidating. A civil war has been taking place in the heart of L.A. for years between rival gangs called the Crips and the Bloods, the former on the east side and the latter on the west side of the city. The Crips identify themselves with blue and the Bloods with red. I've grown used to seeing them and ministering to them, but I still am not used to getting up before a crowd to speak, to teach, and to preach. Yet this afternoon, the Holy Spirit stirs inside of me and pours out. There's a boldness I have as I declare the name of Jesus Christ.

I think I shouldn't even be here. This blond-haired woman from Mississippi who's a pastor's wife. However, this isn't my first rodeo ministering to the deepest regions of the inner city. Back in Washington, D.C., I would dress up as a clown and walk over to drug lords to tell them Jesus loves them. At one point, the little nephew of one of these drug lords attached himself to me, so they issued an order to not touch the white woman. I immediately had my own security team. God gave me favor then, and I know He will continue to do so here in Los Angeles.

Five miles away from the site of the 1965 Watts rebellion, at the South Central intersection of Normandie Avenue and Florence Boulevard, angry protests against the officer acquittals from the beating of Rodney King break out, resulting in all-out riots, killings, and billions of dollars' worth of property damage. Following this brutal devastation we begin visiting five different sites in downtown, housing projects like Nickerson Gardens and Jordan Downs. Thousands are accepting Christ as their savior; more than 50,000 souls will be born again during our time here. I see incredible miracles, things I can't explain that simply come from Jesus. We preach the gospel and see all sorts of deliverance while people come out and gather around us.

Word gets out that there's some woman preaching, that people have to go check her out. A really big rock station starts making fun of the situation, saying "somehow there's this white girl down in Watts" and statements like that, but that only serves as great publicity and causes people to join us. Tonight, while I'm talking to the group in Jordan Downs, I look out to the menacing crowd, and the more I preach, the more agitated the crowd becomes. This doesn't stop me. In fact, it seems to only propel me onward.

"I get amused by people who say I found God. How'd you find God? God was never lost. God found you in a defiled bed. God found you drugging and doping. God found you full of racism and hatred for your brother. Sick and sin-stricken."

I see a young man wearing blue with long dreadlocks staring at me, and at a certain point, he opens up his coat and shows me a handgun nestled in his jeans. The man's name is Dreamer, I learn later, and it turns out his little niece just got killed the day before. This is my signal that enough's enough, to stop preaching, to let God move.

I'm either going to be driven out or I'm going to die.

God gives me favor as always, giving me strength and providing words for this Crips gang member.

There's a young man looking for hope through the barrel of a gun . . .

I see myself standing in between this man and the gospel. So I close my eyes and continue sharing it, talking about the truth and the light. I figure if this is my moment, then I might as well shut my eyes. I keep going.

"There's a reason God brought you here. Nothing is coincidence. Nothing is an accident."

Pastor Paula White, the one people might first see on the stage, is being formed.

When I finally open up my eyes again, I see Dreamer grasping the gun and walking toward me. He gently puts it down on the stage I'm speaking from, then does something else, something shocking.

Dreamer takes off his colors. I know you don't do this, that it's a sign of disrespect. In fact, it can be a death wish. I see the other gang members watching him, but none of them react in a negative way. Instead, they start to come down and take off their colors, too. Soon the stage is awash with blue.

"He's looking for somebody who'll get out of the boat and start walking on water," I say.

Dreamer gives his life to Christ on this day. I later learn he's one of the heads of the Crips, and his salvation leads to many others becoming saved. When word gets out about this, more gang members start to come, to hear what I'm talking about, to hear this amazing message of love. All the while, I simply respect the moment and remain grateful, yet I'm not surprised nor stunned by anything. I will never recognize the gravity of moments like this until I look back in awe of God's love.

Before leaving Los Angeles, I take part in the negotiations for peace between the Crips and the Bloods with gang members and local and national officials. I feel this is my natural setting, bringing people together to find solutions. The credit doesn't matter as long as everybody is marching together in the right direction.

There will be many other supernatural moments, too. While in L.A., we're working around the clock with Operation STITCHES (Saving The Inner Cities Through Christ's Hope Eternal Salvation), asking churches to donate, and even when they do it's still just a drop in the bucket for what these people need. One day I make a pledge to one of the sites where we are ministering that we will feed, clothe, and bring something special to everyone in attendance. We begin to strongly push for donations from all over the nation, going on Christian television and working with other ministries who are supporting these efforts. After sorting through everything that has come in, I know we will still fall short of the amount of people in these project units. I initially start to stress out, then I simply declare: "God, this is not my problem, it's Yours." I have given it my best. We proceed to the sites the next day with what we have been given.

What happens next is nothing short of a miracle. Two tractor-trailers arrive full of everything: toys, food, clothes with tags still on them, electronics, and bikes. When I ask for the names of whom to thank, they don't have any information. We have no way to know who sends this and how it happens.

I will forever remember a small girl whom we give a new dress to. After the five-year-old puts it on, she twirls around as if she's suddenly become Cinderella.

"Look at what Jesus gave me!" she says with this remarkable look of joy on her face.

Another time there's a young boy, perhaps eleven or twelve, who comes in with his head hanging low. We know him from his coming around and playing games with us and memorizing Scripture. I can tell something's wrong, so I ask him what's going on. I tell him to take a toy, so he asks me in a polite manner for the baby doll we have.

"It's for my baby sister," he says. "She's never had one before."

We know how to do the church, but do we know the love of God that commands us and compels us to go outside the church?

Maybe we're the light of the world.

Maybe we're God's answer.

Maybe we're the one to stand between the dead and the living.

There's an irony about my ministry and my speaking taking off in downtown Los Angeles. I remember in eleventh grade, while living in Danville, California, my friends and I take the BART down to San Francisco where everybody would party. I'm the responsible one, of course, staying sober so I can be the one taking care of everybody else. While I'm in the city, I'd walk up to those seven famous million-dollar homes known as Postcard Row. The picturesque Victorian houses known as "Painted Ladies" are side by side and differ in color.

"I'm going to own houses like this one day," I'd tell my friends. "But I'm going to fill them with kids."

All of them just laugh at me. "It's just Paula, making crazy statements like that," they say. And I agree. I've been making those bizarre statements my entire life. But even back then I believed something greater is in store for me. I just know this. I know it even before I am led to the Lord and sent on a mission to tell the world about Jesus.

Everyone is born with a purpose in life; it is your "yes" to your reason for being. God has a specific assignment that is unique to each individual. When you discover your "yes," don't let anyone laugh at your commitment to it. Realize God has set eternity in your heart and the pull to something greater is to come in alignment with what you were created and are being formed for—His purpose and plan.

Don't let your disappointments move you away from fulfilling it.

Don't let others doubt make you forfeit it.

Stay faithful to your "yes."

I close my eyes. For a moment, the 10,000 people sitting in the pews in front of me go away. I no longer see the sea of faces in the sanctuary of Carpenter's Home Church. I've spoken many times before but not like this, not in front of masses all watching and waiting.

The revival that's been happening here at Carpenter's Home will eventually be called the Central Florida Revival. After Pastor Karl Strader invites South African evangelist Dr. Rodney Howard-Browne to conduct revival meetings in the church, thousands of people begin flocking here. Randy and I decide to go and check out what's happening. I'm always curious when it comes to events like this.

What is God's purpose in this? And what do you do when you're done being on the floor falling to your face, when you get up and go back home? What does your faith look like then?

I believe there's always a purpose in things, even misunderstood things such as the "Holy Laughter" that happens at these revival meetings. I see a genuine move of God, with the laughter being true joy.

Pastor Strader heard what I'd been doing in the inner city of L.A., so he came up to me to talk about it.

"I hear you're a good preacher," he says. "Are you going to be coming tonight?"

"Yes, sir."

"Then will you share your testimony about what's happening in Los Angeles?" he asks me.

I'm not sure whether to say yes or no, but I say, "Okay."

Now I'm up in front of 11,000 people, and I'm closing my eyes. Instead of seeing the crowd, all I can think about now is Moses coming to Aaron after the earth opens up and swallows the people, after people are dropping over like flies. It's Numbers 16, when Moses tells Aaron to go to the altar and get a censer and make atonement for the people. "Anger is pouring out from God—the plague has started!" Moses says. So Aaron does exactly this. "He stood there between the living and the dead and stopped the plague."

With my eyes closed, I start to talk. To teach. To preach.

"Between these walls and outside are the dead and the living. So what are you going to do when you get up off that floor? What are you going to take back?"

I'm still not looking at all of them. Not yet.

I don't know what I'm doing here, Lord.

So I tell my story, starting page by page.

"My life was radically changed when I heard the gospel," I say, describing my broken and dysfunctional background. "I don't have much, God. I'm not that smart; I'm not that pretty; I'm not that talented or gifted; but, God... if you can just use a messed-up Mississippi girl, I give you myself."

I tell the congregation I know the pain of walking through life and not knowing the love of an earthly father or a Heavenly Father, and how I know the hopelessness of not wanting to see the sun rise. I ask God if *He* can use anybody and anything, I want Him to use me.

"Can one person make a difference in the world?" I shout.

When I open my eyes, I see faces overcome, undeniably moved by God. Women are weeping. Men are on the floor crying. Hands are raised in the air. I continue to preach, but I don't know what to feel. I'm overwhelmed with fear and a reverence for what the Lord is doing here.

I talk about what I've seen in Los Angeles, about how the fields are not pretty, about the plague in our land, and about how the love of God makes me push beyond every barrier, because I look in the eyes of people who are on their way to Hell who are hopeless and helpless.

"Can one person make a difference? The greatest mission field is in your own backyard. Have you told them? Have you shown them the light of God? The love of God? Will you stand between the dead and the living?"

The fire of God burns inside of me, and I share this. I explain how fire is not meant to be self-contained, how if you contain it for yourself it will kill you.

"Fire is meant to be spread."

Yes, fire is meant to be spread.

After many souls come to saving faith on this night, Pastor Rodney Howard-Browne asks if I can go to Australia and share this message. I say yes, if Randy approves, and he does.

In the next six months, I travel the world over several times ministering to more than a million people. Delivering the same message, I ask them all the same question—"Can one person make a difference in the world?"—encouraging each one of them to yield themselves to God, to stand between the living and the dead.

Early on in starting South Tampa Christian Center, God directs me to start a women's ministry, and I have an immediate reaction.

No, Lord. I can't. You have the wrong person.

God remains persistent, putting this burden for women on my heart. I feel this great desire to see them healed and made whole, yet at the same time, I've never fully known how to interact with women. God still continues to tell me three things:

1. Fill women with the Word of God.
2. Build Godly relationships through fellowship.
3. Spoil them, pamper them, and shower them with good things.

So I begin to meet with women every Friday morning, starting with a group of twelve women who I feel are called to discipleship and are raised up for ministry. This eventually will evolve into Women of the Word on Monday nights, which will grow tremendously and thousands will come from all over to attend.

God isn't finished, however. Around 1998 while I'm in Hawaii teaching and training churches and organizations, I'm walking on the beach when I hear God put another impression on my heart, telling me to go on television. Once again, I know I'm not the ideal candidate for this. Randy already had a TV show, and they had put me on, only to realize I can't do this. It took me seven takes simply to say, "God bless you." I have no experience, but then again, I didn't have experience preaching nor running a women's ministry. God is simply telling me to do this, so I go and tell Randy.

"Sure, go ahead. But the church cannot give you a dime."

I interpret his message as *Go ahead, do it, but I don't know how far you're going to get with this.*

So I mention this to Jim Kirby, who's working with Randy on his book. Jim tells me I need a media agent. So I do some research and find an agent who eventually says he'll make some calls.

"There's a time slot available on BET," the agent tells me. "It's on Tuesday mornings at seven-thirty. It's $23,500 per show for a year contract."

"Let me sign the contract," I say.

So let's see…I've never done a show before and barely know how to say a line when I'm being recorded on camera. I have absolutely no money, and Randy's made it clear there's no budget for this. After years of personally saving I have $10,000. I decide to give it to start Paula White Ministries. Now I'm obligated to more than a million dollars' worth of shows on Black Entertainment Television. Everything in the "natural" is looking like a complete setup for failure. However, I know I've heard the voice of God.

Soon I'm told I'll be going on in two weeks.

The next thing I know we're setting up for my first show in the green room at the church with rented furniture, a single camera, a makeshift black backdrop, and just a few people to help out. I'm the producer, the talent, the director, *and* just about everything else that goes into making a television program. I have no idea what I'm doing, but God does. In time, God will bring people around me who are very gifted and anointed to do a media ministry.

I simply want to show a problem, talk about it with panel guests, then come back after the panel to bring a solution from the Word of God. It is a fresh idea back in the day. We deal with issues the church has shied away from. I want to tackle current societal problems head-on. This is how *Paula White Today* is launched in 1999, and ultimately how Paula White Ministries begins.

After our first show, I go to watch the tape, and halfway through I begin to cry because the quality is so terrible. I don't know what I'm doing and the set is a disaster and we don't have a call center or a post office box, not that I even know to have one back then.

This is crazy.

Jim Kirby feels the opposite. "It's anointed, Paula. And you're saying something. Don't worry—God has you on this. The quality will come in time."

The crazy thing is, once it begins to air, people start bringing the ministry money for the show.

"God told us to bring your ministry this," someone will tell me, driving all the way from Georgia. "Here's ten thousand dollars."

Perhaps after all of the serendipities that God brings our way, I shouldn't feel this is crazy. I just have no idea how it happens, how I'm able to pay $130,000 a month just for airtime.

We will never miss a beat, never miss a payment or a show. The show ends up being successful as I delve into issues like marital problems, money, and the mistakes we make. I can't help being me, open and authentic, so it's natural for me to bring up my past and to also admit my faults. In an article in *Ebony* magazine, someone says, "You know you're on to something new and significant when the most popular woman preacher on the Black Entertainment Network is a white woman."

Bishop T. D. Jakes asks Randy to preach at the Potter's House in 2000, shortly after the 191,000-square-foot sanctuary is built. I've known Bishop Jakes for the past ten years. He's become more than just a mentor; I consider him my spiritual father. I've found much of my spiritual identity in the messages of Bishop Jakes. With similar histories of losing our fathers at a young age and enduring hardships growing up, I truly connect with and respect Bishop Jakes.

This morning while Randy is set to preach, I'm asked to go out and push some products on stage. So I go out there and do what comes naturally to me: talk. The words are fast and articulate, and I'm passionate and communicate everything I need to in a very short amount of time. After I'm finished, Bishop Jakes seems to swirl around toward me and glances at me in amazement.

"You just said more in three minutes than I've heard many preachers say in three years!" he tells me.

I will always remember the words Bishop Jakes speaks to me, as he often pours out nuggets of wisdom over the years. I soak them in and treasure the gift God has put in my life. I recall one that perhaps serves as more of a warning than an affirmation.

"You see the best in everybody, Paula. You promote them based on their potential and not their reality. You see people like God sees them."

11.

SUCCESS

The stadium erupts in raucous applause, the kind normally reserved for professional sports teams and rock bands. The crowd is on its feet, clapping and shouting and raising their hands and thanking Jesus as the pastor extols them to joyfully praise their Savior.

I'm standing on the stage of the Georgia Dome in 2000 and declare, "Come on and really bless the Lord. For about thirty seconds. Let your circumstance know that God is faithful. Let your situation know that you can praise God in the midst of adversity. Let your neighbor know that I'm not ashamed of the gospel or the power thereof. That God's been good to me. He's delivered me. He's saved me. He's healed me. He's stabilized me. He's protected me. He's provided for me," I encourage the audience.

The energy and excitement intensify. More than 80,000 women have packed the Dome cheering and praying as they anticipate the sermon to come. Each one is holding a plastic shovel that reads "Dig It?" These moments are merely the prologue to the preaching, the welcome before opening up the Word of God.

"Look at the God I serve. He is El Shaddai. He is the God that is more than enough. I worship You. That's why David said, 'I'll bless the Lord at all times.'

"This is a good time to let blessing come forth. This is a good time to say, 'Lord, thank you for bringing me to Woman Thou Art Loosed. Many wanted to come, but you chose me. You raised me up for such a time as this. You have equipped me.' Come on and praise His name."

A soaring, powerful voice erupts from my petite frame on the stage. My blond hair is short, cut in a bob with bangs just above the eyebrows. My purple robe is loose and royal; my words are sharp and understandable. There is a rhythm to the sentences I use, a cadence to my words. There is an unexpected fire in my preaching. Christian Broadcasting Network says I'm a "one-woman dynamo who is taking the Christian world by storm." Five years ago I was virtually unknown and now, in 2000, Randy and I pastor one of the ten largest churches in the United States.

"Everybody got a shovel? I don't know what the devil has put on you, but you're getting ready to dig your way out of it. I don't know what life has thrown on you, but you're getting ready to dig your way out of it. I don't know what that man said about you, but you're going to dig your way out of those words that tried to destroy you. Turn to someone today and say, 'Can you dig it?'"

Before moving into my message, I single out the two men whom I need to give honor to: "I am here because God has been so good to me. He has blessed me in ways unimaginable. I thank God for my husband, who has poured much wisdom and love and mentorship into my life. Pastor Randy White is standing by my side continuing to coach me. Will you let the man that I love that has been my best friend and my partner for life know that we appreciate him?"

The stadium gives Randy a roar of applause.

"We're here because of my spiritual father being obedient to the voice of the Lord," I continue. "He didn't have to say yes, but he chose over and over again to say yes, so a word could be deposited in the womb of your spirit."

They know whom I'm talking about, and the applause rises higher.

"He is a great voice for God. I want you to let the man of God know how much we love him, appreciate him, honor him. Everybody from the first floor to the balcony to the fifth tier, stand on your feet and honor Bishop T. D. Jakes."

Everybody shows their love and honor.

"Come on—he needs to hear that. Every man of God needs to know you've got his back. And the epitome of womanhood, the woman who stands by his side. Will you put your hands together for the First Lady Serita Jakes? I believe that beside every great man is a tremendous woman."

I have something important to share with everybody, a resource I'm going to quickly mention is for sale in the back. First, I remind the crowd of my mighty credentials: "My husband's from five generations of preachers. I thank God for his rich heritage. And I'm from five generations of heathens. Thank God for the blood of Jesus. Some of you should have said amen!"

The stadium shouts out a collective "Amen!"

"I've put together packages for you. They're normally valued at a hundred dollars or a hundred fifty dollars. We put them together and made them affordable. They're giving my stuff away! Back there for thirty and forty dollars. So I put the six most important packages together. I'm going to teach on these real quick and then you go bless someone who looks like they're glad to be at 'Woman Thou Art Loosed.'"

I quickly sum up the theme of each message, covering the topics of a half dozen packages of DVDs, CDs, and books. Instantly women are lining up at the product tables purchasing the packages of merchandise. I'll learn that ten minutes into my sermon, more than $121,000 worth of products has been sold. It doesn't even compute.

This is God's will. I'm doing His work.

I deliver an impassioned message, with a voice that almost roars, that drives home points with alliteration and action, that shouts, that encourages every single woman to dig out of their despair and hopelessness. When I walk off the stage to the ovation of 80,000 women, a question still simmers deep inside my heart. Even after I hear how quickly the products have sold and how moved the masses have been, I still wonder something.

Did I do good? Did I get the message across? Did people genuinely encounter Jesus?

Of course, I know the answer, but in another way, I don't. My confidence truly and only comes from the Lord. I remain confident in that truth, confident in Christ, yet I still find room to question myself.

The problem isn't believing whether God can do something; the problem is believing God can do it through me.

Before getting on the Southwest flight back to Tampa, I'm recognized by a woman in the ladies' room: "You're Pastor Paula White!"

Soon I'm encircled by a half dozen women, then more seem to come. The women are thanking me, touching me. It's surreal and surprising. It's wild.

Can this really be happening?

The young pregnant teenager from the trailer…that's just one season of my life. I was also an outsider in California, an athletic overachiever in Florida, and Daddy's girl in Mississippi.

In some ways, five-year-old Paula always returns to the surface of my preaching. Through her I don't believe my success comes from my abilities or anything I've done.

I believe *in God through me*. I can look at the facts and be logical about them. Thousands of ladies moved and praising the Lord and worshipping and crying while I preach. Being thronged by fans in the bathroom. All the places I'm going and the people I'm meeting, and I can be intellectual about it, know my accomplishments, but not try to explain it, because I don't have to.

It's God.

On the plane, as I look down on the grand city of Atlanta, I realize everything God has given me, and I'm humbled and extremely grateful. Every day I truly know that I live and breathe and have my being in Jesus Christ.

I say this from the pulpit time and again: it is God who opens doors. Promotion comes not from the east, the west, or the south; promotion comes from the Lord (Psalms 75). It is God who lifts one up and it is God who sits another down. Psalm 113 says the Lord lifts you out of the dunghill and lifts the needy out of the dust. He sets them before the princes, even the princes of the people. God is the one who positions you, and to God everything is in His timing. That's what the Bible says when it tells us to walk in the Spirit. It means to be in synchronization. When you get into your rhythm, you know how to walk with the Spirit and you don't miss it.

Everything has a time in the kingdom of God. We are told to walk in the Spirit. In order to do this you must "crucify" your flesh. Jesus declares to us in Luke 9:23 (NIV): "Whoever wants to be my disciple must deny themselves and take up their cross daily and follow me."

Since starting Paula White Ministries in 1999, launching on television and speaking at the Woman Thou Art Loosed conference in 2000, God has opened many doors and He lifts me up in ways I could never imagine. In 2001 and 2002, I end up fulfilling between 350 and 400 speaking events each year. There will be more than 3,000 invitations a year. Everything around me doesn't just grow, it explodes.

The church grows to around 15,000 members and 200 ministries. In addition to the six services held at the Tampa location in August of 2002, services for Without Walls start being held on Saturday nights at the 10,000-seat Carpenter's Home Church in Lakeland, Florida. Three years later, our church will purchase Carpenter's Home and rename it Without Walls Central Church. We're one church with two locations.

One of the cities I travel to most is New York City, which is the number one city for Paula White Ministries. Eventually I'm flying there weekly, conducting three services on Sunday for people who line up at six o'clock in the morning to get in the building—regardless of rain or snow. I'll also find myself ministering in other ways, like leading a Bible study for the New York Yankees.

I believe in everything I'm doing. Even the things my fifty-year-old self will reflect back on and would have done differently. I am humbled and grateful, though perhaps I am somewhat naïve. Once I'm on Christian television stations, it is expected for me not only to pay for my airtime, but to also participate in telethons. God greatly favors me, and I'm able to raise millions of dollars to help propel the gospel around the world. I do this out of "purity" and a passion to reach nations with the gospel, not recognizing until much later the false perception and labels it will place on my life and ministry.

Lord, I'm humbled and grateful for your call and anointing.

My journals are maps to take me to that point and place in my life, to remind me how I'm feeling on this day and what happens. My study journal is where I pour my love for God, where I write love letters to Him, where I go over my studies in His Word. My personal journals are details about what happened on this date, where I speak, and who I meet and what happened. Like these from 2002:

September 14, 2002

Lord, I desire for all to be Kingdom-minded and purposed in their heart. I flew to Miami Jesus People Church. Preached P.M. service. Several thousand. Hundreds saved. All I can do is say thank you Lord.

September 15, 2002

Randy preached on the glory of God. It was tremendous. Found myself at the altar. It is so holy. I'm dying right now to self. My heart beats for you. The hand of the Lord is heavy on me. But it's not in a bad way—it's glorious. I'm bored with the world and find it so shallow. There's nothing like Your presence.

September 16, 2002

Fly to Dallas to film five shows with T. D. Jakes.

What a whirlwind—preached Women of Word—people are beginning to fly in for the Bible study. Christina Steinbrenner brought several friends and had great conversation. She's hungry for the Lord.

September 17, 2002

Fly to Dallas—had to film 10 shows—preparing for God's Leading Ladies.

September 18, 2002

People are hurting so badly. I desperately desire for them to receive hope and to be set free with the truth of Jesus Christ.

Balance: it's the key to survival.

Randy and the children are my heartbeat—I love them. How blessed am I to have a husband and pastor who supports me and loves me?

These notebooks will become invaluable for the next few years, because they will be proof that I'm not imagining the whirlwind happening around me. A whirlwind that becomes a hurricane.

"A former staffer of Without Walls International Church criticized it—the part of—you're a part of it—saying, 'It has become all about mansions, planes, money, and fame.' Another detractor says: 'Everything she does is a total act and it's all about money.' How do you respond? Do you have a plane?"

When Larry King asks me this question live on his show on November 26, 2007, there's no way to adequately give a sufficient answer about the mansion we live in or the plane the church owns. Context is everything, but in an interview like this, brevity is also everything.

"Yes, well, not personally, but absolutely, the ministry does," I tell Larry about the plane. Then a few moments later, I briefly state my thoughts about money. "You know, to me, it's never been about money...I don't sit down and say, 'Boy, I'm thinking about getting a great deal of money or I'm not going to have any money.' I believe that money has a purpose. My definition of prosperity would be quite different than what most people probably imagine or think, because I think that it's a wholeness word that means nothing missing, nothing broken. It's not relegated to finances or materialism." It's about the goodness of God.

There's no way to explain my love/hate relationship with money, something I'll end up preaching and teaching about for many years. Money represents freedom, so that can be a good thing or a dangerous thing. Looking at my father, it's obviously dangerous. But money also provides the ability to prayerfully carry out the purpose of God, to do what you're called to do. To help and to be a blessing to others. Money gives you freedom, with which you can either fulfill God's plan or fracture your life and turn it into a train wreck.

From the moment we marry, Randy trusts me financially, knowing I'm good with managing money. I begin to operate on a budget, one where we could spend 3 percent of our income on clothes, for instance. This formula stays the same whether we make $5,000 or $500,000 a year. This is how we accumulated our wealth, even though there were many years when we went without salaries. When money came in, I put it away and invested. Fortunately, God blessed those investments and management.

Five years after the church buys the plane in 2002, I'm still hounded and challenged by it in moments like those on *Larry King Live*. I laugh because if only people could realize that I'm the last sort of diva who demands this or that. I'm just a woman who dreamed of having a family and wanted to stay home with them. Yet as my speaking events increase and my travel schedule intensifies, buying a plane is primarily for practicality. Especially in the year I'm speaking 400 times. On one day I'm actually in five cities! An aircraft allows me to travel with more ease and get back home to my family with more regularity.

The first plane we purchase is an old, beat-up Hawker once owned by John Travolta, for which we pay less than a few hundred thousand dollars. We haven't heard God telling us we need to have a $50 million jet, yet perception will always be reality. In order to get more things done, to avoid a day of travel, then a day of work, then another day of travel, this is the most efficient way to go. There's often a double standard for thriving ministries and companies, and an unrealistic expectation for ministries. Companies deploy private jets or spend money all day long in order to fulfill their mission. However, some people think ministries should be in a horse and buggy, but still be able to reach the world for Jesus.

There is a moment when God commands me to stop worrying about the aircraft, to stop giving it oxygen and to stop feeling anxious about it. Yet the reason has nothing to do with the impression it might give to the rest of the world. The reason comes after surviving an emergency landing in the plane.

One flight while flying over Lake Charles, Louisiana, one of the engines in the Hawker goes out. This is unnerving, of course, but I don't fully panic until we begin our descent and the other engine goes out just before we land.

In the midst of praying and breathing deeply and trying to remain calm, a gust of wind comes out of nowhere on the last part of our descent and manages to carry us down to the runway. I know God has me that day, just as He has on so many other occasions.

The accident does a tremendous amount of damage to the plane, yet our lives are spared. It turns out to be pilot error; they simply forgot to put oil in the aircraft. For a while after this I struggle to get on a plane, yet I continue to so that I can minister. God soon tells me to stop talking about the accident and about my anxiety.

"You still have to carry out your mission to this earth. Stay faithful to your 'yes,' Paula."

October 5, 2002

I should've documented this part of my life years ago but I'm grateful to be starting now. It's an exciting phase of the journey.

First and foremost, I thank you Lord for everything. Words can never articulate nor express my love, appreciation, gratitude and awe of you. You've been so good to me. I'm in my study at our home on Bayshore after returning from Ontario, Canada, and Richmond, Virginia, preaching engagements.

As I spend my morning with the Lord, He tells me He longs for me. I can feel the pull within my spirit. His love consumes me. I long for Him all the more. There's a refocusing in my life. His heart, his cry for the lost souls. At times it's too overwhelming…step by step. His plan and purpose will be revealed. My family is my reward, my bountiful blessing.

I love Randy. When I think of my family and my husband, I say "unbelievable." Yet it cannot be because it is believable. I'm living it—a complete life. So rich and full.

The boys—Brad and Brandon, sixteen and nineteen—are traveling with me. It's a wonderful experience. Thank you, Lord, for all the glory belongs to You.

I pray my life will leave a legacy and history books will be written. Lord, may it be for your glory. Prepare me and keep me pure.

One day I come home from a trip and find out Randy has found a new house for us to buy. It's on the market for $2.1 million even though it's appraised at $3 million. It's no surprise to me it's on Bayshore Boulevard.

"Just because you can afford it doesn't mean you need it!" I tell him.

I give him a definitive, one hundred percent "no" to moving to Bayshore. I can still remember the feeling I had one afternoon while soaking in the Jacuzzi right after we moved to the house in Cheval. Even though we purchased it after a foreclosure, I still question whether it's too much for us. Sure, it's older and needs updating, but I don't feel like it's necessary. I will struggle between what we can do and what we should do at various times in my life.

This will be a moment when I realize God needs to do more work in my life and help me work through the mixed feelings I have when it comes to money and the balance of healthy stewardship. The house and location on Bayshore are too much, in my opinion. At the end of the day, my value system takes precedence as I submit to my husband. Unless it's illegal or immoral, I say "yes" to Randy, even if I'm kicking and screaming in the process. Enough never seems to be enough for Randy. We simply have different positions when it comes to finances.

Moving into the 8,100-square-foot home with a waterfront view of

Tampa Bay doesn't mean it can't be put to God's use. Sure enough, the first Thanksgiving we're there, we decide to host our annual "Table in the Wilderness" meal and have it at our house. Having more than a thousand homeless and impoverished people coming over to the mansion on Bayshore will ruffle almost every single old-money, high-society feather around. The people living nearby become very riled up, but we don't care. This is where Randy and I are radical, where we're rule breakers. An address isn't going to change things. At least, it doesn't immediately.

There's an unspoken code around Bayshore, a high degree of snootiness that we try to ignore. We're going to use it as a blessing to the Lord. So even though I know the perception of having a home like this and in this location, we make use of the space. We do events like this often, opening our home and heart to minister to people.

In time I'll learn an interesting backstory on our house on Bayshore. Missionaries originally owned a small home on this magnificent piece of property. A couple eventually bought the house from them and decided to build their dream home, doing an extensive remodel with additions but leaving part of the original house, including the original stone fireplace. Right after 9/11, the couple decided to move, so they put it up on the market, and we got it at a pretty good price.

Despite my resistance to moving here, I'm glad to hear it has a lot of spiritual roots. When we move in, we dedicate it to God and plan to use it for His purposes. This is a time in my life when I believe we can build big things because they're going to be effective.

You can do this, Paula, so dream big.

But my definition of what's effective will change over the years.

October 23, 2002

Every step creates direction to your destiny or away from it.

Went on TBN—Lord use me. Visited Suncoast Cathedral. I sometimes pinch myself because God is so good to me.

I've thought about this: Psychologists say your life takes on the direction of your dominant thought. I think God is good like a loving, healthy father. And I feel more comfortable walking in His goodness than anything else. I'm confident of who He is.

I don't take it for granted nor demand or feel owed anything. I just know who He is. He is love. That's why I can love myself and others.

Thank you, Lord, for Your revelation and wholeness in my life.

Life is truly a vapor—here and then gone. Don't ever miss your moment, Paula.

I genuinely love God and spend hours in His presence. Fasting every month for a minimum of three days is normal. I don't consider myself "religious," nor are these actions out of the need to do good works. I'm simply trying to go deeper with God, to know Him and His faithfulness.

"You don't need to do all that," Randy will say as he mocks me one day. "That's not necessary. You are relying on your works, by what you do," he says, trying to make me feel like some religious fanatic. Deep within I know better. I know my heart is drawn to seeking God. Nevertheless, his words have a way of deflating me.

Sometimes comments like this come out of nowhere and produce private tears. They have to be private; Randy despises when I cry. I don't really cry for the two decades of my twenties and thirties. If I do begin to cry in front of him, he starts to walk away. So I learned to stop. I don't want him leaving.

"I love doing this," I explain. "I love being in the presence of God."

"But that's not necessary. You're depending on yourself."

"No—I *want* to get into the Word. It's my lifeline." Randy and I go back and forth. The one thing he doesn't get me to budge on is my relationship with God and how I walk it out.

I think about how we used to pray and fast together, about the mornings I would see Randy praying. Neither of those happen much anymore, but I've grown used to this. I've grown used to many things. Like my short hair. I've never liked it extremely short, but Randy hates long hair and won't let me grow it out. He comments on the clothes I wear or mentions that I look like I've gained weight. He points to a laundry basket full of clothes and says, "What's that?" even when I've just come home from a trip.

Nothing ever seems good enough for Randy, and in time, I'll realize this includes me. At the same time, he makes it seem as if the only person I can rely on in the world is him.

"DTA," Randy will tell me, and I'll know what he means.

Don't trust anyone.

"Nobody will love you but me," he says over and over again.

More than anything else—whether it's speaking at Without Walls or ministering to souls all over the world—I pride myself in my desire to be a great wife and a great mother. That's what I try to be.

I'm in Philadelphia for a God's Leading Ladies conference, and I'm the first speaker to come up. Bishop Jakes introduces me to the 17,000 women, and their roar of applause overwhelms me. For me, it's still very intimidating and hard to handle. I still haven't figured out how to receive it; it's so unnatural for me, and honestly a little bit awkward. I'm the first to cheer on others, but accepting those cheers is another thing. I choose to think that they're praising God and not Paula White. I know God has anointed me with a message.

This is the first night of two back-to-back weekends this conference will be in Philadelphia. Different speakers will speak, but I'm a featured one. I'm being courted by numerous publishers, because the market is showing I can sell books. Many people are coming at me, wooing me, giving me advice, asking for something from me. I simply want to do what God is calling me to do and submit to the spiritual authority surrounding me.

The applause I receive on this day goes on and on as if it's not going to stop. It really leaves me feeling uncomfortable and unsure of what to do. When I finish speaking and leave the stage, Bishop Jakes tells me something I'll never forget:

"Never get used to that."

He's giving me valuable insight and wisdom. He's basically telling me this sort of applause is shallow, that it can be very addictive, and that it's not going to last forever, so don't get hooked on it. In ministry, one day people can be praised and then the next day things change and shift and they'll be denounced. Or worse, they'll simply be forgotten.

One day at a service in 2002, God sends a prophet to deliver a message to me. While's he speaking, he looks over at me.

"God's going to use you, Pastor Paula. He's given you nations. And God's going to use your beauty."

In my mind, since I can often be a smart aleck with my humor, I can't help but think, *He better give me more than this.* The preacher continues to talk to me and has my full attention as he discloses a vision I had years ago, yet never shared publicly.

"I see you in this wheat field, Pastor Paula."

Seven thousand people in the sanctuary applaud and cheer him on. I pause for a moment to listen carefully to his words.

"Everything around you will be shaken, and everything around you will fall. But you'll remain standing, and you'll emerge with strength."

The crowd is going crazy now, celebrating and worshipping. But I hear these words as a prophet coming to give me God's message. And the one I'm hearing isn't exactly the kind I'm longing for.

Lord, what is this "everything"? Does it have to be truly everything?

I take a breath in my seat as my eyes stare up at the ceiling in the church. I know in my spirit that this is a "word" from God, but it's not the one I want to hear.

Lord, can this please just be a technicality? Can we send this back up to Heaven?

I'm not afraid; I accept the words and now will wait to see what happens in my life.

Everything that can be shaken will be. The only things that remain are those that have eternal value. I will soon be shaken to my core. God, in His abundant love, will reduce me to Christ, simply meaning the only thing I have left in my life that I can depend on is Jesus. But it's there I will discover His love and His grace in a newfound way. I can't—I won't—forget the good. Those memories and those moments like our first Christmas at Bayshore. I have this profound thankfulness that all the kids are staying with us on Christmas Eve. While sitting at the breakfast table before church Christmas morning, Brad walks into the room with tears in his eyes. He's overwhelmed at how blessed we are. Our family, our health, our finances. It's all because of our Lord.

I write this moment down in my journal so I don't forget.

Jesus, on your birthday, I give you me. I'm your vessel.

I'm excited about our family being here. I love our children. I love my husband. I'm the most blessed woman. Happy birthday, Jesus. Thank you for coming for and rescuing me.

This coming year will be the year of the supernatural. Enemies will rise up but God... You are my strength.

12.

DESPAIR

Be ready, Paula."

I know when God is speaking to me. I just know it. As I always say, it's not an audible voice. It's more than a belief; it's a certainty that is always confirmed through His Word. I believe God reveals things to us. And on this early morning wrapped in the warmth of our bed as I wake up hearing His voice on my heart, I know I should listen.

"You're about to go through something you're not prepared for. You're about to undergo an IRS investigation."

The thought is absurd to the rational side of me, but I don't dismiss it. I wake up Randy and inform him what God is telling me.

"Oh, Paula," he mumbles as he drifts back to sleep.

Randy will often tell me, "You're kooky and a bit crazy, but you're never wrong."

I won't be wrong this time, either.

I simply hold on to this belief and trust that ultimately all the circumstances of God's people are working for His divine purpose.

Purpose...

Four days later, on January 13, 2004, I get a knock on the door at our home. I open it to discover two IRS agents standing next to an FBI agent. They introduce themselves and promptly ask if Randy White is there. I tell

121

them no, but I let them into the house. I don't know I shouldn't be talking to them without a lawyer. I call Randy and tell him he needs to come home.

My initial thought has nothing to do with Randy but rather sports.

We have a huge ministry to athletes who fly down to Tampa for monthly meetings, so we've become good friends with many of them, including baseball players like Gary Sheffield, a New York Yankee. I immediately think about the news a month ago at the end of 2003 when ten Major League baseball players including Gary and Barry Bonds testified in front of a grand jury regarding performance-enhancing drugs. None of the players have been charged, but they're still being linked to a company called BALCO in regard to steroid use. I learn the investigation started with the IRS. At this point I don't have any idea why the IRS or FBI are knocking on our door. I know we spend a lot of money to keep our records precise and we go through massive audits with the best accounting firms every year. So I can't imagine why they've shown up at our house.

When Randy comes home they'll tell us we're under criminal investigation for the years 2000 to 2002. Criminal? I can't fathom what I'm hearing. The IRS is investigating three different things. First, they want to know how we ended up paying for our house on Bayshore. They're also looking into why we didn't have any dividend returns in the last year. And finally, the big shocker is when they say we haven't filed tax returns.

There's no way we didn't file them, I explain. I'm organized to a fault, knowing if you're going to do big ministry that you're going to be under the spotlight. Even though we shouldn't still be talking to these agents, that we should instead be calling our lawyers or finding ones to represent us, I quickly have my assistant pull the files to show them not only the tax returns but also the certified receipts that they were mailed. When I reveal these to the agents an hour later, they can't help looking at each other in what seems to be amazement that we are so prepared. When God speaks to me, I take it seriously.

We have to hire specialty tax attorneys while we're put through an audit.

Basically they look into everything and everywhere to examine our lives. There's not a stone they don't overturn. The IRS interviews everybody they can; all the while Randy and I are personally forced to pay hundreds of thousands of dollars in lawyer's fees just to defend ourselves.

After we work with the IRS and FBI relentlessly, they discover we have impeccable finances and that we handle money with the utmost care. Six months later the investigation is closed and we are found without fault.

The man's words from over a year ago will resonate in my soul:

Everything around you will be shaken...

I wonder if that's the extent of the shaking to come. In time, I realize it is simply the start of the rattling, that this is merely the beginning of the terrible rumblings ahead.

The stress over the course of the following years will at times become unbearable. I know we "walk by faith," but I have come to value and cling to the words I find myself holding on to for dear life during this time. He is "a very present help in the time of trouble" (Ps. 46:1 KJV) and "For we have not a high priest which cannot be touched with the feeling of our infirmities; but was in all points tempted like as we are, yet without sin" (Heb. 4:15 KJV).

When I feel like I have nothing left inside, I'm reminded I am being held. "My grace is sufficient for thee: for my strength is made perfect in weakness" (2 Cor. 12:9 KJV).

The previous year, I had begun to have deeper trust issues with Randy. It's a difficult year for him as he suffers a minor stroke and loses significant hearing in his left ear, along with some of his sight in his left eye. I continue to travel and preach all over the world, and one time after returning from a crusade in Jamaica, where many souls were saved, I arrive home and am surprised to not find Randy there. He is a very routine person—*extremely* routine—so I can't help wondering what he's doing at this time when he would normally be here. When he finally comes back home, the moment I see him I know something's wrong. I know in my heart something is different.

That's not the man I've been married to.

Is this something spiritual? Or woman's intuition? I don't know. I'm not a suspicious or jealous wife, but I realize something has drastically changed.

Later in 2003, I ask what's going on in his life during the afternoon bath we always take together. This is our intimate time, our talk time, the place where we connect the most.

"Have you done something?" I ask him. "Is there something I need to know?"

Something's happened; I can just feel it. But Randy says everything's good, that there's nothing I need to know. I try to get him to open up, but I'm not an aggressive or confrontational person. The last thing I will ever be is some nagging wife.

But I know my husband is keeping something from me.

Not long after the IRS and FBI show up at our door in 2004, Randy and I make another startling discovery at our house on Bayshore. One day after arriving back home from a trip, we discover Brad smoking something on the patio outside the office. He tries to avoid us by running around the house, but we catch up with him and discover he's completely wasted. He's not only out of breath but he seems unnaturally agitated. Wide, glassy eyes stare back at us. We notice his thumbs are all black. When we confront him, he gets angry and tells us the truth.

"You guys might not have noticed, but I've been smoking crack for the better part of a year," Brad says.

Shortly after our discovery, Randy tosses a chair in the library and blames me for this, telling me this is all because I've spoiled Brad, yelling about how much I've failed as a mother. I simply try to hold back the tears, saying I'm sorry, saying I'll handle this, that we'll figure things out. My shock turns to grief and sadness, and a journey begins on this day. Yet it's my son's story to tell, and his alone.

Like his mother, Brad will be embarking on a long journey.

* * *

The package is sitting there under the bench, waiting for me. An anonymous caller tells me to go outside and retrieve a package waiting for me. I walk to the end of our driveway, cross the street to the horseshoe bench area, and pick up the box. As I flip it open, the first thing I see is a photograph of Randy smiling and walking with another woman. The package is full of photographs, tapes, and documents. Everything within me goes numb. I am frozen; it's like I'm living my worst nightmare.

This is the truth I've been wondering about, that I've spent time worrying over. Someone hired a private detective to follow Randy, and it turns out he's leading a double life. There are places he's going that I don't know about, times when he deliberately lied to me when he was spending time with this other woman, along with others that he's publicly photographed with. The worst materials in this are the taped conversations of their phone calls. I listen to them all, as much as I can take, and they devastate me. I feel violated.

They're not full of tawdry and vulgar dialogue, but rather giggling and the innocence of romantic love. Some conversations last an hour, and I'll think, *We've never spoken on the phone that long*. There's this familiarity and this connection Randy and this woman have that we don't have anymore. I begin to wonder if we ever had it.

It resembles a high school love or maybe even a grade school crush. Listening to it overwhelms me.

I don't instantly confront Randy. Instead, I talk to someone close to me, someone who I know will give me the wisdom about what to do.

"There are detectives following Randy." I explain everything that's happening.

I'm stunned when I hear the advice I'm given.

"Call the dogs off."

As if I'm the one who hired the private detective in the first place. The statement isn't some sort of friendly recommendation. It's more of a warning to me. The numbness only intensifies as everything within me is discombobulated.

Ultimately, I go to Randy and tell him that I know about him and what's happening. We get counseling, but Randy never opens up and tells me what's really going on with him. He's learned from his past that opening up and telling his stuff to others can only get him kicked out of the church. We've all seen it happen before, where overnight a preacher and a ministry are done. I don't believe this is how things should necessarily be handled. There are far too many extremes in ministry.

Randy's a survivor. He's not going to let the empire crumble. He's not going to let them take it.

This is the unfortunate thing in ministry. Where is my safe place? Where can I go to ask for help? Where can I find someone who doesn't have an agenda, who isn't going to hurt me?

The only person Randy will trust is me: Batman and Robin. Peanut butter and jelly.

I think about something I just said in my sermon.

"I met a man by the name of Randy—thank you, Jesus. I never thought I deserved a Randy White in my life…you unconsciously attract what you think you deserve. You don't see yourself the way God sees you."

What does all of this even mean now? How should I see Randy, and what does God want in all of this?

He made me a promise before we married. He promised to give me another child.

All the excuses and the reasons and the justification: I wonder if they're all lies. I can hear what Randy's told me time and time again: "I'm afraid I won't be able to hold on to you and keep you."

I'm not leaving Randy. I want this marriage to work. I'm doing the Lord's work. *We* are doing His work. *Surely we will get through this…*

In the silence and sanctuary of my bedroom, I lie on the floor heaving with hurt. This is all beyond disillusionment.

Everything built and everything that exists is centered around God. But my marriage and my family and my ministry…

This feels like too much to bear, though I know God has promised in His Word that He'll never let us be pushed past our limit: He'll always be there to help us come through it (1 Cor. 10:13).

I struggle between pleasing God and pleasing "man." Somehow they overlap and are intertwined in my soul. In my desire to serve God with all my heart, I recognize that is often done in tangible ways by serving others, beginning with my family. What I wrestle with is developing healthy boundaries.

"This is your crux, Paula. Stop depending on a man and recognize it's ME."

I've tried, and I continue to try. The preaching and the ministry—I love serving the Lord, and I've been called, but I'm so exhausted. I'm so tired. But Randy continues to push me to go out and do it. I'll come home frail and exhausted, but my husband isn't sympathetic.

"God's going to take this off of you if you don't go out and do it."

I believe I'm called to preach to the nations to bring deliverance to the wounded and the broken.

But I'm feeling wounded and broken myself.

I also believe in the authority of God and the people He's placed over me.

"I don't want God to take it off of me," I tell Randy.

So I continue to go out and do it. All the while the very foundation of our family is beginning to collapse.

The stillness suffocates. I sit in my study, trying to read, then pray, then once again reading and meditating on His Word. Moving through my morning routine as always. I'm diligent even in the delirium my life has become. The rubble from the explosion of Randy's truth is still scattered all around me, yet I keep moving. It's different, though. Something inside feels like it is dying. I know the landscape of life has changed, and I am not sure what the horizon holds for me.

I continue to think about the packet of material given to me revealing the truth about my husband, a truth that I still can't fully fathom.

I attempt to study God's Word, yet the words I read don't digest. The thoughts I try to organize on paper don't connect. The comments I try to utter to others simply can't be completed. Even two sentences feel like a struggle.

God will give you His strength in your weakness!

I remember the promises I shared so many times with others. That I preached and proclaimed over and over in front of millions.

God will give you His strength in your struggle!

I know and believe this. Yet I can barely move.

The fog of sleepless nights follows me throughout my house. It's been a week since I last found rest. I can hear my stomach rumble, yet physically I can't eat anything. I'm hungry, yet the hopelessness I feel in this moment seems to be shutting my entire body down. I don't have to look in a mirror to know the truth. My normal 118-pound self is starting to wither away. And then I find myself at church, ready to proclaim the fullness of God's truth, spiritually filled yet naturally depleted. But I know there's no way I can stop and back out now.

There are times I feel the blues every now and then or perhaps get a little melancholy, but this is deeper. I always say I'm a twenty-four-hour girl; when I have a bad day, I typically bounce back the next day. This is different. I realize my recent life events have triggered depression. I want to crawl out of it somehow and make it go away, but my reality is I'm covered by a cloud of sadness, compounding my situation.

I do what I've always done. What I know I have to do. I pray. I ask God for the same amazing power He gives others.

Lord, give me strength for every weak place. Grant me clarity for every confused place. Heal every single hurt place inside me. Please, Lord, please give this to me now!

I seek to go to good counseling and find refuge by getting out of myself and serving others. This has always been therapeutic and helpful to my own healing throughout my life. First I go to the nursing house on Gandy Boulevard and ask the manager for five patients who have no family to visit them. I set up Tuesdays to be my day of visitation, taking time to talk, tell stories, play games, and pray over these five precious souls each week. My next stop every Tuesday is Tampa General Hospital, where I visit the pediatric cancer ward. I share with the supervisors of the nursing home and hospital that I'm not doing this for "Paula White Ministries" or as "Pastor Paula," but just as an act of kindness. So I ask to please keep it between us. There isn't much I can do in Tampa without being recognized. I don't want any fanfare but the simplicity of sharing God's love and the beauty of human interaction with a ministry of presence, simply being there for someone.

Still, because I'm often booked one to two years out, and because my responsible side always wants to fulfill my commitments, I ultimately choose to keep following my speaking schedule.

I feel the Holy Spirit, and suddenly I'm an entirely different person. The massive crowd applauds and shouts "Amen!" as I begin to talk to them, as I begin to open up and allow God to speak through me.

"Let me show you the one thing they forgot. You got the same spirit in you that raised Christ from the dead."

This is what I do. This is all I've ever known to do.

This is what I've been called to do my entire life.

"What they didn't know is every time they knock you down, you keep coming back: because you've got a resurrection power in you. You have a spirit in you that causes you to win. You've got a spirit in you that causes you to come back!"

Today, just like yesterday and the day before, I'm talking to myself, preaching to myself, reminding myself.

"Some people left you for dead. They thought it was over. They said you're hopeless. You're helpless. You can't be used. But guess what? Guess what? Guess what? I'm back!"

Every ounce of strength and grit comes from God. I'm His vessel, His voice, sharing His vision with the world.

"You said I couldn't have this. You said I couldn't do this. But while I was going through the valley of the shadow of death, He prepared a table, so get ready!"

I'm ignited by the Holy Spirit, exclaiming His words.

"The table is set. The feast is on. Tell that situation I'm back!"

"I don't think I'm going to make it," Randy tells me.

Behind him, the waves beyond Ballast Point Park still thrash in the aftermath of the violent storm earlier that Friday. Tampa Bay had been in the direct-hit line of Hurricane Charley, yet our city's been spared after the storm shifts east to wreak havoc on southeast Florida. The hurricane ravaging my life, however, has never been stronger and more unstable.

Earlier that day, as the news reported on Charley increasing to become a Category 4 hurricane with 145-mile-per-hour winds, Randy had gone into the office. He wanted to send me to a hotel while he remained at home. This evening, he went out alone for a short while, coming back and asking me if I'd take a ride with him. We eventually arrive at this park, where we stand and evaluate the devastation of our marriage.

"This isn't about you, Paula. I respect you enough to tell you that. It's me. You've been a good wife."

This is the second time he's said that in the past two days. I think of all the things he's said recently, of the comments and the threats and the absolute resignation. This isn't the man I married. His habits have changed, and so has his heart. I picture him driving by our house on his motorcycle racing at ninety miles an hour, acting as if he wants to end it all. Now he's wanting me to just leave.

I believe every word he's saying. And I can't help but think of the last words I ever heard my father tell me.

Just like the details about Hurricane Charley coming in, I've been learning more and more about everything happening in my husband's life: all the different issues affecting him, haunting him, from the stroke from last year to his dependency on Xanax and Valium. Then there's the IRS investigation. Brad's addiction. The revelations of Randy's indiscretions and his diagnosis of compassion fatigue. His self-destructive habits. His suicidal thoughts, such as about hanging himself from a tree in our front yard.

"You can't fix me," he says with tears in his eyes.

"I don't want to fix you. I just want you to be okay."

When we get back to our house on Bayshore Boulevard, we learn that Hurricane Charley has left more than half a million people in southeast Florida without power while tearing off thousands of rooftops and uprooting thousands of trees. As the eye of Charley crosses over Punta Gorda, witnesses describe seeing the sun peeking through.

When I survey the damage brought by Hurricane Charley, I soon discover one of my favorite things about our house on Bayshore is gone. The oak tree in our front yard is destroyed, but the old palm trees I despise somehow remain. The oak tree split because it doesn't have roots, while the ugly palm trees remain because of their deep root system.

Like all the things I preach, I draw from real-life occurrences in an upcoming sermon. How can I not? Ultimately, I'm always preaching to myself.

So I talk about that oak tree. To say it's a good metaphor is an understatement.

"We had a one-hundred-year-old oak in our front yard, huge. In fact, one of my favorite things about the house was the oak tree. It reminded me of Mississippi where I grew up. And there was an old, ugly, skinny palm tree in our yard, too. That thing is ugly. It has holes in it where woodpeckers have pecked it and people nailed into it. It's old and ugly, and that hundred-mph wind came through, knocked that oak tree down, and I looked out into our yard and was really upset, losing one of my favorite views.

"I looked over and that old, ugly palm tree was still standing tall. And God spoke to me. He said many people in my body are like an oak tree that has four-inch roots, and when the storm comes, they're going to fall. They won't make it, but there's a remnant I have raised up that is rooted.

"If you have built your life on the firm foundation of Jesus Christ and His Word when they speak the rumors over you, you're rooted. When he leaves you, you're rooted. When they talk about you, you're rooted. When your money is gone, you're rooted. When your ministry is in question, you're rooted. When your mind is confused, you're rooted. When you feel like giving up, you're rooted.

"And I looked and that old, stinking, ugly palm tree is the only tree standing in my yard, because that storm took out everything that wasn't rooted. When you get rooted, you will have times that life will sting you but it won't kill you, because you're not just going to survive. You're going to thrive. Thank God right now that you're rooted, you're rooted, you're rooted.

"I thank God, I'm rooted and I'm resting in my true vine. I'm resting and His sap is flowing through me, and as long as I have the right roots, I'm going to have the right fruit. Come on, slap somebody upside the head, say you're not just a survivor, but you're going to thrive. Get out of your seat, go to three people, say you're going to thrive. Your purpose is going to thrive. Your heart is going to thrive. Your walk with God is going to thrive. Your mind is going to thrive. Your ministry is going to thrive.

"Come on, I trust you, God."

I'm never preaching anything I'm not living. I'm reminding myself I'm rooted. I'm telling myself that yes, life stings, Paula, but it's not going to kill you.

I'm saying I'm not just going to survive.

I'm rooted in the Lord, and I will thrive.

If everything is torn down, Lord, what will you plant there instead?

Something different... but the same ground.

One morning as I'm studying the word, I hear the whisper of the Holy Spirit urging me to study Jeremiah. The words of Jeremiah 32:14, 15, and 17 (NIV) begin to minister to me, time and time again. I won't fully understand them now, but in time I will: "This is what the LORD Almighty, the God of Israel, says: Take these documents, both the sealed and unsealed copies of the deed of purchase, and put them in a clay jar so they will last a long time. For this is what the LORD Almighty, the God of Israel, says: Houses, fields and vineyards will again be bought in this land."

Let them last for a long time, Lord. Bring your houses and fields and vineyards back to this land, Lord.

"Ah, Sovereign LORD, you have made the heavens and the earth by your great power and outstretched arm. Nothing is too hard for you."

Search my soul, God. Search every dark place. Purify and do what you want.

I know nothing—nothing—NOTHING is too hard for you.

I know if I don't write this all down, I will easily lose the picture.

If I don't pour out these thoughts and impressions of the day, they will be eclipsed by this dark period I'm living in.

Every word and every detail will be almost like a trail of bread crumbs.

I know trauma enough to know how the mind will block out memories. So I will continue to write. Every day and night. Letters sharing my love for God, and lists detailing the hate in my life.

August 22, 2004

Lord, my heart's breaking. I hurt more than I ever have in my life. Please, God, be with me. You're my only comfort and strength during this time. I need you desperately. I was blindsided on this one. Please, I just need you, Lord.

September 29, 2004

Sitting in my study. The word of the Lord came to me.

For the Lord would say to you my daughter of destiny: Be patient and be still. For indeed I will cure and I will heal. For have I not spoken and will I not confirm my word?

You have chosen the higher road and surely your reward will be great.

I will break the neck of the enemy aligned against you. For your enemy is my enemy. Your friend is my friend.

Patience, my dear girl. Patience says the Lord.

Wow... What a moment of peace and joy. I find so much strength in the Lord. So much joy.

It's such a paradox in my life right now. I don't know if my marriage will make it. What will happen with ministry? But I know I will make it.

And the paradox? It took the worst possible situation—Randy and all he's gone through and done—for me to get to the best state of being. It caused me to see the beauty of where I am. The beauty of each day, of each moment.

In some strange way, thank you.

The darkness showed me how beautiful the light really is.

October 11, 2004

It's 4:07 in the morning. I'm in my office to worship you, Lord. Just to give it all to You. For I'm so hungry for Your presence, Lord. You alone are my strength. You alone are my source. Break forth with Your power and Your glory, Lord. I completely surrender myself to You.

Purge me of anything unpleasing to You. Purge me—purify me—cleanse me. I'm your daughter of destiny. I release to You all the hurt and the anger and the confusion. I release it, God.

Will You please put things in proper perspective. At least let there be clarity. For during this difficult season I can only trust You. My life is in Your hands. Deal with every enemy to my soul, with every enemy to my destiny.

The battle belongs to You.

Lord, there are days filled with hope, days full of despair. How will I know when this marriage is over? Let my decisions be completely God-directed in every way and every area.

Lord, I pray for Randy.

His mind is so confused—I don't know if I can help him. Only you can do this. He is yours. Let your love bring him back. Let your love cover us—heal—restore. Not just us as in marriage but us individually as Randy and Paula: Your chosen vessels: Your son and daughter. I rely on you.

Give me love and tenderness and strength. I do love You more than life.

November 17, 2004

Lord, I just returned from preaching in Miami. Quite a move of God—healing for the injured souls.

Today was somewhat difficult for me. I felt a personal attack against me as a woman. Hard to explain but my femininity feels raped. It's as if a big hole is in my chest. Maybe that's why I could minster so effectively tonight to the injured souls.

Randy has days—down days, up days. Today it feels as if it's over.

He torments me on days like this. It's so hard to understand.

I just rest in You, Lord. I rest in You. You're my hiding place. Please cover me and protect me.

I need You, Lord.

This has gone on for six months. I really desire Your wisdom for direction.

If You say stand, I'll stand. If You know the inevitability, then please release me. Heal me. There's no need for prolonged pain.

Please speak to me, Lord. This is not a time for silence. I give the hurt and anger to You. Put Your peace and love in my heart. I yield myself to You.

Surround me with the right people—it's crucial. I love you. Really, really love you. Was my heart destined only for you?

I stare at the ink on the journal page, the stark black against the white. I look out the window, knowing a new year is coming, knowing I truly need to be surrounded by the right people. I think about something a colleague recently told me: "When everything falls apart, you'll find out why people are there in the first place."

There have been many words, harsh and cutting and brutal, yet today they stop me from breathing for a moment: "You're not going anywhere. You're a porch dog, Paula. I can walk all over you and you're still going to be there."

Porch dog.

I'm left alone to contemplate Randy's remarks. They're not only offensive; they're outrageous.

I'm not a porch dog. No.

On this day something inside of me changes. I suddenly can feel the shattered parts inside of me being forged together through fire and pain.

You're mistaking my loyalty for weakness.

He feels he can walk all over me, and I'll still be there forever. He's always said I could be on an island full of a thousand naked men and not do anything. "You're loyal," Randy says. He knows this about me.

The picture gets clearer. "DTA," and "Me and you versus the world," and "The Oz," and "Nobody will love you but me." He's been brainwashing me for years, and I have no boundaries. I bought into it all. I've put up with this sort of abuse too long.

The old brick building from the 1960s is the only eyesore residing on Bayshore Boulevard. One day Randy takes me there up to a condo that reeks of smoke, with baby blue sinks and green linoleum. It's worse than the trailer I lived in with Dean.

Randy is pleasant as he talks to the real estate woman. He acts as if this is an investment we're making, but the truth I will discover is this is where he's planning on putting me. He tells me that I can live here while he lives in our home. I am speechless and appalled.

The walls seem to smother me. I walk into a bathroom, excusing myself so I don't make a scene in front of everyone right before bursting into tears.

What is happening with my life?

Like the rust and lime circles in the toilet bowl, my entire world feels in a tailspin.

God, please stop the world. Just let it stop.

But of course the world isn't going to stop. It never stops. My world is going to keep going, and I'm going to keep putting one foot in front of the other as best I can.

I see Randy peer into the dimly lit bathroom and catch my reflection in the dirty mirror.

"You better stop now," he says. "Pull it together."

I'm mortified when we leave the building. "This is ridiculous. There is no way I am going for this," I tell myself.

February 18, 2005

I just got home after meeting with Donald Trump tonight. Even after knowing him for several years now, he really went out of his way with complimenting my ministry. Melania was with him. She's a sweetheart.

I must say, when he began to share with me how impactful I've been, it made me feel good. It's good to hear good things said about you when you've been torn down so much the last ten months.

Randy isn't doing so well. He went Tuesday for a massage with ——. We got into it pretty ugly. Today he talked to me from his heart in the parking lot at Starbucks. Says he loves me too much to hurt me anymore. He's always loved me. Emotionally abandoned, etc. Not true. The problem is, I don't know what to believe anymore. Said he wanted to separate, it escalated that night pretty bad after finding a gift he bought for ——.

I'm thirty-nine years old, lying on a picnic bench alone in a state park in Tampa, just stretched out staring up at the sky and thinking. I feel alone, and desperate for answers, asking God to show me a sign. The world around me spins while the blue sky above remains steady and watchful.

I need something. I need to know You're with me.

I'm struggling to face the fact that my marriage might be over, because I believe in the sacredness of the institution of marriage. It's difficult to know when to actually cut the cord. On one hand, you're praying, believing in God for some sort of miraculous restoration; on the other hand, you are faced with your own daunting reality. The suspicions hadn't just been true; they're far worse than I could have ever imagined. Every single thing I see in my life has been charred and lies in the ashes, yet the rest of the world only sees the fire burning in front of it.

As I sit up on the picnic table, I hear a voice speaking in the distance. It's an audible voice coming from the speakers of a car probably parked close to mine. For a few moments, as I hear the words booming over me, I can't help thinking how familiar the speaker sounds.

Then I realize the obvious, ridiculous truth: the voice is me.

Someone in the lot is detailing his car while blaring one of my messages. In this most surreal moment, I listen with a dumbfounded fascination. It only takes me a minute to recognize the sermon that's playing. The voice—*that* voice from *that* woman who never planned on being all *that*—has hit its stride and found its rhythm:

"It's very clear Isaiah chapter fifty-four was written for you. It's very clear that Isaiah chapter fifty-four was written for us, the redeemed ones. Somebody look at someone and say, 'You better sing, girl, you better sing.' Now He's talking to us. This promise is for you. This is not for many centuries ago. This is not for thousands of years ago. This is your word that God's getting ready to release you into what He's promised for you."

I remember very well giving this sermon recently.

"I don't know who's been barren, but I'm getting ready to show you your breakthrough. I don't know what you went through, but God said it's a setup. I have a word for His church and for your elevation, for your advancement. Your trial will not be wasted. Your pain will have purpose. God's gonna use everything the enemy meant for bad and He will turn it around for good. He shows us very clearly that beauty is to follow affliction and peace is to follow tempest and disturbance."

I can't help but smile as I listen to the sermon.

"I know it's not popular, and you're not gonna stand up and shout, but you will give God some praise for some things that cause you some headache and some heartache. You're gonna look back and you're not going to thank God for everybody who just cheered you on. But you're gonna thank God for Judas that kissed you. You're gonna thank God for every enemy that betrayed you because had Judas not kissed you with his nasty breath, you would have never been put in the position, you would have never been put in that place. And had Christ not gone to Calvary, then He would not have had a death, and we would not have had a resurrection."

The message is called "Your Friend Judas." It's a profound message God gave me about how Judas is needed in your life to get you to a place of purpose.

This is a moment. One of those moments. Not the kind that are bread crumbs for the trail we're journeying down. No. These are lightning bolts. The kind where God shouts, "I'm with you and I got you." When He says, "I've got you, Paula. I have all this."

That voice...I sound different on tape; I never listen to myself.

Today, the miraculous happens when God speaks to me *through* me. How crazy is that? He tells me one thing over and over again: "You're gonna thank God...for people who walked out on you and broke your heart.

"You're gonna thank God...for people who talked about you.

"You're gonna thank God...for every trial and every test you went through."

In fact, "You've been praising God for some of the wrong things. You've been thanking God for everything, like when you got the promotion, when you got the house, when you got the hot date—come on! But you gotta thank God for when they walked out on you.

"You gotta thank God for when they told you you'd never make it—you wouldn't become anything.

"You gotta thank God when they spoke against you. You gotta thank God that everybody gave up on you. For if God be for you who can be against you?

"You gotta thank God for every demonic assignment, because the devil doesn't waste stones on dead birds.

"You gotta thank God. You better look at somebody and say 'I'm going somewhere.'" The words are now heard, not just spoken. Ultimately all the circumstances of God's people are working for divine purpose.

Purpose...

I've always known mine. And I've always believed with all of my heart that God does have something greater in store.

I still do.

13.

DEATH

I'll always say it, time and again: the greatest blessing in my life is that God loved me enough to reduce me to Christ. These aren't mere words; they are my life's story, the mystery of my worth. They are the truth of the transformation God began inside of me in 2003 and continued through 2008 and beyond.

The first part of this transformation is already begun when life crushes against me, when I'm hit in exactly the right place from something totally out of left field. When I stand there like a deer in the headlights, not wondering whether I'm going to be struck but worrying whether I'll survive. I'm forced to leave the known world of my comfort and convenience for a place I've never been. Some things I bring on myself. Other things, people's decisions, impact me greatly. Some things are direct demonic attacks, while others are simply "life," where it rains on the just and the unjust. Regardless, my world gets rocked. Not everything is "God-sent," but it all can be "God-used" if I allow it to be.

From this I go to a second place, a radical disorientation for creative transformation. Everything around me that's been created begins to fall apart. Chaos comes in every sort of form and covers every single fragment of my being. The idea that life is neatly packaged, always stable and reliable, is an illusion. The landscape of life can change in the blink of an eye. I have wanted change, prayed for change, but suddenly find myself in a discombobulated state because I didn't realize that all change initially feels like loss. I'm dying to who I was but haven't come forth to who I will become. This is where faith has an opportunity to really function. Faith is the willingness to experience life as it unfolds with all its pain and still trust God's plan of promise for you.

One of the greatest truths I discover during this time is that God is with me even when everything is falling apart. I become intimately acquainted with Psalm 23:4 (NIV): "Even though I walk through the darkest valley, I will fear no evil, for you are with me."

Ultimately this difficult and turbulent period will bring me to a third and final place, a place of return. This is where I come back to my authentic self. A place where my genuine self will be discovered. I am a spirit being having a human experience. A metamorphosis will finally occur if I allow the process of becoming what I've really been all along. This is where the greatest potential and power comes forth for the glory of God.

In 2006, I'm only midway through my journey of transformation. The Lord knows I hope the worst days are behind me. But my metamorphosis isn't complete. I have fully surrendered to God and trust Him even when my mind struggles to understand everything.

The message I preach near Easter weekend of 2006 is given to me from God, and it's for myself as well as others. I will have to remind myself it's not over many, many times in the dark months to come.

As I stand behind the pulpit, I tell everybody how honored I am to be here, and how honored I feel to have Dodie and Lisa Osteen among the many guests.

"You know how much I love Ms. Dodie and how honored I am that you've been with us, and Lisa, and all the ministry you both have done. Every single person, I just stand in awe at the goodness of God. Sixteen years ago, the Lord gave me a word. He said, 'There will be ministry gifts that come and sit at the feet of this ministry, and your mouth will drop in awe at the caliber of people that I will bring. And here we were with five people in a storefront, and really just believing God to do big things. He said, 'You'll see nations being shaken,' and if God can use a girl like me, God certainly is getting ready to use you."

I honestly don't know how long I will speak, whether I'll be here for two minutes or ten or thirty. God gives me a word today as well, and over and over again I declare it to the spirited and hungry crowd: "It's not over."

"God's getting ready to push you into a new season. Weeping may endure for the night, but joy cometh with the morning. I came to tell you, God has ushered a new season into your life."

Acts 14 is on my heart, so I share about the apostle Paul and Barnabas speaking in Lystra, with the former eventually being stoned and left for dead.

"Hey, you better get verse nineteen. There were people that stoned Paul supposing he was dead. There are some people that think it's all over for you. There are people that have tried to already mark your ending because they looked at your beginning. They have persuaded other people that you're not going anywhere. They think it's over. They think because you went through that divorce, you're not ministry material. They think that you should've lost your mind. They think it's over, that the best part of your life has been lived out, but the devil is a liar. They drew you out of the city, away from the power, away from the provision, away from the blessing of God, and they left you for dead. But something is getting ready to hit you called a resurrection spirit; the same spirit that raised Christ from the dead is getting ready to raise every dead place, and you're getting ready to rise up, and go on. 'It's not over.' You better get out of your seat, say, 'Don't you judge me just yet. It's not over. Don't conclude anything over my life just yet. It's not over.' I know you think the best has already happened, but it's not over."

My heart is open and raw as the words flow out. Once again, I fall into a rhythm, with that progression and cadence and flow. There is no filter in my message, however. I don't share the Scripture simply to show how many verses I've memorized; I want them to know I *live* the Scripture. They're not mere words in my head; they're something that changed my heart and my life. I don't simply rattle them off to rap to the crowd; they are what I depend on to walk through every day. It's living Scripture as an epistle where your life is a handwritten letter for others to read by the Spirit of God. God doesn't want us to have head knowledge of Him without heart knowledge. The children of Israel knew the acts of God, but Moses knew His ways. He is continually asking us, "Will you come up higher in order to know Me?" There is a place in God that few people ever seek or ask to go to. Nevertheless, He is ready to reveal Himself if you are ready to ascend.

Inside the sermon, this unexpected message, are pieces of my vulnerable soul, pages of my story. Some of the congregation may perceive them, but I'm talking about God and me. I'm always talking about this amazing love story we have going on.

"It's not over. I believe God because of Him. He is able, He is willing, He is going to do it. It's not over; 2006 is going to be my best year ever. My season is getting ready to change. God is going to accelerate my destiny. He's going to send an angel of assignment to me. He's going to increase the more and the more. According to Psalm 112, He's going to bless me and my horn or authority will be lifted high in honor. He's going to shield me in. He's going to protect me. He's going to allow me to spend my days in prosperity (His goodness and grace) and in pleasure and with long life."

I believe this with every ounce of my being. I'm still believing God for more in my life, for my marriage to still survive, for my children to be saved and to serve God, for my ministry to continue to thrive, and for my voice to reach nations that will be shaken for the glory of God.

"And when the devil said, 'You're finished with'—he told me three years ago, he said, 'I'm going to silence your voice and destroy you.' And I went through an eighteen-month period, and I decided, at the end of those eighteen months, 'It's not over. It's not over. It's not over.' And a boldness hit my spirit, and an authority in the name of Jesus, because I decided to pursue His passion and purpose, and that resurrection spirit hit my spirit, and I said, 'Devil, you are a liar. It's not over. My best days are ahead of me. They are not behind me.'"

The words are true. My best days will simply take a little longer than I hope to arrive. Yet that boldness and authority won't disappear. In fact, they will only deepen inside of me.

The news at the end of 2006 doesn't make sense at first. It doesn't seem real. How can Kristen have a malignant brain tumor? The oldest daughter of Randy and his ex-wife, Debbie, is only twenty-eight years old. She seemed perfectly fine at Angie's wedding a short time ago. The tumor is diagnosed as terminal, and they only give her a few months to live.

Her cancer becomes a dark shadow over our family, even darker than the breakdown of my marriage. Yet in the midst of this chaos, the one shining light is Kristen. The hope she carries will sustain her two young children, Drew and Emma, and ultimately it will help to transform me in ways nobody else has.

To write the story as it unfolded back then, as Kristen briefly beats cancer and is allowed to live another seventeen months, would involve a myriad of emotions and rough moments we all have. The truth as I will see it later in life is that we all handle her battle and her death in different ways.

Kristen is the oldest of the four children between Randy and me. She lived most of her childhood years with Debbie and her husband, Eric. We are a blended family that shares holidays, summers, and life together. We go on outings, do events, and share the parental duties and responsibilities that come along with co-parenting. We never view our children as "his" or "hers," but rather as "ours." We always want the best for them individually and collectively. Initially, we had our challenges, but eventually we all found a way to come together as one big family with love and respect. Ultimately, all of the children, along with Debbie and Eric, move to Florida, making it their home. The kids live between our two homes and sometimes venture out on their own. This is where we are all living and working, with the exception of Brandon, who has taken a traveling position with a worldwide ministry, when we receive the devastating news of Kristen's cancer. No one can ever be prepared for that moment. It's shattering, numbing, and surreal. This can't actually be happening—not stage three to four cancer in our daughter.

Randy refuses to give up on her and pours himself into caring for her in his own way. One thing he has always been is a fighter, so Randy goes to battle, but this is one that he has never been in before. The siblings—Angie, Brandon, and Brad—all share such a tight bond as they rally around their sister. Each of them is so amazing in their own way, so during this time they have a right to be angry with the mess that's spilling out from the tensions between Randy and me. The timing of so many things collapsing cannot be worse. It all feels so unfair. We are suffocating from the perils of all that we are going through. We want to breathe and process and "land," but we can't, not with one blow after another.

It's tough and it's hard, yet everything Kristen says and does makes it feel the opposite. Before she undergoes radiation treatment, Randy takes Kristen to a place she's always wanted to go: Hawaii. Angie, of course, will accompany them as well. It will be a lifelong dream that she gets to fulfill.

Thirty-nine different events and nineteen life crises. Such is the summary of this period of loss in my life when it feels as if the very fabric of time and space are being torn apart, allowing unexpected events to occur.

God, I turn to you. I need you. I want you. I want to laugh again. Remove any poison. Heal me.

The private hell I've been living in has bled over into other things. Randy and I aren't the only ones struggling. Along with Kristen fighting cancer, other family members are struggling as well. Our personal lives and the ministry have undergone public scrutiny with the vicious attacks from the *Tampa Tribune*. Randy has made it clear to me the sanctity of our marriage isn't worth fighting for. Perhaps the only fight he has left inside of him needs to go toward his daughter.

I've been left exposed and vulnerable way too long, Lord. Please cover and soothe my soul.

Getting through this chaotic transitional period in my life will involve facing many ordeals and facing the facts of life with both eyes wide open. One of those facts will be painful to realize. At the end of a Creative Summit meeting for Paula White Ministries, I come to see that my life no longer belongs to me. In the midst of doing God's work and fulfilling my purpose, and while being the visionary sitting behind the driver's seat, I suddenly ask a question of myself: *Have I become a commodity?*

During a meeting with colleagues and friends, I have a moment where I'm hovering over myself as well as hearing all the talk about Paula White, the woman, the brand, the image. I never lose sight of my love for God and the desire to bring people to His salvation knowledge. It's always been my core, my heartbeat. Throughout my ministry, I predominantly had my hands on the steering wheel. With the devastating blows we are going through, I find myself having to shift my time, energy, and strength to personal matters. Somewhere in all of this the "business side" of ministry has to be sustained. After all, there are missionaries to support, orphanages and schools being built, churches being planted, wells to be dug, prisoners to be visited, the poor to be fed, and the gospel to be preached. My personal crisis doesn't stop the commitments and demands of Paula White Ministries.

It hits me over the head when I hear someone summarize this brand in a succinct and matter-of-fact way.

"Paula White's a wife! She's a mother! She's into health and wellness! She's a bit playful and humorous! She has a vitamin line! She's hopeful but not sentimental."

How was all of this created? And why is there so much chaos that I'm feeling? Like my marriage, and like so many other things in my life, I wonder how it got to this point, and how in the world it's ever going to change.

I can't see that this is the force leading to the breakdown of old systems, a breakdown that will lead to unexpected breakthroughs.

Remember, Paula, in darkness what God spoke to you in light from Isaiah 57:15 (MSG): "I live in the high and holy places, but also with the low-spirited, the spirit-crushed, And what I do is put new spirit in them, get them up and on their feet again."

God is with us when everything is falling apart.

I'm in my car driving. I once again think of the familiar passage from Jeremiah. I reread it this morning from *The Message:* "Life is going to return to normal. Homes and fields and vineyards are again going to be bought in this country."

This continues to be the only word God is giving me during this time, this season of my life. It partially feels as if Heaven is closed; I only wonder how long it will remain that way.

God, why are you quiet? This is when You should be talking to me the most.

I miss the turn I'm supposed to make because I'm deep in thought, and as I pull into a parking lot to head the opposite direction, I think of a GPS that guides me in a car. Instantly the analogy seems perfect.

We put our destination in the GPS, and it will tell us only the critical things to get us there. It will say things like "take a right in one mile" and "your destination is on your left," but for long stretches of time it doesn't say a word to us. The GPS doesn't tell us which radio station we should listen to and whether to turn on the air conditioner. Those are our preferences. When we ask ourselves if we're about to run out of gas or if we really should be driving to this place, the GPS tells us nothing.

God is the master of GPS. He doesn't always give us details as we move toward our destiny. Faith is having total trust and confidence in Him. That's our walk and our journey with God.

He wants your total trust, Paula. Your absolute trust.

It's easy to trust God when you're happy and your life is coasting and you're in love and you have money and all of those good times. Total trust is when everything looks like a contradiction to His Word. Imagine what Mary and the apostles thought while standing at the cross.

God's ways can be confusing. Yet there's no confusion about what absolute and complete trust looks like. It's continuing to drive down the road, knowing where you're headed, knowing eventually you'll arrive.

* * *

There are ugly moments between Randy and me, the sort of stains I wonder if we can ever get out of our souls. During a particularly heated argument that unfolds in front of the kids over a recent revelation, I go upstairs to find Kristen in tears, beside herself. I no longer see this strong, joyful woman, but I see this heartbroken, scared child, one who has experienced enough pain from the divorce of her parents from decades ago. She's weeping because of seeing what's happened in our marriage. Angie is next to her in the bedroom crying as well, but the pain spilling out of her sister is like a break in a giant dam. She is sobbing, saying how bad this hurts, that I am her mom, too, that it's all too much to handle. My heart is breaking in more ways than one could imagine. As I try to comfort and console them, telling them things will be okay, I make a decision right there.

I can't do this to Kristen and to Angie. To the rest of the family. I won't.

I can't put myself in situations like this anymore. I can't make Kristen's last few remaining days on this earth a living hell. I have to remove myself from the situation. There will be many times I talk to Kristen on the phone or pray with her alone, but I decide to subtract myself from times with Randy and the children. It's the respectful thing to do, especially for Debbie. She's Kristen's mother. It's the right thing to do, even though the children won't understand why I'm not there at times.

The strain in our relationship has turned tense and ugly and malicious. Our kids despise how we're acting, and I don't blame them.

I hate this chapter in my life, but I never stop believing my story can turn out well. I will finally realize that story doesn't involve Randy.

This place of complete surrender reveals that I'm not going to compromise myself in any way. I keep trusting God.

There can be beauty that comes from these ashes.

At any point, we can call it quits on everybody, including God. How many people do call it quits on God?

During this time, I allow God to prune me and purge me. I am and always have been a work of God's amazing grace.

I can point the finger and I can assign the blame, but I'm not perfect and without some responsibility for the failures and shortcomings in my life. When something falls apart, people often look for the one thing, the reason it went wrong. It reminds me of the man blind from birth that Jesus passed by, recorded in the book of John, chapter 9 (KJV), where the disciples asked him, saying, "Master, who did sin, this man, or his parents, that he was born blind?" Jesus responds that it was neither. People, especially in the church world, will put pressure on you for that one reason that things didn't work out. Whose fault was it? Who messed up? The reality is there are probably many reasons that you are in the situation you find yourself in when facing devastation, loss, and brokenness. No one wakes up and wants to derail their life.

I cling to hope, perceiving something not visible, clinging to a mental picture of a better future, a place where my whole self can continue the vision I have inside, the purpose God put in me.

It's March 24, 2007, our seventeen-year anniversary. Randy tells me he loves me but also tells me he's not going to change his lifestyle or his actions. I refuse to live like this. I can't and I won't.

I understand what Sheronne Burke once told me years ago. She's a great businesswoman who runs many of our operations, so she knows what's happening. Sheronne's always been very respectful of Randy, and she knows the sting of divorce, since she's been through one herself. She can see my daily, silent torment. One day she pulled me aside and looked right into my eyes.

"You'll know when. Don't let anyone tell you when. You'll know. God will speak to you."

At the time she says this, I give her this look as if to say, *What are you talking about?* But she knew better.

"Paula, they don't want your husband," Sheronne said. "They want your life."

Even though I've never said a word publicly about what's happening in our marriage, I will soon be faced with an ultimatum, a line I will not cross. I genuinely believed there would be repentance to God to bring restoration and wholeness for my marriage; I have been praying and hoping for our family. A divorce isn't just between two people; it's your kids and your family and your church and everything else. Yet I can't tolerate his behavior any longer. How can I when I'm told that he wants an "open marriage"? It's a line that I will not cross.

Randy refuses to quit with his behavior, and I refuse to quit with my beliefs.

"If we get divorced, you're going to lose everything," Randy says.

"I might lose everything, but I'm not going to lose me."

I'm really fighting for my purpose.

All along I've still clung to hope. I've still tried. Since 2004, I've simply assumed this is my life. I still believe in marriage; it's always been crucial to me. I will always be able to authentically say that I would have stayed married.

At this point, Randy is renting a house in Malibu, California. He tells me he is working on himself. When he stays away, I'm in Tampa and New York. Paula White Ministries is succeeding more than ever before. Does it become my mistress, as Randy will often say in public? Yes, absolutely, in some ways. Randy demands that I leave the ministry all the while sending me mixed messages. I don't trust his intentions or ability to make good decisions at this time. One day he begs me to keep everything going, the next week he tells me I need to stay home and quit ministry, then the next week he reminds me as he proclaims to the world on a TBN broadcast of *Praise the Lord* that he owns me and created me.

I continue to say nothing in public. For years I've patiently endured the harassment and abuse while going through a lot of counseling and therapy. I still believe in the institution of marriage. I've simply gotten to the place of asking myself, what do I need emotionally? Physically? Obviously, spiritually? Financially?

God gives me a gift when Randy makes it clear he is not going to change his behavior. God releases me.

Like so many other things he's done, Randy's announcement about our divorce surprises even me. It's August, and I get a call before our Thursday night service at Without Walls International Church.

"You better get over here. Randy just announced to the staff that you guys are getting a divorce." The gut-wrenching reality sinks in. I've held on with some small thread believing this would be a blip on the radar screen and eventually we would "land," that our marriage would somehow make it.

When I get there, it turns out all the media is waiting, including CNN and MSNBC. An hour into the service, a somber Randy invites me to the podium to help him deliver the news.

"We have a very, very difficult announcement to make tonight before Tim preaches, and that is that we are going through a divorce," Randy says. "It is the most difficult decision that I have had to make in my entire life. And I came to you tonight, to first let you know that I take full responsibility for a failed marriage."

As he talks, I can hear audible cries of "no" and see the shock on the faces looking up at us. The tears on their faces pierce me.

I'm choked up and look as if I'm in a daze. I can barely talk.

"This has been an ongoing process and journey," I tell our Without Walls family.

If you only knew...

"While this is a chapter that has closed in our life, it is not the end of the story for Randy or for Paula—or maybe even Randy and Paula. And we stand in full cooperation, in full support of each other, and especially for the cause of Christ."

My faith and my hope in God's plan and purpose in my life haven't wavered. Even in my shock of having to stand here tonight and make this announcement, my desire to speak to others is still within my heart.

"God is always faithful," I declare. "God always carries you through the dark places of life."

September 23, 2007

Well—how did I get here? What is here? I've had a pit in my stomach. Chest pains. Sore throat. A ringing in my ears.

I won't live like this. Figure it out, Paula. Find release. Find it fast.

I feel like I can't breathe. Just want to breathe. I'm suffocating. It feels like someone's shoving a sock down my throat instead of giving me an oxygen tank. I couldn't remember my mom's number yesterday. Still can't. That elephant is still on my chest. Why, I should've butchered the sucker!

On plane flying to Texas. Randy major pressure. I'm so done. Would rather be dead and that's pretty serious since I love life. (There's my warped sense of humor.)

I will adjust in a different way. Everywhere I turn people are talking. Sure is hard. Just want a normal life to breathe and enjoy. Really tough for me. I'm responsible for changing that thought. Inside myself is a place where I live alone. And that's where You renew Your spring that never dries up.

As the tears flow down my cheeks at the table in Applebee's in Ocala, a hand reaches over and grabs mine. I apologize.

"It's okay to cry," Kristen tells me.

I see her pale hand on mine and then see the joyful smile looking at me. A heart waiting to hear more about *me*, about *my* life, about *my* pain. Kristen is patient and keeps telling me how much it means to hear what I'm sharing. She understands the pain of broken love.

My daughter is battling a fatal disease, and yet here she is, letting all of that go and being in the moment. It astounds me.

She doesn't care about having a career or looking too far into the future, a future she can't control, a future she's given over to God. She can just let it go.

Can you just let it go, Paula?

Not once—ever—has she complained or questioned this disease. She's never shown any fear. Surely she has fears. She's not superhuman. Yet every sign shows no trace.

That's what real faith looks like.

This is a precious experience, the moments that will mean something to me for the rest of my life. Teaching moments. The kind where God's getting my attention and telling me not to process everything and not to let the anger of others distract from the love right in front of me. We laugh and we cry, and I discover that it doesn't have to take you fifty years to learn how to live life with grace and with gratitude. It's only taken Kristen twenty-eight.

I've been writing my book for the last several years—all the while believing that someway, somehow my marriage will make it. Finally I have a release date, and my book tour is set to include ten cities in three days. Ironically, and despite the hope I'd had for us, I start the tour right as Randy announces our divorce.

Even though my new book, *You're All That!*, is written to equip readers to conquer pain and build a strong sense of self through principles that have transformed my own life, most everybody I meet seems to want to help *me*. Woman after woman greet me not as if they're at a book signing but rather as if they're standing in line at a wake. Many will give me a popular marriage book as I sign my new release for them.

"Pastor Paula—you gotta stay married!"

All I can do is smile and say thank you. Those who know Randy and me, the so-dubbed Ken and Barbie behind the pulpit, are mourning. They just don't know I've been doing the same thing for the past three years.

It's hard to be promoting a book encouraging others to live a bold and dynamic life filled with love and joy when it seems like my own life is anything but.

Naturally the media wants to raise questions. Most will come from the venomous ink printed by the *Tampa Tribune,* which is waging a war against

Randy, slamming him. Forty-nine articles, to be exact. All of them mention me, of course, since I'm his wife and a public figure. There is a lot of slander and malice with an occasional bit of slanted truth. A woman who formerly worked closely with Randy for years and who had a falling out with him has gone to the *Tampa Tribune,* so the attacks seem personal in nature.

The irony of our divorce is all the people who don't even realize I'm married. Randy is never on my program and he's rarely around, so unless you're a local in Tampa, you might not even know we were a couple to begin with. But this doesn't stop the media from asking the same sort of questions as I'm promoting the new book. In my live interview on CNN with Larry King, he addresses all the big ones.

"What did end the marriage?" he asks.

"Oh, boy, that's a large question. But I think—"

"Because you didn't answer it in the address, did you?"

"No. But no one goes into a marriage—when I went into my marriage eighteen years ago, I thought I'd end my life with Randy. And the divorce is nothing that I ever wanted to happen. And so when you say, what made it, I don't know if you can say this was the one thing. Because even—there are crucial things that cause fractures, breaks, whatever in relationships. But no one throws a life away, Larry."

It's not only impossible to explain everything in an interview like this, but I'm not going to say anything or even give hints for others to speculate about. I can't go into the account of Noah and his sons—Shem, Ham, and Japheth—and how you can't uncover your father's nakedness (Gen. 9:20–27). That would take longer, would be out of context, but that lesson is what I believe. God is the judge. I'm not going to judge Randy or anybody, because I don't judge myself. It's not my place to destroy or dishonor Randy and bring our family further hurt, so I won't.

The other questions arise as well, ones that have nothing to do with my new book. There is the familiar comment about my appeal to African Americans. My political stance. And then there's the big one I knew would be coming up.

"Senator Grassley, as you know, is investigating many televangelists, especially those who made a great deal of money, and the question of whether they should get a tax break," Larry King says. "A former staffer of Without Walls International Church criticized it—the part of—you're a part of it, saying: 'It has become all about mansions, planes, money, and fame.'"

This inquiry was only announced three weeks ago. Six ministries including ours have been asked to divulge financial information to the Senate committee to see if any of the funds have been inappropriately used. I reply in a broad way, talking about the current laws and the legal jurisdictions, about how everything we do is legal and can be justified. At the time, none of us knew what brought this targeted inquiry on. I'm advised by my attorneys not to speak about it. We are fully compliant and give them everything they ask for. It is a public relations nightmare, not financial impropriety. We ask for the judicial branch, which should have proper oversight, to come take a look. There is nothing to hide and no wrongdoing, but perception can be more powerful than reality.

Years later, I discover the truth of what a bitter person who is out to get someone can do to others. Eventually we are all advised to submit ourselves to a Christian organization to hold ourselves ethically accountable, and that will be the end of it with a wake of damage done in people's minds that find you guilty, not only before you are tried, but when there isn't even a trial.

Even when I'm finally able to talk about the book, the subject veers back to money.

"Does it ever bother you at all to know that your organization makes a lot of money? Does that bother you, as opposed to an oil company or a bus company?"

"Larry, to fulfill what we are called to do, if you go on the website, you will see that over eighty cents of every dollar—I think it was maybe eighty-three cents to eighty-seven cents—went straight back to missions, outreach, and evangelism. So if I really believe that we are blessed to be a blessing..."

I sum up a small percentage of what we're doing in the community and with children and with the poor and with prisons. They're simple sound bites. The stories that are being told with the lives being helped—that is the reason and the purpose. I tell these stories all the time. They are the stories that matter, the lives that are being changed and transformed by the power of a loving Savior. Nevertheless, they are not the stories people want to hear.

The lyrics from Don Henley's "Dirty Laundry" are ringing in my head: "Kick 'em when they're up, kick 'em when they're down..."

People want the juicy, the dirty laundry, not the truth or feel-good stuff.

I explain to Larry, "If you look at major companies who are doing wonderful things, and they give their portfolio billions of dollars that they make and they give away ten million dollars or so, when you start putting the percentages there, what we are doing is significant."

"You have nothing to be sorry about?" he asks.

"I have nothing to be sorry about. In fact, the very opposite. I'm extremely proud of the ability to really go forth and minister."

The climax of everything seems to be hitting me at once. I can't breathe. I feel like I'm being asphyxiated. I'm spent. I'm so exhausted. I'm so distraught over Kristen.

For a brief moment of time, our family is elated to hear that Kristen's tumor is gone, but only weeks later the doctors discover the cancer in her brain has intensified and spread all over. She goes to spend time with Debbie in Ocala, but soon her situation is so critical that Randy and Debbie decide to get her down to Mexico for the absolute last option in getting help.

On the recommendation of my attorney, after the divorce and facing an unknown Senate inquiry, I moved to Texas. On their way to Mexico for a desperate and hopeful medical treatment, Debbie and Kristen fly into San Antonio so I can see them. Kristen is mostly paralyzed. I don't realize this is the last time I will ever see her conscious. Only a few days after reaching Mexico, Kristen falls into a coma. And after getting back to the U.S., to hospice care in Tampa, she remains on life support for the remainder of her life.

All of this leaves me devastated and drained. Yet this only makes me think of those times I've been on the phone, saying the same thing to Kristen. Her voice would always sound so natural and normal on the phone, just like any conversation we'd have over the years. She'd ask me how I was doing, and I'd tell her how tired I was and how I was having a tough time with everything. She'd listen, and then eventually she'd be talking and slip in how she needed to drop off Drew and Emma and then go get chemo. I'd feel my head and heart drop. I'm preaching and flying to four cities and I'm tired?

How can she possess such joy and embrace it? How can my daughter minister so much to me in her greatest time of need?

With so many things in April of 2008 hitting and attacking me, I put the internal brakes on. I finally say NO. So many issues and problems, including the Senate inquiry into Without Walls, have to be dealt with. But I can't do everything. I can't say yes to everything. Not now. Not anymore.

While spending some time with Kristen back in Tampa, I'm still aghast at the life that's being taken from her. She is dying quickly before our very eyes, yet life outside of this room continues and makes its selfish demands.

We all deal with life crises in our own ways. I just know my life belongs to you, Lord. I love you, Lord. That is a fact that will never change no matter what crisis comes.

Randy and I are not on good talking terms at this point. I'm trying not to become bitter or bruised over all that has happened. I pour out my toxins in my journals and give them over to the Lord. Daily. Hourly.

My heart is broken because of Kristen. Yet she reminds me I need to deeply appreciate life.

April 29, 2008

I'm sitting in hospital with K. We bring her home tomorrow. My heart is heavier than it's ever been. I really feel like I've aged—I need to get it together and move on with LIFE. Because I do have a life and I can move on.

I CAN move on.

I look at the pictures in her hospital room, ones when she had a life.

I promise... I will preserve those memories.

She can't move on, so I sit here with many mixed emotions.

Why do I fret over things that don't really matter? Why do I choose to live less when I have more?

I still have life and that in itself is a gift. I still feel even if it's pain.

I hurt, but that gives opportunity for God to heal.

I want to navigate this course set before me successfully.

I want to be able to see with clarity the end and chart my course appropriately.

So paint a picture, Paula...

Brad is my heartbeat. He knows me fundamentally so well. He's not aware of all the details so he misprocesses and misdiagnoses me at times, but he sure does know me. I'm proud of him. He's strong. He has an inner fortitude and stamina. His dark side scares me sometimes. Only from concern and fear. I want the best for him. He is so dang smart. Really smart.

Angie is amazing—I genuinely respect her. She's truly a nurturing caregiver—how blessed Kristen is to have her. My Goodness—I can only imagine what Angie's going through. She's Kristen's love, her anchor and her other half. She's amazing—I deeply love and respect her.

Brandon—I am very proud of him and the man he is becoming—sometimes I'm scared for him—I see the shell that he wears at times. I hope he finds his substance. It's there. It's in him. He is searching and longing. God show him who he is, be with him, and keep him always. May he find his own way and fulfill his purpose. I love him so much.

I love my kids. I really, really love them.

I wonder if I was in that bed what would the dynamics be? Good question.

Lord: My numero uno. I love you. We got a thing going on. Keep me. You know I'm yours. I love you forever.

P

Kristen passes away at 2:32 p.m. on April 30, 2008.

The memorial for her is beautiful in many ways. It's held on the beach. I will always remember the white carnations, the sunset, the slide show, and the tension.

They play her favorite songs. There are so many smiles. Angie looks as beautiful as her heart when she stands and talks about Kristen. Brandon and Brad both have joy on their faces even during this heart-wrenching time. I know Randy is carrying hurt and guilt that I can't imagine.

Yesterday, Brandon asked right after Kristen passed away if anyone had any regrets. I'm never sure how to handle that question. I've always tried to do what I'm capable of doing in life with where I am or what I know. But regrets?

Do I regret putting all my eggs in one basket? Loving a Lord so much and so hard that I missed some of the other moments because I wasn't more evenly distributed? Or do I say I've had something most people won't experience in a lifetime?

Where does my life go? How will it end up? All I know is that my life belongs to the Lord. It's not random, but it's fabricated and fashioned by God.

Kristen's life shows me that I need to fulfill my life's purpose and to embrace its beauty. And to never, ever settle.

I need to live life to its fullest. To choose never to live beneath but to take the path to the top.

I love and trust the Lord.

On my way back home from Kristen's funeral, I am in the back of the plane by myself with tears running down my face. I'm emotionally exhausted, feeling like life has been drained out of me with the death of our daughter.

My assistant, Andrea, is sitting near the front, letting me grieve by myself. Brian, who's been my pilot forever, is in the cockpit hearing my heaving, heavy cries.

It's so unnatural for a child to die before you do.

This is an area of my life I won't talk about, that I will put in a vault and lock away. The pain and the ugliness and the mess and the sadness.

Kristen's life shines bigger than that. Her Lord and Savior bursts through the ugly muck and grime.

Sprawled out at the back of the plane, in one of the deepest pits imaginable, feeling this searing pain inside, it all overcomes me. The loss of Kristen and the disintegration of my marriage. All the tension. All the lies. All the ridiculousness. I know there will be moments I can never get back.

Then all at once, just like that, peace pours over me. I don't instantly stop crying, nor does the grief simply vanish. Yet I'm covered with this blanket of calm. I understand more than ever before what a peace that passeth all understanding truly means.

In a moment where I'm lying on the floor, experiencing as overwhelming a sadness as I've ever felt in my life, a kind that makes everybody else afraid to even be near me, I am suddenly overcome with tranquility in a truly supernatural way. My assistant and the pilot can see what's happened, that something divine has occurred.

This is not Paula emerging from the ashes. This is God's Word alive in me. There's always something that's going to cause it to come out. There will always—always—*always*—be the comfort of the Holy Spirit. There is nothing else that can take away the depth of this pain.

Kristen...your life teaches me we're never guaranteed any moment. It will cause me to wake up every day with gratitude. Even on those days when I'm off, I'll be able to say my issues out loud and be done with them. I won't hold things in. I won't let them stew inside. I have to move on. I have to let things go.

I will strive not to fret over things that don't really matter and to appreciate all the good things. And I will thank God for all the good things in my life. Just like Kristen always did.

14.

LIFE

Life will constantly remind you what you long for and what you lack. The little things you never got to see. The love that somehow kept leaving you behind. The light that doesn't wait at the end of the tunnel, but rather exists right there in your living room.

On Christmas day of 2007, I'm in San Antonio spending the day with friends at their house. Brad is with me, but our other children are back in Florida with their father. I miss them dearly.

In the afternoon, I hear the familiar chords of "Sweet Home Alabama" and walk into the living room to see everybody gathered around a large-screen TV. They're watching a video that someone made. A man in his forties and his twenty-something daughter are having fun, dancing to the Lynyrd Skynyrd song and playing air guitar while cracking each other up. It's an incredible sight. This is the power of music, the beauty it brings, its ability to cause people to come together and make memories just like this.

Watching the video of the daddy-daughter dance containing so much life and levity and laughter, I have this realization that stings my soul. There, right in front of my eyes...

I've been looking for this picture all my life.

The father is giddy as he guides his girl along while jamming to the song.

"Sweet home Alabama. Lord, I'm coming home to you."

Watching their interaction overwhelms me. It's a bond I've never, ever known.

Paula, I'm so sorry you missed so much of that, I tell myself.

I didn't know what it looked like, so I tried to design it, but how could I? I'd never seen it before.

That eighteen-year-old girl holding her precious new son. I wanted to be a mother, to be a wife, to have a family. That twenty-four-year-old woman embracing her precious faith. I still wanted to be a mother, to be a wife, to have a family, and to do it the *right* way as directed by my Heavenly Father. To have stability and to be strong. But I began with so little knowledge and information.

Even as a forty-one-year-old, I realize there's so much I don't know. So many things that are still foreign, that my entire childhood missed: the love of a father. The smell of home-cooked meals. The warmth of a family. The joy of a clan. What a kitchen full of family members is all about.

That is life.

Teach me, Lord. Teach me. I want a real experience of what you designed as family.

I think of what I said in the introduction to my first *New York Times* best-selling book, how I'll consider myself successful if my husband stands before God and says, "I have a great wife." And my children call me blessed. My greatest desire wasn't for a career or a ministry. I never thought I'd have any of that. I loved God and wanted to be a wife and a mother.

I know it sounds crazy after everything that's happened, but I still long for that, God. It is what it is. I love you, Lord. Thank you for everything.

It's pitch black and barren just beyond my backyard. The steady wobble of the Texas cicadas sounds like my thoughts, never silent, never bothering to stop to rest. I stare out into the wilderness with wonder, wonder at God and how He works and how He woos me.

I think of how far I've come since I stood at the pulpit before 11,000 people for the first time at Carpenter's Home in 1993. I closed my eyes and saw

Moses standing between the dead and the living. I asked the question I find myself asking again: "Can one person make a difference in the world?"

I've tried to, Lord. I've tried.

I'm a long way from the shores of Tampa. The hill country home forty minutes north of San Antonio is a perfect place for this time in my life. I've converted one of its two bedrooms into my office. This is a sanctuary during this period of mourning and transition. It's the summer of 2008. I'm still grieving the loss of Kristen and, really, the loss of a former life. The brokenness during 2004 and 2005 were the toughest years for me, so the divorce in 2007 wasn't as shocking to my system as it was for others. But the impact and strain of the split won't go away for years.

I think of forty-year-old Moses, only a couple years younger than me, escaping to the wilderness to live out his days on the backside of the desert. What happens during the next forty years of his life? Why is it undocumented? My take is God basically is telling us, "That's none of your business." I wonder if this will be my gap period, too. And if so, will it last forty years as well?

There are many nights when I cry myself to sleep. It's not the same sort of cry I had in 2004 and 2005. It's a kind brought to the surface by the end of an era, by a closure to many things. My entire environment has changed. My family and friends are no longer nearby. I've never been alone since I married at eighteen. For the first time in my life, I find myself on nights like this in the wilderness by myself. Just God and me.

Maybe that's what you want, Lord.

Paula White Ministries is still functioning. I'm still being strategic, regularly going on live TV to preach to the general public, just to show them I'm still here and I'm doing okay. I'll do a certain number of appearances where I simply focus on the Word. I still need to remain out there in some capacity. By now I know something in ministry and in life. You can never assume you're not dispensable. You're *absolutely* dispensable to people, not to God.

I think about being eighteen and seeing all the nations shaken when I open my mouth. So when I begin to preach and when Without Walls becomes bigger and Paula White Ministries explodes, I assume this is the way it will happen. This is how God is going to do that. But now everything's being shaken in other ways.

So how's God going to do it now? How's He going to use me?

I know I'm a child of God. That's solid and that's never been questioned. And I know God's ways are not our ways.

But my purpose...

I've been so used to knowing it and walking in it for so long.

I don't recognize it and realize it at the moment, but I'm in a radical disorientation that will bring a creative transformation in my life. Like every birth, there will be some pain and labor involved.

Alone in Texas for a year, I will begin again.

I will ride horses and simply breathe in the air outside and embrace the sun settling down on my skin. I start to feel again, and feeling is part of healing.

I ride motorcycles and even buy a Harley. Day by day I feel a little less numb. The anesthesia is wearing off. My head is finally starting to get straight again. It's never been off with God; during the hardest times, I ran toward Him. I also had my mom. She is there every step, supporting, encouraging, and loving me. Sometimes we talk ten times a day. She visits often, or I will go visit her.

I still make my trips to the church in New York every month. I'm preaching several times a month, but this is quite different from having four hundred speaking events in a year. I realize there are many other ways to do ministry. The year 2008 *could* be my year of starting an Angry Women Against Men ministry, because so many supporters of mine are suddenly showing up and sharing their fury at what's happened in their lives. But I won't go there. Maybe I'll go back and finish my degree in psychology, then open a counseling office. Or perhaps I'll open a shelter for abused children. I know ministry is a lot more than being behind a pulpit. I will figure it out.

Some things don't change, of course. Like my time with the Lord every day. Studying and journaling. I also continue to read. After the divorce, I walk away from everything except my books. I have to keep those. I continue to pore over self-help and entrepreneurial books I've never read while rereading the favorites I do every year. Resources like *Boundaries* by Henry Cloud and John Townsend, *The Pathway* by Laurel Mellin, and *The Lost Art of Listening* by Michael P. Nichols. Even though this is a transformational time in my life, I still can't force myself to read a novel. A book still has to have a tangible takeaway for me; the book has to inspire readers to do something.

How in the world would I ever begin to write my own memoir? How could I compose a book without creating discussion questions and bullet points?

Life is more enjoyable, and I try to accept that. I go out to eat more and have my first glass of wine in 2007. I never go crazy. That's not in my DNA, whether God came into my life or not.

I'm working out every side of me. Maybe in some cases, I'm making up what I feel my pregnant eighteen-year-old self might have lost by not going to college and not experiencing adulthood on my own. I never veer off the deep end. There's no wild sex escapades, or parties, or drugs. But okay, fine, there will be some rock and roll. I will be out of character, because for once in my life I won't have a set and rigid schedule. I work from home in my sweatpants and no makeup. Randy would tell me to get ready and put some clothes on if I ever dared to do that when we were married. *Everything* is changing with me.

This is the third phase of my creative transformation, the phase of my return. The person I am isn't the same one who left on a radical journey years ago. I'm becoming someone else, someone authentic, someone truly me. This true self is valuable and unchangeable. I have authentic wisdom to share with others. Not just biblical knowledge and God's heart inside of mine, but I have the story of the work God has done inside me that He will continue to do through me.

Out of this journey, I finally find true strength to offer others for a common good. I find my way to the true Paula.

It's amazing to think of the people God brings into your life and the moments He chooses that to happen. In the middle of the circling winds of change in Texas, a stranger will contact me out of the blue and give me one of the greatest gifts and blessings I'll ever receive.

Henry Dodge is a wealthy businessman from Tupelo who owns a collection of convenience stores/gas stations. He is also a strong Christian who happens to own the church Elvis used to be a part of. He's heard of Pastor Paula White but only recently realized I'm the daughter of his childhood friend Peckie. When he calls me, he explains that he and my father were once best friends.

"I've heard you tell your story publicly," he says to me over the phone. "I feel God told me to show you who your father was."

After Henry flies into San Antonio to meet me, he says he's felt this responsibility to give me some insight into my father and to share how deeply he loved me, so he's put together a video on Peckie's life to share with me. Even though he and my dad drifted apart after high school, Henry was heartbroken when he learned of my father's death. He spends a lot of time and money years later investigating whether Peckie did indeed commit suicide. He'll confirm the truth I already know, that my father had gotten himself into a very dark place before he took his life. Yet when I sit down and watch the video with Henry, I see a celebration of a life.

A life I've never known.

Suddenly I see pictures I've never seen and hear stories I've never heard. I've grown up with barely any photos or anything belonging to my father. Now in this video I'm seeing so much and hearing from childhood friends talking about Peckie with fondness and admiration.

I've always wondered where I came from and why I acted the way I did. I've always felt like some kind of alien in a land where I don't belong. Yes, I've done things my way, diving into this faith with a drive that won't be stopped, with a passion that makes them think I'm a Jesus freak. I've understood that part of myself because it's my mom.

Now I know the other side. I've always understood the left hand, but now I can make sense of the right hand that comes from my dad. Peckie, the big giver and the big lover who would always buy everybody's meal and always was generous. The one to win over everybody in the room and probably buy them a drink. Yes, there was a dark side to my father, but the enemy can find all of our dark sides and make us bleed if we're not careful. Peckie's dark side wasn't a mean one. Lonely? Yes. But always the life of the party and always caring.

Things make sense. So much sense. Questions that have lingered in my heart suddenly become answered. Pieces fall into place.

My father grew up always having a caretaker. He lived in a house that people always took care of. He always had new toys, even when grown, like a new car and membership to a new country club. He's the life of the party, the instigator, the rebel with a cause. Sure, he's six feet, two inches tall, a good-looking and charismatic man. But now I really understand how he won over my brother and mom and married her in ten days.

I hear how my father used to sneak into the black dance halls. It was segregated Mississippi, yet my father didn't see African Americans as any different than himself. Again, this explains how colorblind I am when I look out at the world. And why I love to dance so much.

At the end of the video, as I wipe away the tears and look at the photo montage, the stirring "Clair de Lune" by Debussy plays in the background.

I get it all now. I get it.

I thank Henry Dodge for this incredible gift. He has brought closure to so many questions. The video is not only cathartic, but it's insightful. For so many years, I've been haunted with all these questions. Who was he, and how'd I get to be like this? But now I understand. I have a greater understanding of who I came from. I get it. I get it all.

Like everything God does, there is a purpose in the timing of this.

The video Henry Dodge shares about my father makes me look at my own life, the story of the last twenty-four years.

Since I was eighteen years old, I feel God put a "Not For Sale" sign on me. I feel I've known my place and purpose. God tells me to document my life, so I pour into my journals on a consistent basis. The first $10,000 I can ever borrow, I do, and I invest in a Christian learning library filled with commentaries and books on biblical history. Those who know me think I'm crazy, but I tell them I know where I'm going, so I have to prepare. I'm going to see nations shaken. At the time, I remember very clearly God telling me something:

Don't ever let anybody own your voice.

I've always believed I was advancing the Kingdom of God, that I was making a difference for someone. All of a sudden, I find I'm not just fighting for my marriage and my ministry. I discover a war is being waged for my purpose.

My greatest blessing will come with the ground beneath me rumbling and the walls around me shaking. God loves me enough to allow every temporary thing in my life to crumble enough and reduce me to Christ.

At the end, when I'm threatened that I'll lose everything, I know this one fact: I won't lose my identity. I still have a plan and a purpose. I still serve a loving God.

On a beautiful and peaceful day in San Antonio, not long after learning so much about my father and letting it sink in, I finally realize the truth.

For so long I've been wondering how things are going to turn out now that I'm not performing and trying to land every single jump I'm making for God. But I'm reminded it's not about me and my works.

For so long I've realized every time a chapter closes in my life, I go out and write another one. That's why I've been struggling so much since coming to Texas.

Forty-two years, and I can still be so thickheaded. So many years, yet I'm still figuring out the obvious:

What God wants most is me.

All this time, I've been wondering what's going to happen next. What if I don't preach again? What if I never build up His church again? What about the mission God gave that eighteen-year-old girl? What about the promises He put inside her heart? Those ten thousand what-ifs that I'm wondering whether I'll ever do... These rocks of questions I think I've been building to cross to my next place of purpose have actually only been constructed to be a towering wall around me. And in an instant they tumble down like a stone wall crushed with a battering ram.

I am reminded once more. Yes, oh yes, God really does love me.

God is where He has always been. He's not shutting the door and leaving me. Instead, He's torn down these self-imposed walls I've built around myself, rendering them into dust and letting me see His sweet smile and loving arms when it finally all settles.

"I'm the one who decides where the paragraph ends and where a new chapter starts. I'm the one writing the story. Don't ever forget, Paula."

PART THREE

A DIVINE PURPOSE

15.

CONNECTION

This is one of those moments; seemingly minuscule at the time in 2001, it is monumental in the bigger picture that God allows me to see. Danny Withum, my executive director at Paula White Ministries, or PWM, walks into my office in the administration building of Without Walls International Church. He oversees all the media and basically everything happening at Paula White Ministries. We're the primary people running PWM, along with the CFO and COO; Danny reports to me.

Sometimes the Holy Spirit taps your shoulder and tugs on your arm. It's gentle, like a loved one's hand guiding you through a busy crowd while crossing a Manhattan street. The problem is most of us can't feel this because there's too much noise in our lives.

Noise is something I'm starting to know quite well. To say there's a lot of it in my life is an understatement. Ever since signing the $1.2 million contract with Black Entertainment Television in 1999, my face and my voice are starting to show up everywhere. *Paula White Today* has become a hit on BET, and Paula White Ministries is buying a significant amount of airtime that will eventually lead to spending about $8 million a year in airtime reaching 98 percent of the households in the United States and hundreds of millions of homes around the world. Our efforts here are going to build to produce five programs a week, with two secular shows and three Christian shows. In many ways I'll be oversaturating the market, in which my show is broadcast everywhere from FOX, WGN, CTN, and daily on TBN, Daystar, The Word Network, and many others. We hit a variety of demographics, from country music fans watching CMT to younger audiences tuned in to MTV and Spike TV, to women watching Oxygen.

We're still in the beginning of this incredible growth. The commotion and clamor are out there, but for me, God is keeping those things at bay.

God says, "If you prepare, I will send opportunity to you." I know the key to having vision is receiving spiritual eyes from the Holy Spirit.

This is how I approach PWM from the time I start it in 1999. Two years later, I still make decisions with a step-by-step process that matches our mission statement of transforming lives, healing hearts, and saving souls. So when Danny first asks me whether we should pick up another low-powered station, I instantly disregard the notion. My very human side weighs in on the decision, as I doubt whether it will be worth the cost.

"Where's it shown?" I ask him.

"Fort Lauderdale, West Palm, and some lower parts of South Florida," Danny says.

"We're talking TVs with rabbit ears," I reply, speaking from my pragmatic mind and heart. "How much is it?"

"Three hundred a month."

For our ministry at the time this isn't a big expense, especially considering that putting our show on BET every Tuesday morning at seven-thirty a.m. costs $23,500.

I just laugh. "Danny, you know me. I don't care if it's three dollars. I'm not spending three hundred dollars a month if we don't need to."

Both of us know I will always be a good steward with my money, and that goes back to when I was five years old and suddenly our family lost everything.

But Your way, Lord, and not my way. It's Your thoughts and not our thoughts.

Then as Danny walks toward the door to leave I recall everything in an instant, about God telling me to go on television despite all the odds stacked against me. I did this in obedience to the voice of God.

God says to prepare not for where you've been and not for where you are but to grab a hold of something that's bigger than you.

"Danny, come back here."

I feel the Holy Spirit telling me this is important, as clearly as I felt Him telling me to step out and go onto television, and as vividly as I felt being called to reach out to BET.

"Let's sign the contract."

God says if you prepare, He will send opportunity to you.

Every time I fly into New York, it takes my breath away. I am inspired and awakened when I see the sprawling metropolis's skyline, considering how imagination, dreams, and determination built one of the world's most populous megacities—an international cultural, financial, and media hub. I feel a spark inside the moment my heels hit the city sidewalks. This is my safe haven, a place where I ultimately find myself. I regain my confidence here. During the height of Paula White Ministries, here is where I end up rediscovering myself during such a critical time.

There's an irony to this: I find peace in the most chaotic city. I love this place.

You can't help but notice the name Trump is present on so many buildings. Fourteen years before he is elected president, I meet Donald Trump.

God uses him greatly in my life, just as I will be used in his.

The director of my executive office hand delivers this opportunity one morning. To say this comes out of the blue is quite the understatement.

"Mr. Trump's on the line," Stacy Crane tells me.

I can't help but laugh, thinking this is some kind of joke. "He's on the line? Yeah, right."

I'm used to getting calls from famous people. This isn't something I've ever sought. Becoming a pastor, starting a ministry, and going on television, I've never pursued the company of notable athletes, musicians, or any public personality. The celebrities I've already met are no different than anybody else. I respect their gifts and talent and the work it takes to succeed in their industries. I come to have a special spot in my heart for them after seeing how lonely and often misunderstood they can feel at the top.

When I answer the phone, Trump's receptionist, Robin, is holding for me to get on the line. She connects me and Mr. Trump.

"Paula, this is Donald Trump. I just wanted to call and say I think you're fantastic. I've been watching your program. You have the *it* factor."

The last thing I could have imagined when I woke up this morning and had my quiet time with the Lord was having the businessman behind all those skyscrapers and hotels and casinos telling me I have the *it* factor.

What in the world is he doing watching Christian television?

"Thank you," I say.

"I really enjoyed your recent sermon about vision. Vision is the bridge that takes you from the present into your future. How you have to write out the vision and make it clear and then you have to implement it."

He's literally quoting my sermon.

I grab a legal notepad and start jotting down notes as he is talking to me. Trump mentions two other recent messages of mine and is able to quote them almost verbatim. Part of me still half believes someone is pulling my leg, that this is some elaborate joke and the punch line is coming any moment.

"I love listening to Billy Graham and Jimmy Swaggart. They're some of the best preachers I've ever heard. Norman Vincent Peale is another. I've been to his church in the city and I've gotten to know him."

Trump starts to tell me about very specific sermons Peale has preached, giving specific illustrations the preacher used almost verbatim. His memory amazes me.

"He has to be one of the best storytellers and orators to ever get behind a pulpit, the way he makes the Bible come alive," he tells me. "Some guys aren't like that. I go to their church and they are done in seven minutes and, quite frankly, they're boring." I am smiling as he dissects different preachers, their delivery, and the impact each one made on him.

Praying at a service at City of Destiny.

Dad and Mom in the early 1960s.

A day with Jon and Journey.

Archbishop Duncan praying over us at our wedding.
(Credit: Jensen Larson)

Asher's Baby
Dedication.

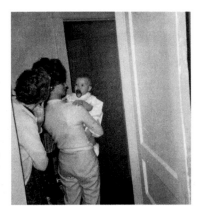

Paula, Mom, and Momma Annie.

Brad's Graduation from UT
in 2008.

Baby Paula, always destined
for television.

On my fifth birthday, Daddy gave me a ballerina cake and a jewelry box. Four days later, my life would change forever.

Eric and Lara Trump and me at a Journey concert.

Fun teenage days!

Family together at
Mom's house.

First female clergy to pray at
a presidential inauguration.

First trip on Air
Force One!

Thad Riley and me at our tenth-grade prom.

G-Pa and his little chef, Asher.

Uncle Butch, who led me to the Lord when I was eighteen.

Having fun with my grandson Nicholas.

Six-month-old Brad and me.

Ivanka Trump, my friend and world-changer.

Dean with two-year-old Brad.

Jon and me ministering together—Restoration—God is faithful!

Jon and me on the Journey and Def Leppard Tour in 2018—over one million tickets sold!

Jon and me visiting President Trump in the Oval Office.

Jon wiping away my tears of joy on our wedding day.
(Credit: Jensen Larson)

Junior high school softball.

TBN with Zonelle Thompson, at the Hope 4 LA Crusade in 1994.

My family's Christmas picture in 2003.

My mini-me, Asher, and me.

Me holding baby Nicholas, my heart.

Ministering in South Korea, 2017.

Mom and me in Memphis, ready to go antiquing.

Mr. Trump, Melania, and me in 2004—one of our first meetings.

Pam Anderson and Kid Rock backstage at my LA Crusade.

Our first wedding—Ghana, December 2014.

Los Angeles Life Design Crusade, 2005.

A water baptism on Power Night at City of Destiny.

President Trump and me at the Kennedy Center.

Shooting a *Paula Today* video with Sheila at a New York photo shoot.

The glamour photo shoot—
a gift from Tyra Banks.

A photo shoot is a wonderful gift from Tyra Banks!

Ministering at Woman Thou Art Loosed, 2000.

Safari Nights Charity Ball.

Paula White Ministries Magazine, 2007.

Taping *Paula Today* in New York with Mr. Trump and Robert Kiyosaki.

The Girls: Rachel, Mom, me, and Rachael.

Altar call at a Life by Design crusade.

Praying for a young man at a Table in the Wilderness Outreach—Tampa, Florida.

White House listening session, 2016.

Ronnie, Mom, and me with Rachel and Brad.

Brad, Rachel, and Asher, with Nicholas on the way.

Me on *The Steve Harvey Show.*

Praying over my grandchildren—dedicating them to the Lord.

Vacation with "my baby" in St. Barts.

There's something unique about the way I deliver my messages that strikes him. From a theological standpoint, I know I stand somewhere in the middle between Swaggart's *fire and brimstone* and Graham's *only by the grace of God*. I personally believe that what Trump finds intriguing is simply God's presence in my sermons.

We talk for a half hour about spirituality and God. As always, just as I'd be with anybody calling to talk about their lives, I remain respectful and I listen more than I speak.

"We went to First Presbyterian Church over in Queens. I was confirmed there. My mother gave me my first Bible when I was eight. We went to Sunday school every weekend. Later on we started to attend Norman Vincent Peale's church. We never missed a Sunday. There was no one like him. He made the Bible come alive." He continues, "Did you know Robert Schuller came out of his ministry? Have you ever seen the Crystal Cathedral? It's amazing."

Beneath everything spoken, I can sense his fascination and how he's drawn to spiritual things.

He's longing to know more.

I speak to the man on the phone. That's the only aspect I can talk to. Not the business mogul calling from Manhattan. A feeling of excitement fills me. Our conversation is genuine and enjoyable, leaving me supercharged; I know not every conversation will do that.

"Are you ever in New York?" Trump asks.

"Yes. I'm starting to come there more often. I've been doing a small, informal Bible study with some of the Yankees."

"Next time you're up here, I'd love to take you to lunch."

Before he hangs up, I can't help asking him one of the many things I'm curious about: "Did you catch my show up in New York?"

"No. I watch it when I'm at Mar-a-Lago. I was changing the channels late one night and I saw you preaching on some local station."

When I get off the line, I am energized and encouraged by the unexpected phone call.

God's using Paula White Ministries to bless someone like Donald Trump.

I smile, knowing God always has a plan. I believe good things are to come with our thriving ministry.

"I need you to set me up etiquette lessons," I tell my assistant one day not long after talking to Trump.

She smiles and asks me why.

"Because God is preparing me for places. And because I don't believe in coincidences. Nothing is coincidental."

This is shortly after talking with Donald Trump on the phone and shortly before learning I'll be having lunch with him at Jean-Georges. When my first meeting with Trump is set, I can't even pronounce the name of the restaurant at the Trump Hotel where we'll meet. Jean-Georges Vongerichten is a two-Michelin-starred chef, which only serves to make me more anxious about how little I know about this world. It's *way* out of my league, so I diligently do my part to prepare for this meeting.

I'll always be the girl waking up at four in the morning to practice my back handsprings until I master them. This isn't something I will master immediately; the environment and culture will take time to absorb and understand. All I can do is my part to learn more about it.

After I meet Trump and his staff in his office on the twenty-sixth floor of Trump Tower, we leave for the crowded restaurant, where he knows everyone. My assistant and his security accompany us to Jean-Georges and sit at a separate table, while we are seated at a center table.

When I open the menu, I don't understand any of it. When I'm not familiar with something new, I learn by watching those around me. Yet Mr. Trump asks me to go first when the server comes to take our drink order. There is an extensive wine list, but when I'm asked whether I'd like any, I politely say, "No, thank you." When I do, I notice Trump's expression seems to say *that's interesting*. The server doesn't ask whether he would like wine, and as I'll later learn, Trump doesn't drink.

I don't do this just because I'm a pastor or simply because I'm religious. I've never had a drink in my life up to this point, nor have I ever smoked a cigarette or touched a drug.

The menu seems to be in another language. Nine courses? I let Trump order. With all these forks, spoons, and knives in front of me, I still feel unsure about what to do—despite the etiquette lessons. I just know the food that comes is amazing. And I'm not sitting here by coincidence.

In the Hebrew language, there's no such word as *coincidence*. As a believer in surrender to the Lord, I believe God orders our footsteps. If every day you bind yourself to the will of God, and if every day you say, "Not my will but Your will be done," then God will truly align you with His purpose. He is the one who determines the purpose and intention He has for us. Our decisions largely determine our destiny.

The lunch with Donald Trump is just one more way God is allowing me to accomplish His purpose and the assignments He has for my life, though I won't know the full context of it at this point.

During one of our first meetings, I am bold and surprisingly candid with Trump. We laugh about this now, how up front I was back then. When Trump calls me into his office, I carry the same sort of image many have of him: the powerful, brash business mogul. So I walk in and make things very clear.

"I don't want your money; I have enough of my own. And I don't want your fame, because I have more than enough of that, too. Mr. Trump: I want your soul."

This is not how I normally approach an early meeting with anyone. In fact, this is a very unusual thing for me to do.

My desire with Trump is the same as every other person I meet: to help them know God, and if they already do, then to help them know and love God more. But this feels different. I feel God saying that Trump is "a spiritual assignment for me," that I am to pray over him daily and show him God. So I do. I put his name and those close to him on our prayer cards at the church. I stand at the altar and lift his family up to the Lord in prayer continually. Every year, our church will pass out a card titled "Top 10" where an individual lists the ten people they are going to target "for God." Without fail, Mr. Trump's name appears on my card every single year.

When I first meet Trump in 2001, my ministry is exploding and my life will soon go from craziness to chaos. I'm at a point where I feel like every person who calls, who emails, or who comes near wants and expects something from me. They want me to help solve or fix a problem. We have hundreds of staff members who are running multiple "corporations."

Deep inside of me, I want someone to simply ask, "How are you doing, Paula?" On occasion, I desire someone who doesn't want me for prayer or for answers or for a check or for anything else. Yes, I'm a pastor and a leader, but those aren't my only qualities.

To Trump I simply want to be a friend and spiritual leader who doesn't want anything. I decide with myself right away that I'll never, ever take a dime from him, nor will I ever take advantage of anything he has.

16.

CELEBRITY

In February of 2004, I hear Brad's steps pounding down the stairs and racing toward me in the kitchen.

"Really, Mom," he says, tossing a magazine down on the counter next to me. "What are you doing in here? You're my *mom*."

I pick up the *Maxim* magazine and see one of the recent photos taken in the fashion shoot I had courtesy of Tyra Banks. The accompanying article's headline reads "Sexy Televangelist."

I can't help but laugh. This only reiterates the title others often use for me: *celebrity pastor*. As far as I'm concerned, I'm just Pastor Paula.

The first real exposure I will have to celebrities occurs when professional athletes begin attending services and Bible studies at the church. Tampa is a hub for athletics, with the Tampa Bay Buccaneers winning the Super Bowl in January 2003, and the Tampa Bay Lightning capturing the Stanley Cup in 2004. Even though the Tampa Bay Rays haven't won a World Series, they have a lot of fans, and the area is full of many Major League baseball teams that come down for spring training. A lot of these players enter the doors of Without Walls.

With our church only a short drive from Raymond James Stadium, Tampa Bay Buccaneers Hardy Nickerson, Derrick Brooks, and Michael Pittman attend services, the latter two of whom played on the Buccaneers'

Super Bowl–winning team. When they begin to come to the Monday night Bible studies, other NFL pros begin to follow, some even flying in, like Deion Sanders and Michael Irvin. Players from baseball's Major Leagues also begin to come, and I develop friendships with many, including Darryl Strawberry, Gary Sheffield, Carl Everett, and their wives.

Doors and connections are natural. Like a woman I meet named Christina who lives in the Bay Area and brings several friends to my women's Bible study. We have a great conversation, and I can see she's hungry for the Lord. At the time, she's married to Hal Steinbrenner, who will go on to become the general partner and co-chairman of the New York Yankees. Not long after Christina begins to come, I'm asked to start doing a Bible study for the Yankees. Later on, that will expand to the Mets and also NBA and NFL teams. One door will open another as I begin to minister in these tight-knit circles.

There's an obvious reason I'm mentioned in the magazine and become known as a "celebrity pastor." Only a couple months earlier in December 2003, I visit Michael Jackson's Neverland Ranch and decide to take Darryl Strawberry, along with one of our associate pastors. Someone had introduced me to LaToya Jackson earlier in the year and I've ministered to her. We're invited to attend a gathering called You Are Not Alone to pray over and minister to Michael after he's charged with lewd and lascivious conduct with a child under fourteen. Around six hundred people attend the event—a combination of celebrities and a who's who of pop culture and sports—to show love and support to the entire Jackson family.

I don't go to Neverland Ranch to be seen with this group of celebrities but to offer spiritual care. Randy will articulate this quite well in an article, after being asked about our supposed support of a child molester.

"If he is guilty, he needs some type of ministry and counseling," Randy says. "And if he's not guilty, he needs some kind of ministry and counseling with all he's been through. We are not the judge. We are waiting to see the outcome."

When I arrive and meet Michael, I can see his pain. Standing in front of me is a little boy, the guy who writes songs from a tree. A part of me wonders whether he's stuck inside that eleven-year-old kid just trying to figure out life.

I'm already quite familiar with Los Angeles from my trips here during the riots a decade earlier. There are a lot of famous people at the ranch, but what surprises me is how many people seem to know me. I even see a few people looking my way whispering, "There goes Paula White." Up to this point, I haven't recognized how well known I've become. It's one thing for women at a conference to know me, since I'm speaking at the event. But these are well-known celebrities singling me out. I come to know quite a few of them, and I never make a big deal out of it.

Many times, I'm prompted by the Holy Spirit to simply ask the person if I can pray over them. That's my signature, placing my hands on someone and praying over them. I've never been shy about doing that. And it's not just the so-called famous that I experience this with. I always try to be grateful, to stop and thank people despite who they are and what they're doing. I've never known why I've been given this calling and life, but I respect it and try to steward it well. The key in life is to recognize what you've been given; out of recognition comes respect.

Growing up, the very first thing I would do after moving to a new neighborhood was to go out and find new friends. At the core of me, I've always been a relationship person. Every aspect of life is seen through these filters. God is about community. He's about relationships. I genuinely care about people and desire for them to know God in a deep and intimate way.

Life is all about your relationship equity. Want to know what your net worth looks like? It's the people around you; it's the quality of the relationships you have.

Everything to me in life boils down to relationships. First between God and me, and then through the relationships I have with others. This is the way I think and see the world and process it. I don't think, *Can I build a big church building?* I'm always asking, *Can I build up a person?*

This is how I approach ministry. I shouldn't be here only to "bless" others. If I simply bless you, I've miserably failed the will of God. If I meet you momentarily and if you leave feeling blessed, that's great. If you don't, that's okay. What I long for and desire is to build you, to disciple you. I'm here to help you locate your supreme reason for being, to discover your "why" in life and then help you fulfill it, which can only be fully revealed by the Holy Spirit.

So the whole way I think about relationships and process them is probably different than many others. This world and life and people…it's *all* about my relationship with God and with humanity and extending that to others. This goes back to those strong core values I have. In the right context, it's a beautiful thing. I have often said when I'm walking in the Spirit, I operate as a restorer; when I'm walking in the flesh, I operate as a rescuer. It can be a fine line for me. If you cut me, I bleed loyalty and commitment, which can be good qualities. Nevertheless, throughout my lifetime as I've unraveled the dysfunction of codependency, I can overextend my shelf life in some relationships and go far beyond their expiration date. God might have released me, but I don't always hear that. I have been stuck, much like Abraham was with Lot. I've had to learn some people are only for certain seasons in your life. If you try to hang on to what has been released, it's like the rocket boosters on the space shuttle. Rockets allow a spacecraft to lift off the ground by burning fuel to give it a strong enough thrust to get it into space. As the shuttle nears its orbit, the rocket boosters have to fall off or they will bring the shuttle back to the ground. Not everyone is meant to be in your life forever. This is hard for me, as a loyalist, to accept that some people are seasonal.

There's a reason I've kept the same cell phone number for twenty years, because of the plethora of people who know they can reach out to me. I tend to have really long relationships. I believe in people and always want to lift them up. For those searching, all I want to do is come alongside them and listen. For those believers seeking God, I want to ignite a fire inside them. I want everybody, both the destitute and the distinguished, to come as they are.

* * *

One day while riding with Randy, he shocks me by blaring this blistering song where someone comes screaming through the speakers introducing himself: "My name is Kiiiiiiiiiiiiiiiiiiiid. Kid Rock."

I'm mortified for a moment, because Randy's never listened to music like this. It's one of the early signs that something's going on in his life, that some sort of change has occurred. But like many of the surprises in my life, I can't imagine one of my many close relationships will be with this guy belting out, "Bawitdaba da bang da bang diggy diggy diggy shake the boogy said up jump the boogy."

Kid Rock is the persona and professional name for Robert James Ritchie, but I'll forever call him Bobby. Randy first meets him in February 2006 at one of his concerts. After that, Randy wants to introduce me to Bobby, so before another show I get to meet him. The first thing I notice is the tattoo on his left bicep that simply says "Paul." I look in his eyes and introduce my-self, then open up with him as if I've known Bobby all my life. I tell him my story automatically, about my father's suicide, and my coming to Jesus at eighteen, and everything. I can't explain why this happens. It's simply a door swinging open and boom! In two seconds, I'm deep into conversation with this long-haired rocker telling my testimony.

Bobby is really quiet and listens attentively as I share with him. Usually it takes me a while to open up to people, so this is very unlike me. I tend to be very observant and extremely guarded, yet now I'm open and honest and vulnerable with this stranger. Perhaps it's because I want him to hear about the ministry he's had in the lives of Randy and me.

"I have to tell you something. I owe you," I say.

"Why's that?"

"Because last year when Randy was going through some rough times, he listened to your song 'Only God Knows Why' over and over again. Your song helped to soften and open up his heart."

Randy will eventually write about this part of his life in his own book.

During the period of time in 2005, when Randy feels as if he's drowning, he could have called any pastor in the country to ask for help. Yet instead he ended up finding hope in the most unlikely place. That's often how God works, isn't it?

"So, I owe you," I repeat to Bobby. "Nothing could get through to my husband, but your song did."

I'm sure this singer would be surprised to hear about all the insane things that have happened in the lives of two pastors from Tampa—the moments Randy felt like ending it all, all the times I needed to help him navigate through a life-and-death crisis. Then again, Bobby seems to be a caring and perceptive soul. I doubt much will shock him.

I ask if I can pray over him like I do with many. Before the end of our conversation, I can't help looking at his tattoo and wondering about the story behind "Paul." Perhaps in time God will allow me the opportunity to ask him about it.

I'm scheduled to preach in Detroit at Bishop Keith Butler's megachurch with more than twenty thousand members, Word of Faith, when I receive a phone call from Bobby asking if Randy and I would come be guests at his home and meet his family. We agree to go. I'm scheduled to fly out from New York while Randy is to fly up from Florida and meet us, but he gets detained by a storm. He insists that I go, so I call Bobby and say I would be honored to meet his family on one condition: that he would go to church with me. He agrees. When I arrive, he introduces me to his family and close friends who also work with him, like Shakes, the road manager who's been with him for a long time. Shakes's mom makes us a wonderful home-cooked meal as we sit around and talk about life, God, politics, music, and ministry. I go to the guesthouse for an early night's rest knowing I want to be refreshed for the morning service.

That Sunday, Bishop Butler sends a limo to fetch us. I jump in the car while waiting for Bobby and his security to join me. Bob's usual attire, aside from his stage clothes, is a white T-shirt and jeans, but not on this day. He gets in the car all decked out in a baby-blue tuxedo with a white shirt and a top hat to boot.

"I got dressed up for you and God today," he declares.

"Yeah, I can see that."

He has a genuine excitement about going to the house of God. It will be his first time to hear me preach and a while since he's been in church. Before we take off, he requests to go pick up his brother Bill. We swing by, grab him real quick, then off and away we go.

When we arrive at church, the praise and worship is in full gear. Vickie Winans gets up to sing. Suddenly she looks down to the front row and yells out, "Whhhaaaaaaatt?" only as Vickie can. "Is that Kid Rock up in the house?" The place erupts as Bobby is taking it all in. I know it's a divine appointment and setup from God. I get up and preach on Jacob, a sermon titled "Not Until He Blesses Me." By the end of the message, the entire place is in a Holy Ghost frenzy. Bobby's brother lifts his hand and receives salvation at the altar call. There is still an electric feeling when we jump back in the limo and proceed to Bobby's house for lunch.

I turn to him and ask, "Well, what did you think?"

Bobby grins. "It felt like when I first fell in love with music."

Since I've spent a lifetime on a stage and behind a pulpit speaking into a microphone, people might naturally assume that I enjoy that spotlight. Actually, what I really love is being behind the scenes, helping to connect and bring people together. I want to give a big party, but I don't want it to be about me. So when it comes to relationships with those in the limelight, I've always tried to remain obscure.

This is one of the reasons why, I believe, I've been able to have so many relationships, like the ones I've had with Trump and Bobby. I'm comfortable sharing about both of them, but there are so many people whose stories I'll carry to my grave. Part of being a pastor to them is becoming a vault. I believe that's why God puts me in some of their lives. Over time and testing, they realize they can trust me as I can them.

Whenever I meet anyone, I always ask God to give me a word of knowledge. To give me discernment. I ask Him to give me something so that I can reach them for Him. A nugget of truth that applies to their life, so they can know God is real. God will reveal in order to redeem.

Sometimes God gives me more than a simple word. Sometimes I feel Him give me an assignment, the way he does with Donald Trump, and the way he does with Bobby. Over time, as I get to know the talented Kid Rock on a personal level, he enjoys introducing me as his pastor. I've watched him "bet" someone that he'll give them a million dollars if they can guess his pastor. Some of his friends won't believe I am an actual preacher. "You don't look like a preacher." The stereotypical mold in many people's minds begins to melt away as God begins to work on their hearts. I always know my lane and lines. I'm not trying to fit in, but to pave a path for them to walk down and discover a new life in Christ. I am comfortable being the "church" outside of the four walls of the church. This is actually my favorite "pulpit," going into the highways and hedges and compelling people to come in. Over time, I find myself backstage praying over Bobby and his band before they perform, sharing truths from the Word of God, being that listening ear with a heart of compassion to reach them where they are with the love of Christ.

All the moves during my youth and all the experiences I've been through have helped to shape and mold me. Meeting people is easy, and I've always been adaptable. I get both enjoyment in talking with strangers and comfort in listening. That's both my mother and father in me. I don't try to be self-righteous or judgmental. I accept people as they are. All I can do is try to convey the same grace I've experienced in my life.

"God's after you because He has this abundant life for you," I will share with individuals. "He can't bless this mess. He's trying to get you to a place where you can live in peace and joy and no matter what's going on out there, internally the Kingdom of God is joy, peace, and righteousness."

There will be many leaders in all walks of life—entertainment, business, politics, sports—who reach out to me and whom I encounter. I've always been very cognizant that it's not me they're attracted to; it's God in me. There's no confusion in my mind that this is what my appeal happens to be. They're not seeking me out because I'm pretty or smart or can talk—they can easily find all sorts of people who are smarter and better looking and more fascinating. I know I'm a bright light because of God in me. This is what separates me and why they keep coming back.

This is why someone's background is so important. It truly forms them to be the person they are. I've never been caught up in the trappings, enamored by the success, money, and fame. I never longed for it and eventually saw the dangers it brings. I'm not against it, if it is useful in fulfilling the purpose of God. All I want is to serve God, fulfill His purpose, and have a family and meaningful relationships. Now that's a full life.

I'm always fascinated by the public and private personas of people. When Bobby isn't touring and making music, he's a very normal and stable guy. As I get to know Bobby, I see he's a guy who will wake up early at home, cook Junior his breakfast, and take him to school. He's a solid dad with his family nearby.

On the day of Bobby's wedding to Pam Anderson, an event I perform at a restaurant, the reception for this notable event in 2006 takes place back at his house. Everybody's dancing, and I finally feel comfortable enough to ask him about the name "Paul" that's inked on his arm.

"Paul was my father's name," I say, telling him why I'm curious.

Bobby opens up to me and says Paul was the name of his cousin who ended up taking his own life. He was very close to him, like a brother, so the loss was really tough to take. I can tell he doesn't usually talk about his cousin, but he feels comfortable sharing it with me.

The last thing Bobby reveals amazes me. It brings this little story back full circle. He says his cousin's suicide was part of the reason he ended up writing "Only God Knows Why."

This is exactly how God works: in ways we can't even begin to fathom. Sometimes we see the bread crumbs He wants us to see. In this case, God draws me to a special spiritual assignment, and as details of our lives overlap, the bonds that are formed bless us mutually.

God is constantly writing our stories. Most of the time He writes them in invisible ink, but every now and then we see the unmistakable proof and stand amazed by all the things God knows. He knows why. He always knows why. And we should listen and respond to Him. If not, we might sometimes miss the assignment He has for us. This happens to me in the summer of 2009. Randy calls me and asks me if I can come back to Without Walls Church. The membership is down to only 800 members and the building has gone into foreclosure. Randy is still dealing with the grief of losing Kristen, so he decides to step away for stress and health-related issues. After much prayer and seeking the counsel of others, I can see it's the right decision to come back as the senior pastor.

I plan to fly back to Tampa on the last weekend of June to take over the reins at Without Walls. Then on Thursday, June 25, I learn that Michael Jackson has died. I spend a long time on the phone with LaToya, ministering to her during this incredible loss. We all feel the devastation of his death.

When I get off the plane in Tampa two days later, I discover Randy has set up a press conference announcing my return to the church. This sends me into a panic, knowing I'll be walking into a firestorm and will need to deal with the ramifications of this. I don't know what to expect. So when I get a voice mail on my phone from LaToya Jackson asking me to call her back, I decide to put it off until I'm back in Texas on Monday.

I just spoke with her and I have all this mess I'm needing to deal with. I'll call her when I'm back to normalcy.

I feel guilty for not immediately calling her back, and I know it's the Holy Spirit nudging at me, knocking on my heart. But I try to justify my procrastination. *I've been talking to LaToya throughout the week*, I tell myself.

Sometimes in life, you know you've missed a moment and another one like it will never come around. This is one of those cases. When I finally call LaToya back, she sounds disheartened.

"Oh, Paula. We wanted you to do Michael's funeral, but since I couldn't get a hold of you, we had to get someone else. They needed a final list of who would perform at the funeral this weekend."

I just gasp.

"LaToya...I am so, so sorry."

There's a sick feeling in my gut, the kind that knows, the kind that has no excuse.

I just missed God.

I know this is a battle the enemy has won. The world has lost an icon like Michael Jackson, and I'm given this incredible moment to share the hope of Christ with the world. God *wanted* me to have that moment. Not for Paula White's glory but for His. And I missed it! All because of my focus and cautiousness related to everything happening in Tampa.

There's nobody else to blame but myself.

I call up a friend and describe what happened. "You won't believe this," I start to say. My friend simply wants to be encouraging to me.

"It must not have been God's will."

"Are you crazy?" I reply. "It absolutely *was* God's will! It was God's will to put me in that place to minister for His glory from the very beginning. You can call it Satan or whatever. But that was *my* irresponsibility."

Honestly, what I want is a little comfort. Someone to simply sit with me and let me grieve this missed moment. I call another friend and tell her the situation. Once again, my friend tries to be sympathetic.

"Oh, Paula. I'm so sorry. God will open up another door. Another opportunity will come."

"'Another opportunity'? Seriously? There's Elvis and there's Michael. There's not going to be another opportunity like this in my lifetime! *I just missed it.*"

It's easy to make excuses for missing moments of purpose, times when God opens a door but we remain too skeptical, too preoccupied, or too stressed out to take it.

I repent and pray I won't miss another "God" moment again.

Good communication means being a good listener, being able to *really* hear people. Most can't suspend objectivity or hold back emotional reactivity. We often quickly utter the next thought we have in our minds. It takes a certain ability to simply suspend your thoughts and to really hear what someone is saying. It's not just *what* they're saying but *how* they're saying it.

One day I meet a Jewish woman who works closely with Tyra Banks. Out of the blue she says, "Oh, I get it now." I'm not sure what she's talking about, so I ask her what she means.

"I get it. I understand why now. At first, I didn't get all the money and how famous you are, but I totally get it now."

I still don't know where she's coming from and what exactly she's finally understanding. So she continues to explain.

"You couldn't reach some of the people you reach if you didn't have all of that. The name and the status. There are some people who wouldn't pay attention to you. God must trust some with money and fame because there are people He wants to reach. So I finally get it. Sometimes God will bless people and put them in the same world as others so they can be impactful."

This is an interesting observation. In some ways, I agree with this woman's assessment. I'm in those people's worlds, but I'm not compromising myself. I'm just Pastor Paula. I'm the Paula from the trailer and Paula from Bayshore. I see beyond the money and fame. I respect gifting and talents. I could have millions of dollars today and it could all be gone tomorrow. In many ways, the massive Paula White Ministries does take a hit over the next decade. That doesn't matter, because I know I'm doing what God has called me to do. He has always provided for His purpose in my life. The door opens and people come in. I always try to leave them with something tangible to lead them to God.

17.

POTENTIAL

New York—July 23, 2007—Bestselling author and life coach Paula White's "Life By Design Empowerment" conference was an over-whelming success with over 3,000 in attendance and nearly 3,000 people were turned away because the seating was at capacity at the Manhattan Center's Hammerstein Ballroom in New York City...

...Says White, "This is a clear indication that people want to live a life of wholeness—spirit, soul and body and want to understand their unique purpose in life."

White was joined on Sunday, July 15th by some of today's most powerful gospel recording artists such as CeCe Winans, and DeLeon Richards-Sheffield...White used practical applications and illustrations in teaching individuals how to discover and appreciate their unique gifts and purpose.

Webwire.com

My life in 2007 resembles the title of the Charles Dickens classic *A Tale of Two Cities*. Like the famous opening lines, "It was the best of times, it was the worst of times," New York represents my season of light and my spring of hope, the place where I find my voice and do the final shedding necessary in my life. As I've said, I find peace in the most chaotic city. Every time I come here, I'm inspired to write a sermon or imagine the impossible. Whenever I stare out at the endless sea of skyscrapers, I feel alive. I feel a sense of grandeur.

People with a dream and a vision created this.

This city is a reminder of my dreams and my vision. It's a hub for my ministry, a place where I'm preaching at crusades and having partner lunches and launching a church located at the Manhattan Center, with overflow crowds in the connecting hotel, and where people line up at six a.m. in the freezing cold just to hear the Word preached and experience the movement of God. We host three services a day, eleven a.m., three p.m., and six p.m. People pour into the building filled with faith and expectancy, as each service is uniquely distinct with a manifestation of God's Presence. They come from near and far, from all different walks of life, for an encounter with God. The worship is heavenly as it envelops the venue and the hearts of people who reach for God and press into "throne room" ministry. Ministering is so easy and effortless in this atmosphere. I am simply a conduit yielded to the Holy Spirit moving at His desire.

God has a place for every assignment in a person's life. Geography is important to Him. He is the one who chooses your location, and when you discern and obey that decision you will see His fruitfulness. New York is an "open heaven" for me. These buildings with fifty, seventy-five, and even one hundred stories—each one pointing toward the heavens—are examples of possibility and potential. They represent the power of what humans are capable of doing.

So how much more can God do through us?

I'm witnessing the fruits of that in my life. One day I'm in jeans and tennis shoes helping those in need of food, clothing, and shelter in downtown Tampa. Or, I'm in the Appalachian Mountains or across the world in Africa. The next day I'm in a skirt and heels preaching before a crowd of 28,000. There are accolades that I'm humbled to receive, like the Trailblazer Award from Jesse Jackson and the Rainbow Coalition in 2006 and the 2009 Humanitarian Award of the Trumpet Award Foundation. In 2008, I'm invited to perform the invocation for the fortieth anniversary of Dr. Martin Luther King Jr.'s assassination in Memphis, Tennessee, and also to present at Maya Angelou's eightieth birthday tribute in Atlanta, Georgia.

New York shows me there is more favor in my life and access to the promises of God. The towering monuments tell me again how nations will be shaken with one swoop of His hand.

I recall standing on the sidewalk of Bayshore that overlooks the beautiful Tampa Bay, and I heard the devil whispering, "You're not going to see it." Yet I began to walk again, eventually picking up my pace to a steady jog, telling myself to look at these legs of mine, declaring how these strong legs have carried me through my life. And soon I find myself running. I get my step back. I run every day to remind myself, "You can do this, just keep running." The fire and the spirit of the Big Apple allow God to fuel my self-belief.

It turns out this big melting pot of a city loves this Mississippi girl.

After spending time around Donald Trump I find myself inspired by his vision, thought process, keen insight, and overall discipline. He's a brilliant thinker who tends to walk several steps ahead of the masses. I want to share his wisdom with the world in my own way, so I show him my broadcast schedule and ask if he will join me for a program. "Sure, I'd love to. Anything for you, Paula." He will soon discover just how much impact the show has. I sit in Central Park, one of the prettiest places on earth, and reread his book *Why We Want You to Be Rich* to prepare for the upcoming interview on my show:

Ask yourself why you like a certain place. Sometimes it's obvious—it's beautiful, it represents holiday time, it's romantic, or whatever. But if you keep asking yourself the reasons why, very often you'll hit on something that could open a door for you to a new idea or career.

When I read these lines from Donald Trump in one of his bestselling books, I don't have to ask myself why I love New York. It seems like I've always felt this way, even starting with the very first time I visited the Big Apple.

In 1990, I end up taking a memorable trip to New York City to work with Bill Wilson and his worldwide ministry to children called Metro World Child. His heart is for helping needy boys and girls in the inner cities of all continents. Since we can't afford the airfare to New York, we take an old yellow school bus that somehow manages to arrive in one piece after twenty-five hours on the road from Florida. I'll always remember sleeping on the gym floor of Bill Wilson's place and hearing the rats skittering across the floor in the dark.

"You can't go outside at night or you'll get shot," Bill warns us.

Bill's simple roots of going to the streets had the type of raw tenacity that I liked and related to. It took me back to my D.C. days where I dressed up in costumes carrying a bullhorn skating through the "war-torn" drug areas shouting "Jesus loves you" at nine a.m. on a Saturday morning. By 2005, Bill and his ministry dubbed "Sidewalk Sunday School" will reach more than 30,000 children, with two-thirds of those in New York.

Even though my accommodations aren't exactly four-star (or even one-star), the experience is thrilling because I'm out here living and working and breathing ministry. There's something about this city that feels so familiar, that seems to fit. I come alive with a passion that burns within me. Back then I can't identify it, but I sense there's a story waiting for me to unfold here.

Years later, Donald Trump will see this feeling whenever I'm in the city.

"You really love this place, don't you?" he says one day.

"I do. I love the grit of New York, the fact that it's so diverse. It's the best of the best and the worst of the worst."

"Well, it loves you, too, Paula."

In a city where I find myself, I'm also able to momentarily lose all those trappings that come with being Pastor Paula White and simply enjoy being Paula. I can ditch my security detail and decide to walk around New York; one particular day I'm inspired to walk across the whole city for twelve hours. I can sit at a café and watch strangers pass by while sipping on an espresso. New York is different than other cities for me. When someone recognizes me I'm usually greeted with a respectful, "Hey, love your ministry!"—not a bunch of fanfare or prejudiced opinion. It's the city of tolerance, acceptance, and authenticity for me. That's something I've always longed for and valued. Every living creature has an environment it thrives in. If you put a fish on land, it won't survive very long. Fish were made for the water. I discover my transformation, the cocoon that God has chosen for me to come into my being is the Big Apple. After having been trapped in someone else's set routine for many years, I've discovered spontaneity. I take ballroom dance lessons, and I read books simply for enjoyment.

I'm rediscovering how to enjoy life again along with fulfilling my purpose.

By now I'm spending so much time in the city that I begin to think it'd be a good idea to get a place since hotels are so expensive. I know by now why Trump is successful in his hotel business: their service is impeccable. After spending many nights at Trump International Hotel and Tower, I feel as if the staff is family. The bellman knows my name and has a key waiting for me upon arrival. Whenever I stay at another hotel in New York, even a highly rated place, it never feels the same.

One day while visiting Trump and talking about hotels, I tell him I really need to get a place up here in the city.

"I have a place," he tells me.

Of course he has a place. Donald Trump has *many* places. At that time, as the chairman and president of the Trump Organization, he's known as the wealthy real estate mogul who stars on *The Apprentice*. He's seemingly helped to build half of the buildings in New York City.

He takes me down to Trump Park Avenue and shows me a unit. The walk from Fifth Avenue to Park is two blocks over and usually takes about five to seven minutes, but not on this day. We exit Trump Tower, take a right, where he first greets a vendor with a friendly "hello" and everyday chitchat. As we proceed to Park Avenue we pass two more construction sites, where the guys stop their work to shout out, "Hello!" or "Trump!" or "Good to see you!" He shakes their hands, gives them a pat on the back, points out different aspects of their work, and proceeds to talk construction with them. He is clearly comfortable on site and genuinely appreciative of their work even though these are not his own buildings. I realize this isn't just business for him; it's a passion and love of his. He notices details that most of us would miss. His eye for craftsmanship is impeccable. Before leaving he compliments them again, asks a few more questions, and walks away with his usual thumbs-up, wink, and nod.

We arrive at our destination. This building is one of his favorites, a true gem he's immensely proud of. Located on the corner of Park Avenue and 59th Street, the former Hotel Delmonico was bought by Trump back in 2001 for $115 million. It's a hotel the Beatles once stayed at and where they hung out with Bob Dylan.

When I walk into the corner unit, honestly...I feel home. Unlike other places I have lived, I feel like I belong here, as if I'm taking a step that has already been ordered by God. Every ounce of my spirit just knows this is going to be my shelter. It's crazy, of course, but no more crazy than anything else in my life. I tell Trump how much I love it. I won't even look at other units. There is no need, since sometimes you already know in your spirit.

When I call the real estate agent to ask about the property, the woman tells me how much it costs. I knew it would be pricey, but this wasn't about a real estate investment or a deal—it was something deeper.

My business side instinctively kicks in as I ask, "Does Mr. Trump ever negotiate?"

"He doesn't need to. I've worked with him for thirty years and have only seen him come down in price once or twice on a project like this."

The remodeling and renovation project has just been completed in 2004, so nobody's lived in this unit. The real estate market is booming, and so are Mr. Trump's businesses.

"Okay," I say. "Can you do me a favor? Can you put me down for the unit? And can you give me thirty days to figure some things out?" I feel this overwhelming peace that I'm to purchase this unit.

Moments after talking to the real estate agent, Trump calls me.

"So you like my place?"

"Yes, sir."

"Name your price," he says.

A panic clamps over me for a brief second. This is the gentleman whom I told it's not about fame and not about money. The one whom I told, "I want your soul." The one about whom Christ said, *Show him who I am.*

"Mr. Trump, please don't do this to me. You know I'm a good businesswoman. I told you it'll never be about money."

"Name your price, Paula."

I sigh. "Please don't do this to me. Put it at list price. I won't go under it."

I can't say exactly what Trump is thinking, but I know for me, this is a real test. Will I stick to my guns when it comes down to it? At the time, perhaps, he won't be able to figure out why I won't compromise. When I've faced difficult challenges before, he has asked me in an almost fatherly manner why I didn't call him to let him know. I tell him I fight my own battles; I can take care of myself. He knows that, and I believe he respects that about me.

I come to the realization and understanding that if I'm going to buy this place, if I'm meant to be here, then God will make it happen.

As Trump writes, "Don't underestimate yourself or your possibilities."

Before I get ready to fly back to Tampa, I go to Trump's office and by chance meet Bill Zanker. Bill created and runs The Learning Annex, a leading company that produces seminars, lectures, and workshops all over the country. Along with Trump, some of their notable speakers have included Tony Robbins and Robert Kiyosaki, author of *Rich Dad, Poor Dad.*

"Bill, do you know Paula?"

"No."

"She's the best!" Trump says, starting to sing my praises as he does for so many. "You should hear her speak! She fills stadiums. Destiny's Child watches her videos on their tour bus. She's fantastic."

They tell me Trump is speaking at an upcoming event and invite me to come, so I decide to attend. When Donald sees I'm there, he once again brags about me to everybody and makes an impromptu request for me to come up to the stage and say a few words.

"Guys—if you think I can speak, wait till you hear her. Now she can speak."

I only talk for five minutes, but when I get off the stage the people go wild, and Bill Zanker rushes over to tell me what a great job I did. He's more than animated; he's as excited as a kid on Christmas morning.

"You really are great. This is as good as Tony Robbins!" he tells me. "I need you! I need you!"

"Tony Robbins—wow, now that's a compliment, Bill. Okay. What do you want me to do?"

"I want to sign you," Bill says.

"Call me in a few days."

When I talk to him on the phone, I ask what he wants me to talk about, and he tells me the seminars are about empowering people financially.

"Well, I really have a message about the spiritual side of money. It's more about emotions and spiritual. It's not just fiscal, like, can you add two plus two? There's an emotional side. I always ask people, 'What's your earliest memory of money?' There's a spiritual side that most people don't recognize."

"Oh, my—I love that," Bill says.

The lineup for the conference tour is top-notch, with the best-caliber speakers within their field of expertise. *New York, New York* reports, "Donald Trump will make a cool million dollars for one hour's work speaking to the crowd... That's $16,000 a minute."

I'm not Donald Trump, but when Bill ends up drawing up a contract, he signs me up for a year with a deal that almost makes me feel guilty. *Almost.* At the time, all I can think is *wow.* This money was not expected, and once again I see that God is making a way for something I don't fully understand yet in my life.

This isn't a time when I want to build my net worth and my assets. This is a time when I'm learning to breathe again. And in this city where dreams may come alive or be killed, mine have come alive.

* * *

In New York, a healing and renewal process starts that continues when I'm in Texas. Both of these places give me the strength I need to go through the divorce, the losses, and the changes of everything around me. I cling to my core, my relationship with God, finding myself digging deeper and deeper to unravel the mysteries and sacred secrets of His Word. In many ways it is a sabbatical for me. I never leave my purpose, but need to realign myself and allow God to course correct any and all areas necessary in my life. Not only that, but my vision and the belief in my life's potential will expand, thanks to Donald Trump.

Ever since meeting Trump, he gives me access into his world. He has an open-door policy. He describes himself this way: "I know that often when people think of me, they think, 'Oh, the billionaire,' and it's a bit like having the door shut in my face. My son, Don Jr., has said that I'm like a blue-collar guy with a big bankroll, if that's any insight into my persona. He's spent a lot of time with me, and he knows I'm pretty simple at my core."

This is true. Trump might be simple in some ways, yet he's also extremely smart and observant, always studying people and situations.

He invites me to an *Apprentice* finale, asking me to pray over everybody. When I arrive on set, I'm blown away by an entire production with sound guys, and assistants to sound guys, and assistants to assistants. There seems to be 350 people working on the stage and forty cameras. As I take in this well-oiled machine that's working for a single purpose of delivering an entertaining show to America, I can't help but get visionary thoughts of my own.

If they're doing this for the world, how much more can we do for God's Kingdom?

Any time I spend with Trump, I do a lot of listening and, in turn, a lot of learning. Putting me front and center with so many influencers, Trump is always generous to me. Opportunities like *The Apprentice,* when I go to the NBC set and meet all these executives working for the network. Every time the opportunity comes, I ask God to give me wisdom. I know God is opening these doors for something greater. Exposure will expand you if you allow it to.

Your résumé is being built by your experience, Paula. You know this because you preach this: it's not learning Scripture; it's living Scripture.

When it comes to bringing a guest in with me to meet Trump, I'm always very selective. I witness so many people wanting something from him with little or no concern about giving back. I watch people, from the most famous to the ordinary, line his reception area to stop in for one reason or another. More seem to be takers than givers, to me. One day I invite my friend Debra to come with me and meet him in his office. Trump asks her what she does, so she explains that she runs a ministry to prostitutes. She'll go on the street and take care of girls who've been battered and abused, ones who have been victims of trafficking. Right as she's in the middle of sharing a story, Trump stops her.

"Rhona!" he says to his assistant who's been with him for many years. "Bring me my checkbook."

In just moments he's sitting in front of us writing out a check to Debra for this ministry. "Now, that's real ministry!" he exclaims. It isn't the only time I witness his generosity. He gives often and significantly, never letting anyone know all he does for others.

Ever since he first called me out of the blue, I've been praying over Donald Trump and have been a part of his life. He doesn't bring up faith with me simply because I'm a pastor. Faith is important to him, something he writes about:

My mother was a devout person, and she lived her faith. That was a great example to me as a child and as an adult. She was very strong and yet very gentle, and she was also very humble. She gave everything she had without reservation. So when I speak so highly of my parents, you can see that there is good reason to. My mother's advice was simple but wise. It cuts to the core and keeps me focused and well-balanced.

"Trust in God and be true to yourself." It doesn't get any better than that (from *Why We Want You to Be Rich*).

Trump's mother had a tremendous impact on his life, and so has mine. In fact, during these years, my mother is not only a major part of my life, she's my best friend. During some of those really difficult days, Mom carries me and keeps me on track. God isn't just writing a new story in my life; He's also writing a whole new book for my mother as well. The wonderful thing is when we're both on the same page in those stories.

Even though my mom lives in Memphis, she visits me often in New York, where we go shopping and spend time truly bonding. We laugh together, and I listen to her tell stories I've never heard. For my thirty-ninth birthday, we go discover Paris together. She travels with me to the Bahamas and Hawaii, and we take precious mother-daughter vacations where memories will be forever forged in my heart and soul.

It's funny how time can give you the gift of perspective. As I gain a better understanding of what my mom went through when she was younger, she also better understands what I've been going through. What I didn't listen to when I was eighteen years old, I try to receive at forty years old.

This lady's a lot more wise than I thought, and she is really fun to hang out with.

I cherish our time together and recognize I'm a lot more like my mom than I had realized.

After my divorce, I conclude one prayer and desire as a newly single woman:

Lord, I just want to die whole.

For the first time in my life, I'm not focused on everyone else or what they need. I'm taking a long, hard look at myself. I am determined not to compromise or settle for anything less than what God has for me. I'm shedding the thoughts that previously bound me in codependent, unhealthy relationships. I'm on a mission to be the best version of myself. I no longer feel I have to prove anything or earn anyone's approval. I am ready to live a life that illuminates the beautiful reality of who I really am—a designer's original, a handcrafted, fearfully and wonderfully created daughter of God.

I don't know if I'll ever marry again, and as for dating? I don't know how that's going to work. *It's difficult to date as a high-profile pastor,* I tell myself. I know deep in my heart that marriage is God's best, and I also know that unless God gives you a grace for being single, His will and His Word are for us to be married. I don't believe it's my grace to be single, yet I'm not out there pursuing anything.

I'm actually enjoying this time to myself. I can come and go as I please. I am fully dedicated to my calling and serving God and His people. However, this doesn't stop my friends and family from always trying to set me up with that perfect somebody. My son Brad teases me that he is starting a website and managing applications for possible prospects.

"You're going to be a very difficult person for someone to marry," Trump tells me one day.

"Why? I'm a really good person."

"I know. But you have no needs."

"I have needs," I say.

I don't need someone to pay my bills, nor do I need someone giving me compliments all day long. But I long for someone to share my life with who is compatible and is called to walk with me in purpose. I feel I have all this love pent up inside of me, waiting to be shared with the right person. I desire someone with whom I can share my dreams, my vision, and my intimacy. Someone who is my counterpart.

I wonder if this someone is out there.

On Friday, October 6, 2006, I interview Trump and Robert Kiyosaki on my television show, *Paula White Today,* and we discuss *Why We Want You to Be Rich: Two Men, One Message,* which they've co-written. As I welcome both of them, I introduce them as two of the most successful people who have been raised for such a time as this.

There's always been a practical side to me, even after becoming born again and pursuing a life with and for Jesus. I know the value of wisdom and learning. I have seen the fruit of hard work. So being able to interview leaders and thinkers and doers like Trump and Kiyosaki is truly a blessing.

"We're going to give people tools to transform their minds," I tell my audience, "because if you want to change your way of living, you have to change your way of thinking."

As we talk about the financial state of the country and how we're quickly starting to lose the middle class, Trump talks about a lot of his friends who didn't make it along the way and ended up going bankrupt.

"So why did you make it?" I ask.

"I think because I never, ever quit," Trump says. "I don't give up. You have to be born with something. God has to have blessed you with a good brain. When I make speeches, I start off by saying most of you shouldn't be in this room because most of you won't be entrepreneurs. The people I'm doing that speech for—they never love it when I'm telling them they probably shouldn't be entrepreneurs. With that, you have to be born with something."

We talk about the book and the lessons inside it.

"I've read it cover to cover, and it's one of the greatest books," I say. "You not only give that explanation, but you also give the philosophy—the way you need to think—you give the principles. You really teach people self-empowerment, begin to take control, here it is simply broken down."

Trump nods. "A lot of people give up. And they don't have the courage or maybe the fortitude or whatever it is. If only they would keep trying, they'd be a lot better off. Maybe it's not something so expected—but they give up, they quit. And a quitter is always a loser. We discuss that. A quitter is always a loser. I've known so many people over my life—in sports and in business and everything. Anytime you're a quitter, ultimately you're a loser."

We talk about issues like the power of perseverance and thinking big. It's easy to see why I connect with someone like Trump so easily. He's all about purpose, vision, tenacity, and sheer determination.

"Did you always know you'd succeed?" I ask Trump. "Did you always know you'd win?"

"Well, I always felt I was a winner. I always strove to be a winner. But your question about 'can anybody be rich?' Probably not. The fact is some people can be rich, but they can be rich in other ways. And they can certainly live better. It doesn't mean they're gonna be multimillionaires or billionaires. But they can certainly be better and do a lot better."

As always, near the end of the program, I put my teaching hat on, though I don't need to today since my guests are doing a great job already.

"You have to believe in yourself," I say. "All behavior comes out of belief. And if we don't change the way we think, we'll never change the dynamics of our life. You learned that philosophy through life lessons. Talk about sports—what your parents taught you—what the education system taught you."

Trump says, "In my case, I have a father who was successful. He was a builder in Brooklyn and Queens. And he loved what he did. It wasn't that he sat and told me, 'I love it, I love it, I love it,'' 'cause that doesn't mean anything. But I saw that he was happy and he was always working. He'd work seven days a week. Today, you go out and play a round of golf or you do something else. He didn't know about that. And yes, he was very happy. I'd see his friends and other people—I'd watch older people when I was young—and they would take two-month vacations and everything else. They were always the most unhappy. My father would never—I can't even remember him taking a vacation. Let's assume he'd take it for a day. But he was just really happy.

"It wasn't like he told me 'just work work work.' He just set an example for me. I watched it and I saw his life. And he led a good life, and he led a happy life. And he did nothing but work so we talk about that."

This is great stuff. I nod and smile.

"Find your passion in life," I say. "And figure out a way to make money."

"That's the key," he says. "You have to find something that you call passion. I say you have to find something you really love. If you don't find that, you have a problem, because you're never going to be good at it and you're never going to be happy."

I ask about Trump's study habits in college, about how he always did a little more, something he shares about in his book.

"I went to the Wharton School of finance and, believe it or not, I really was a good student," Trump says with his familiar grin.

I begin to summarize our conversation before our time is over.

"It's not too late. You can change it. It doesn't matter where you start in your life, but it matters where you finish."

I know because I'm talking from experience. From many experiences.

"The only limitations in our life are the ones we put on ourselves. So when we change our way of thinking, we change our way of living."

I've changed my thinking and my way of living.

"It comes with educating ourselves. The Bible is all about empowerment. It's about God's instructions. It's about taking control."

So are you remembering that, Paula?

"When you give up your decisions, you give up your destiny," I tell the audience and viewers at home. "I am blessed to be a blessing. And today, I can realize my dreams. I can have the future I deserve."

As I say these words, they come from my spirit, the place I fully trust. As much as I know God has sent me into Donald Trump's life to pray for him and his family and be a person who wants nothing from him but to show him God, I am beginning to realize that he is being used in my life to help restore my confidence after some pretty shaky years.

"Robert and I want to expand your thinking," Trump says. "We can all benefit from the wisdom of Descartes: 'I think; therefore I am.' Think bigger!"

There's no city bigger than New York, and no businessman bigger than Donald Trump. They allow me to see God and His purpose and plan in my life in a bigger and bolder way.

From the very beginning of our friendship, there is a cross-pollination between Trump and me. Obviously I bring something to his life spiritually, something that extends to his family and staff members. Some of them I grow close with. All the while, God is once again solidifying my value to me. I'm seeing my purpose in a new way. And I'm seeing the value of casting a grand vision. I air the show on October twenty-second, with some stations carrying it the twenty-third through the thirtieth. Mr. Trump starts to see my value, too, maybe in a different way than I do. He sends me a handwritten note on the broadcast schedule I had sent him:

Paula—You are an amazing woman—book went to #1 after 31 minutes.

Best, Donald.

One of the last lines Trump writes in his book carries a mighty grand vision in the big picture of things: "Have you thought about 2016 yet? We have. Stay tuned. As Henry Kissinger knowingly said, 'History knows no resting places and no plateaus.'"

18.

HOME

As I gallop on a beautiful dark chocolate mare along the soft white sand of
Montego Bay, my guide whistles and points into the pristine turquoise waters, signaling me to go in for a swim. I'm already riding bareback and decide
to take my experience up a notch to amuse my adventurous soul. With a
small pull on the right side of the rein, the mare starts to glide in the shallow
Atlantic waters.

"How awesome is this?" I shout back to my friends who watch from the
shore.

I'm breathing in the fresh, salty aroma of the summer breeze with the heat
rays of an early morning gently covering my back. It feels like paradise. The
horse surges forward, paddling through the water with ease and enjoyment
to the rhythm of the rising waves, lifting her head up slightly over the break.
It is surreal and euphoric to me until without warning I hit a sudden drop-
off of the bottom of the ocean. Upon the initial kick of the mare, I grab
her mane, pulling, tugging, and holding on for dear life. The waves begin to
swell and intensify, bashing burning salt water against my face and filling my
nose and mouth. My peace turns to panic as I clutch her mane with all my
strength. We are no longer in sync but resisting each other. In a matter of
seconds, my mind flashes over my life.

Really, God? Not like this.

I bargain with Him.

We have a deal. I made a commitment to purpose, which makes me useful for your Kingdom.

As I'm being tossed around by both the ocean and the horse, I tell God, "This is not even cool." It's not like I'm on a missionary field or being stoned like Stephen in the book of Acts where the glory of God is manifest in his life. I'm simply riding a horse in Montego Bay. Similar to the many occurrences in my life such as seeing Dreamer in L.A. or standing before 10,000 people at Carpenter's Home Church, I shut my eyes, surrender, and let go. As soon as I do, the mare surges under with the incoming wave and emerges with perfect cadence to the rhythm of the water. The mare knows how to swim in deep waters.

I feel the Holy Spirit whispering to me.

Don't resist, Paula. Just flow.

It is a life lesson I live by. I don't force what doesn't fit.

This voice from the Holy Spirit can come in seemingly minor and insignificant moments, too, like something as simple as booking a short flight.

I believe in flow. Usually when a door shuts, I don't try to push it open. The difficulty is discerning whether God or the enemy is shutting it. When God shuts a door, no matter how much you try to pry it open, kick it down, or barge through it, nothing is going to open. When it's demonically closed to resist you and the mandate on your life, we need to respond just as Paul and Silas did in Acts 16 when they prayed and sang praises to God. The foundations of the prison were shaken, and immediately all the doors were opened.

I'm settled back in Tampa now as the senior pastor of Without Walls International Church and need to go to Texas to take care of some business. No longer having a private jet—which was sold after my divorce—I'm accustomed to taking the easiest, least expensive route to San Antonio, a direct Southwest flight at nine a.m., noon, or five p.m. Weeks out from the day I'll take it, I call my assistant and tell her to book me on the noon flight.

"Sure, I'll take care of that," Rachael says.

She calls back a few minutes later. "It's shut. There are no seats available on the noon flight, but the morning and evening are fully open, so I booked you for the five p.m."

"But that's not what I wanted. Try again."

An hour or two passes before Rachael calls again to inform me the noon flight is oversold. "There's nothing available."

For a week, then another, I continue to bring this up, insisting on taking the noon flight. There is no rhyme or reason for my unusual persistence about being on this particular flight. I don't have a speaking engagement or an appointment where I have no flexibility. I'm simply matter-of-fact about being on the noon flight. Once again, it's as if my spirit has knowledge of the future that my mind struggles to comprehend. People often joke that I have a "sixth sense," but it's no joke to me. I have learned there is a frequency of the spirit realm where I zone in to see and hear from a heavenly perspective. God puts eternity into our heart, and when we are sensitive to follow, it directs His will in our life.

While I'm at a doctor's appointment on the morning I hoped to leave, Rachael decides to try one more time, calling Southwest to see if anything is available. She soon calls me, excited to let me know they have one seat that just opened on the noon flight.

"I have your bag packed; just drive to the airport and I'll meet you there," she says.

"Great, I really appreciate it."

For some reason, I just know I'm supposed to be on this flight.

When I arrive at the gate to see all this commotion happening around a group of men, I can tell some famous people are flying on the same flight. It only takes me a few moments to see they're in a band. As it turns out, there are actually two rock groups unexpectedly flying Southwest, with not only their band members but their crew. I don't recognize any of them, but I would recognize all their songs. I've grown up listening to their music.

Southwest is open seating. With all my miles and preferred status from frequent flights, I always make the A-list section, so I never bother to look at my boarding pass until the last minute.

End of B group? What the heck?

I tell myself I'm just grateful to be on the flight and hope that I'll get an aisle seat.

As I board the packed plane, I spot an aisle seat open midway back. Carrying my usual overstuffed bag and packed carry on, I struggle to lift it to the overhead. A nice gentleman seated across the aisle unbuckles his seat belt and offers a helping hand.

"Thank you, sir," I say while grabbing half my office out of the bags and putting it beneath my seat.

"No problem," he replies as he sits back in his seat and seems to be occupied working on something, just as I intend to be. Now if only those rowdy guys around him would cool it a bit.

As I take out my computer from my case, the book I plan on reading drops out into the aisle. The nice gentleman who helped me picks it up, stares at it for a moment, and then hands it back to me.

I'm wearing my usual travel clothes of jeans, a black shirt, and, of course, my four-inch Fendi short boot heels. Ah, the shoes, a trademark I have become known for. I love my heels and wear them practically everywhere.

"Nice shoes," he says. "I think you dropped this."

God seems to be winking at me, showing His sense of humor, though I don't know this at the time. The book is *Calling in "The One": 7 Weeks to Attract the Love of Your Life* by Katherine Woodward Thomas. A friend gave it to me, so I decided to start reading it on this flight.

"Can I ask you what you do for a living?" he says.

He has a gentle tone and a Midwestern accent. When I look into his friendly eyes, there's something inside of me that feels compelled to give him an answer I usually don't give others.

"I'm a pastor."

"A preacher. Really?" he says with a kind smile.

I nod. "I am. Totally true."

I typically don't tell anybody I'm a pastor for many reasons. Revealing who I am usually results in two hours of counseling or two hours of debate. Most of the time I simply want to have a little bit of private time, reading a book or writing in my journal. So instead of saying "pastor," I'll usually say I'm a motivational speaker. Then when they ask what kind of motivation, I'll say inspirational, and when they ask what sort that might be, I tell them, "God."

I guess all roads in my life lead back to Him, don't they?

I don't mind sharing this today, however. The man across the aisle introduces himself as Jonathan Cain and tells me he's in the band Journey. They normally don't fly Southwest, but they needed to be in Texas for a business dinner, so they took an earlier flight.

He has his laptop open in front of him, so I ask what he's working on.

"I'm writing a memoir. I've been working on it for years. About growing up in Chicago."

Jonathan opens up his heart in the next two and a half hours, sharing his life like an open book. He tells me as a young boy he wanted to be a priest and he would pretend to pray over communion using his father's golf trophy as a chalice while draping his bed blanket around his neck as a robe, reciting Latin and making the sign of the cross until his mom came in and busted him. I'm chuckling on the inside, thinking how a rocker wanted to be a priest and how a pastor wanted to be a rocker. If only I could sing. We continue to exchange our life stories, finding similar tracks, experiences, locations, and likes. Our lives have run parallel paths, making it like we're two old familiar souls intersecting at this kairos moment.

Halfway through the flight and conversation, which glides by with ease, Jon begins to tear up as he shares about surviving a horrific school fire at his Catholic school, Our Lady of the Angels, in Chicago when he was in third grade, a fire that ended up killing ninety-two children and three nuns.

"I was born in February, so I was too young to attend the year before. Otherwise, my class would've been on the second floor, and I would have been in those flames."

His father tells him that God has spared his life as an eight-year-old because one day he's going to be a famous songwriter. Jon is not sure about that, but his father's belief in him never wavers, and one thing Jon is sure about is his father. His father loves him unconditionally, teaching him how to pray.

As Jonathan shares his story, I can feel the hurt and pain in his words and tone. They're cloaked all over him. Talking about his father and the tragedy at the school makes him talk about God, about how confused he was at everything.

"I felt abandoned by God," he tells me. "It didn't make sense. Two-forty p.m., I'm staring at my Mickey Mouse watch thinking just twenty more minutes and we wouldn't be here."

He tells me he gave up his desire to be a priest and instead turned his drive toward becoming a musician. In turn, I begin to share about my father's death, how I was sexually and physically abused, and how a divine encounter with God led me to find the love I had been looking for. Jon is fully engaged. Talking to him is effortless with a sense of familiarity, though we have just met.

"You're deep, Jon," I eventually tell him after we've talked for a while.

He chuckles. "I'm not deep."

"You're very deep in the Spirit."

He seems to be surprised to hear me say that. Eventually as he continues to talk about things that have happened in his life, events and circumstances I can relate to, he asks me an amazing question.

"Is it possible that I can go back to how I felt as a boy? To know the Jesus I knew as a child?"

"God loves you and He's after you," I say. "He's been chasing you for a long time. The Lord definitely has something for you."

These aren't mere words of encouragement I'm giving to a stranger. I know I'm meant to be on this plane, sitting in this exact seat. As our conversation unfolds, I sense this very strong spiritual connection with Jon, as if I've known him all my life. I realize he's a kindred soul.

"You are going to get your story published," I tell him without a doubt in my mind.

Like some kind of spiritual planner God is unfolding inside of my heart, I am given three very distinct words. I can see the book, and I see the studio he is dreaming of building. Then I see a date, too, and I know what it means. I can't tell him that, however.

Lord, what are you trying to tell me here?

This encounter is unlike any I've ever had before. This is different from first meeting Donald Trump, or being introduced to Michael Jackson, or sharing my story with Kid Rock. My mind cannot wrap around what I feel in my spirit.

I open up about some of my own mess in the middle, about my public testimony, along with my divorce. I've been on a similar journey, and I know something by now: God never tells us all the details. We want the whole plan, but honestly, we can't handle the whole plan.

"God doesn't give you details to your destiny," I tell Jon. "He tells you the end from the beginning, but he doesn't show you all the mess in the middle."

"Is it too late for me to return to the Lord?" he asks me.

Before we leave, I tell him the faith he had as a child can come back. I will repeat the theme of my life to him.

"When everything in my life fell apart, I clung to my core. I never lost my love for the Lord. That childlike faith in God did not waver. It doesn't have to waver for you any longer, Jon."

Years later, Jon reveals in an interview that he never felt understood by a woman like he did that day. Our God is omniscient and will fill our hearts and mouths with His wisdom and love when we open ourselves to manifest His mandate in the earth.

Not long after meeting Jon on the plane, I wake up one morning with a song. I've never written a song in my entire life, but God urges me to get out my notebook and begin to write. I don't know what I'm doing, yet the words rush out of my heart.

My soul's journey home
A place I want to be

Wrapped in His love
Is where I find me.

False illusions
Pains from my past
I struggle to leave it all behind
I pray these fears won't last.

Finding my way through the darkness of the night
Guided by His glory
Captured by His light
I'm coming home
I'm coming home
With blessings beyond anything I've ever known
I'm coming home
I'm coming home
To that place where I belong.

The voices in my head that keep me bound
I'm fighting back this time
I'm not backing down
On the wings of His sweet grace
Ready to take flight.

Emerging to the beauty
A dawning of new light
Finding my way through the darkness of the night
Inspired by His glory
Guided by His light
I'm coming home
I'm coming home.

The day that I was gone
I never felt alone
Shine Your Heavenly mystery
Down on me
More than I am
More than I've ever been
You've opened up my eyes
To the road You've paved for me.

Emerging to the beauty
A dawning of new light
Finding my way through the darkness of the night
Inspired by His glory
Guided by His light
I'm coming home
I'm coming home.

I keep in touch with Jon over time, occasionally sending him a Scripture or a prayer. I send lots of people messages like this every day. Jon sometimes sends me back a nature photo he's taken while on the road where He feels God is revealing Himself to him. So after I write my song, I decide to tell him what happened.

I guess you're inspiring me in some way because I wrote a song this morning.

Send it to me! Jon writes back. Do you see it being a ballad and do you have a melody in mind?

I never think Jon would want to see it. This is the man who wrote "Faithfully," and who co-wrote "Open Arms" and "Don't Stop Believin'" with Steve Perry and Neal Schon, and he wants me to send him these song lyrics I scribbled down.

I don't even know the difference between a ballad and a melody.

I send him the lyrics and describe a little of how the words make me feel.

217

I'm very intimidated. It's personal and intimate, like opening up a part of me and letting him inside. Jon quickly gets back to me with his input.

It's really good, Paula. You wrote everything—the chorus, verses, even the bridge.

Thank you! I write back.

I'm going to change a couple words and put music to it.

He does and sends me back the completed song. It's amazing to hear him singing those words, the very ones I had to get out onto the page.

Now as I look at it, the song is epic. I didn't realize I was prophetically writing our story.

How amazing is God? How cool is He?

I have found my way through the darkness of the night. It is a true dawning of a new light.

Yes, Lord, you've found a way to bring me home.

By this time I've truly come into my own, confident and honestly content in my singleness. I know that I'm not going to settle in my life, and marriage isn't something I'm looking for. I love fulfilling purpose, and that's exactly what I'm doing. My prayer is to die whole, and I'm finally comfortable in my own skin. In a straightforward manner, not a sad one, I ask myself, "Will I be the girl that loved the world but never has an intimate love?" I just know I'm not going to ever allow myself to not be valued and respected "as is"! I march to the beat of my own drum, and that beat is God's Word in my life.

We don't know all the steps we need to take, the bridges we need to cross, and the intersections we need to go through before our destiny can be revealed. The pain and struggle Jonathan is going through with his divorce and the conflict with his children helps create a bond between us. I understand, having been there myself, and know that only God can really bring us to the other side. The landscape of life will change but it doesn't mean God is finished with us. In fact, new beginnings with greater beauty and light can spring forth from our darkness if we allow them to.

They say opposites attract, but in Jon I find likeness much more appealing and satisfying. Our lives were very much identical but within their own distinct manner. Jon makes me laugh, he brightens my smile and helps me to breathe more in life. He gets me, as I do him. He understands and supports my purpose on earth, a rare thing to find in a lifetime. There will be long talks, romantic walks, photography, cooking meals together, going to baseball and basketball games, skiing, diving, horseback riding, gym time, meeting each other's friends and family members, and lots of prayer time together. Jon grabs my hands one day and starts praying over me. I melt and feel a floodgate open in my heart and soul that brings strength, joy, peace, and safety.

Is this what a "husband" feels like, God? I can do life with this man...

I help Jonathan find the faith he lost in his life, and he helps me find the fullness I've always longed for in mine. I don't know if I believe in the concept of a soul mate, but if there's such a thing, Jon is mine. I know it's the most ordained relationship in my life outside of having Brad. There is no doubt in my mind it was God's intention for us to be together.

Jon wants to meet and be baptized by a spiritual mentor of mine, Archbishop Nicholas Duncan-Williams. I'm so blessed to be able to see a supernatural and spiritual breakthrough happening in Jon's life. Archbishop Williams sees Jon's repentance for wasted years and sin he had yielded to in his life along with the work of the Holy Spirit taking place in him, too. Jon's hunger for Jesus is infectious, causing a renewed passion and fire in my own life.

"This man should not have been set loose," the archbishop tells me. "You have made Hell furious that they lost him."

I look at him innocently, smile, and shrug my shoulders as if to say, "Take it up with God." He asks me if I love Jon, and I say emphatically, "YES!"

"Then we will do the work," he declares.

I understand what he is conveying to me. I know Jon by now, and I see his desire to serve God forcefully and in complete surrender. I also recognize the last thing I need to do is "pastor" Jon. He wants someone to disciple him and teach him the things of God. Jon dives all the way in, wanting God deeply and desperately. This makes him all the more attractive to me.

Very soon Jon asks me to marry him. The bottom line: we want to do the right thing. We don't want to live in sin or even dance too closely toward that sinking line. At this point we know and believe we're meant to be together.

Jon arranges a trip to Memphis to meet with my mom again. We had gone to a few Grizzlies games and a Journey concert together. I am thinking we are going to dinner and will spend some quality time together, as Jon knows how close I am to my mom now. He asks her for a recommendation in Memphis and she suggests Chez Philippe, a gourmet French restaurant at the Peabody Hotel; she calls her friend, Andreas Kisler, and arranges for a private room.

After Jon orders a delicious meal and we savor it, he suddenly looks to Mom and asks her for my hand in marriage. My heart feels like it is going to explode. In true Janelle fashion, she gives him that Southern-charm smile.

"Well, I hope you'd better dang well asked her," Mom says. "I would be honored to have you as my son-in-law."

We burst out laughing, pick up our glasses, and toast to the love we have found in each other and the life we plan to build together. Mom and Jon become very close with a special bond. She can talk sports better than most men, enjoys being a history buff, reads more than 200 books a year, and has a strength and grit that Jon says he both loves and respects.

While being greatly influenced by his dad, Lenny, Jon is honorable when it comes to class and courtesy. He goes to my son, my board, and those who have spiritual influence in my life to share his desire to marry me. They give us wisdom, insight, counsel, and their love for the union and covenant about to be formed. We both have come from broken marriages, yet deeply respect the sacred covenant we are making together. We desire the blessing of God and man.

There is a lot of prayer—hours, days, and weeks of prayer—and many trips to Ghana to spend time in counsel before the Lord. Brad takes a liking to Jon immediately. This is not the norm for someone who had to grow up really fast and become fiercely protective of his mother as the man in him emerged. He has seen the best and worst of human behavior, and with a keen sense of discernment, he sees the sincerity and authenticity of Jon.

I am encouraged by someone close to wait a while. "You've got to let your base date him," I'm told. "You both have a lot to gain or lose." He reasons that since I had never showed anything in public about my failing marriage with Randy, the divorce felt too sudden and traumatic. I understand, and I would never want to do anything to bring offense to anyone.

But do you live by image, Paula, or do you live with reality?

I know in my heart and by the Word of God I have to do right with what He says. We don't want to waste any time. Jon and I want to be right before God. We have peace and blessing from everyone in any authority position in my life. We took heed to the wisdom and introduced Jon to the congregation I pastor, we went on double dates and posted our times together on social media. When God is in your relationship, there is no need to hide or work in darkness. We date before the world and then end up having three weddings.

Our first wedding is in Africa in December 2014, which holds a very special place in our heart. Our next wedding takes place in April with 150 of our closest family and friends at the Ritz in Orlando, Florida. It is a day of perfection and beautiful in every way from start to finish. The next day we have a wedding at our church. I figure this marriage is sealed in the name of the Father, the Son, and the Holy Spirit. Jonathan designs a wedding ring for me, with red rubies representing the blood of Jesus and black diamonds representing His spiritual authority and grace. It means everything to me.

Life is not about the size or about the status. It's not about the price tag or about the popularity. Life is about relationships. It's about having a relationship with Jesus Christ and about building relationships with others.

The first third of my life was spent in search of those relationships. The next third was spent trying to grow those relationships and create more. Now in this new phase of my life, I realize why they're so important to me, why they're so natural and why they happen.

Maybe I've become that safe place for many people because deep inside I wanted that safe place. You usually give love the way you want it. Or you become what you want others to be to you. With Jon, I find the safe place I've been looking for, and I receive love the way I need it.

We all need to be heard, and we all want validation. For a lifetime, it feels as if I've listened to people and loved them and poured into their lives. God's amazing gift is to bring a man who listens to me and accepts me as I am. Without trying to fix anything. He is the home I've been looking for my entire life.

19.

HOPE

God, I thank You for bringing new life, in Your way and in Your timing, for You are good.

On April 26, 2015, a day of love and celebration and God's goodness, I'm reminded of the power and the promise of Ephesians 3:20–21 (MSG): "God can do anything, you know—far more than you could ever imagine or guess or request in your wildest dreams! He does it not by pushing us around but by working within us, his Spirit deeply and gently within us."

God heard and answered the longing of my heart. He lavished me with love when Jon and I sealed our hearts and holy purpose before Him.

Today is a day to celebrate God. His love for us and for the love He has given to Jon and me. For the love we receive from our family and friends joining us for our sun-soaked and windswept wedding day.

"Marriage is a commitment to God and life. To the best that two people can find and bring out of each other. To supporting being whole and complete individuals while loving and fulfilling purpose together."

I had meticulously labored over every word of the hour-long sermon that Pastor Doug Shackelford would deliver. As a pastor, weddings are one of my favorite occasions to fulfill. This was not any wedding or any sermon, but it was Jon's and mine. I locked myself away in prayer and fasting for two straight days, taking more than fourteen hours to construct the sermon. I wanted God's Word, His heart, and His thoughts for Jon and me. As always, He spoke and I wrote.

As Pastor Doug delivers the sermon, I stand next to Jon, hand in hand, listening while looking over to the amazing man I'm marrying. Jon's solemn expression shows how serious he is about the vows we are taking, and also reveals the obvious emotions he's holding back. The same feelings of utter gratitude toward God.

"Your life has so much meaning to so many people," Pastor Doug tells me. "We can be in the most intense meetings, and when Jonathan walks in everything shifts. It's amazing to see how happy Pastor Paula is. Your life has been so worthwhile for the masses. I'm glad you found that one person."

This is a day to celebrate my gladness, to celebrate the joy of these moments. Like Brad walking me down the aisle, his smile so bright and infectious. He is joy and restoration in physical form. Seeing Brad saved and serving God is one of the greatest joys of my life. I won't ever forget lying on his bed for hours praying and praying for him.

God, you are so great.

"And, Paula—the man who you've chosen above all others now stands before you. Do you take Jonathan, whom you hold by the hand, to be your beloved husband? To—"

"I do!" I interrupt, suddenly looking like a grade-school girl speaking out in class. Everybody bursts out in laughter.

"She's ready to say I do," Doug says with a grin. "I'm almost there—four more words."

Once again, there's that girl. The one who never stops talking in Ms. Shealy's class, and the one who leads the students in singing in Mr. Sheridan's class. Yet as I take my vows, facing Jon and holding both of his hands, and as my emotions start to spill out in tears, something unexpected happens.

"I vow to be there fo you always," Pastor Doug says.

"I vow to be there for you always."

Jon moves his right hand and slips it into his pocket.

"When you fall..."

"When you fall..." I repeat.

Jon brings his handkerchief up to my eyes and wipes my tears away. Gracefully. Gently. Proudly. Lovingly. Confidently. Servant-heartedly.

Faithfully.

"I will catch you," Pastor Doug says.

The unexpected arrives as I barely manage to say the words because I'm so overcome with emotion.

"I will catch you," I whisper through choked words.

In this moment, I know.

I am enough.

This is what is right about me.

Two and two do add up to four.

That handkerchief softly sliding my tears away is real, and this is all really happening, and I am loved. God has given me His gift, a husband, a strong man who loves me in every way.

"Angels put you on a plane from Memphis, Tennessee. From across the aisle, you saw the man that I could be."

He sits behind the instrument he knows so well, his fingers moving over the black and white keys they're so comfortable with. He sings to the girl in ivory who leans against the pillar that's always been there her whole life.

"I never settled, never gave up on my heart. Unafraid to dream what only Heaven knew. From the first look—yeah, I knew it from the start—God gave me you."

Like he's done his whole adult life, Jon gives me the gift of his heart in a song. Except this song belongs solely to me.

After Archbishop Williams serves Jon and me communion, he makes a decree for God to bless this union, asking Him to allow us to make a difference in others' lives. Then as he prays a mighty prayer over us in the name of Jesus, I look up to see the clouds in the sky shifting and swirling as if they're in a tense struggle.

"We raise fire walls over this union. We raise prayer shields around this union. And declare that the adversary would not access this union. That he would not engage any one of them. In the name of Jesus, I declare above all other things that this union is not just about love or affection, but it's about your original intention. It's about a divine agenda to impact nations. To transform communities. To touch lives. To bring glory to God. May your lives impact many. May you bring glory and honor to His name."

All these moments will remind me of Psalm 133:1 from *The Message* that was quoted during Pastor Doug's message at the wedding: "How wonderful, how beautiful, when brothers and sisters get along!"

It is a first for both Jon and me, perfect harmony with everyone who attends. We carefully selected our closest friends and family to keep it intimate. There is nothing pretentious; everything is pure about this wedding and union.

My soon-to-be sister-in-law, Tyra, and niece, Brittany, create a masterpiece of beautiful makeup and hair. It's the first time they have ever fixed me up, yet it feels like we have known each other for a lifetime, kindred spirits and souls. With each brushstroke I feel love and the genuine desire for me to be the most beautiful bride their brother-in-law and uncle has waited for. Jon's brothers, Tommy and Hal, love me like the sister they never had. My mother smiles with a love and deep peace that radiates through her being of an assurance that her baby girl is finally in the right arms. She has adored Jon from day one and cannot be happier for this joyous time. My son and daughter-in-law, Rachel, are nearby, and I feel completeness for me and for all of us. We are a family. There are joy and love for the celebration of two lives that are divinely orchestrated into one union.

Jon and I have attended to every detail of our wedding together. Our theme is "Piano and Heels" with a massive red piano cake topped with five-inch heels displayed as you walk into the stunning Ritz ballroom for the reception. From the meal to the band capping the night off with "Faithfully" and "Don't Stop Believin'," it is truly magical, romantic, holy, and fun.

I love watching our blended family and friends celebrate. The cheers given to us during the reception will be incredible blessings of affirmation to Jon and me. Like the blessing from Jon's son, Weston.

"When I sat down for the first time at dinner with you guys, Paula told me something. That you guys didn't need each other, that you guys were better together. That resonated with me and it has further, 'cause individually you guys are beautiful, amazing people, but together you guys are like this perfect unit of just being one. I love you both, and I'm happy for you guys."

Brad jokes and entertains the crowd before becoming serious and sharing his love to Jon and me: "Our family walks around with our wounds visible for everyone to see. Imperfect humans. You embrace that. You are that. You accepted that as a couple, the grace that God bestowed upon you and on this family, and we're so glad we're one unit now. Thank you for showing that off to everyone. We love you."

One of my best friends since eighth grade, Candace, will honor me with her words: "Pastor Doug really hit it for me when he said, 'Paula you have touched so many people and meant so much to so many people.' It just makes me want to cry. I have to be honest—there's nothing lovelier that could be said about a human. I'm so happy that was said and meant about you. Thank God for you and thank God for you guys being together. I'm so thrilled to be here to toast both of you. Cheers."

Then finally, Rosa, Archbishop Williams's dear wife, sends us off with an amazing affirmation of grace and hope: "How amazing God can take and connect seemingly disparate pieces and people and mold them together into one for his divine plan and purpose. Pastor Paula, a vibrant woman of God on fire for the Lord and a leader in the Kingdom. Jon, a gifted musician, rock star, celebrity, an icon in his genre and generation. Two worlds apart. Two seemingly different people who meet of all places on a Southwest airline. Pastor Paula preaching about her journey. Jon part of a famous music group called Journey. And God taking them on a new journey that's not even on a map."

Both Jon and I smile, knowing the words are absolutely perfect as Rosa continues, "Walt Whitman said 'the strongest and sweetest songs yet remain to be sung.' And more importantly, God said to prophet Isaiah, 'Behold, I will do something new, Now it will spring forth; Will you not be aware of it? I will even make a roadway in the wilderness, Rivers in the desert.' How wonderful—how miraculous Jon and Paula followed God's leading to each other. Jon and Paula, we raise our glasses to celebrate your purpose and holy union, with the highest hopes for your happiness and assurances of God's blessing and favor."

Amen!

20.

PURPOSE

God has something greater for us. We all have dreams yet to fulfill, promises waiting to come to pass, songs and books yet to write, companies to build, families to start, sermons to preach, and seasons to weather. We are the only ones who can forfeit what God has for us. No enemy, no devil, no one can take it unless we give it up. So, no matter how it looks or feels now, we must hold on. Quitting is not an option, even when chapters of our life story are unexpected and not desired. We stay the course with a full assurance that somehow, some way, God takes what the enemy meant for the bad and turns it to the good for those who love God and are called according to (which means in harmony with) His purpose.

The graveyard is filled with unrealized potential, possibilities, and purpose. It is the wealthiest spot on planet Earth, where people are buried with the greatest books that won't be written, inventions that won't be created, and ideas that won't come to fruition. People keep dying with their treasure. We are not supposed to die until we are empty. Let's die finished! Life is evidence we are not empty yet. When the apostle Paul stated, "I am now ready to be offered up," he was literally saying, "I am dispensed, my life and purpose have been poured out like a drink offering." While most people are trying to get filled, the true goal for a person who understands purpose is to be emptied out; to realize that our life experiences have all been part of the development process to build and release through us something greater, something that will outlive us and continue to make a difference in generations to come.

While building a new life with Jon, my own life becomes revitalized and focused thanks to my husband. In turn, his life develops new purpose, and after so many songs written, God fills him with a renewed spirit to write new melodies, ones that lift up Christ's name. Songs that God wants to hear. Like so many amazing things God does, Jon will discover this new calling in the most unlikely of places: on a cruise ship.

In 2014, shortly before a cruise to the Bahamas where I'll be ministering to 200 women in ministry and leadership, I discover we don't have anybody to lead worship. So I go to Jon and tell him the situation.

"Can you bring your piano and learn eight worship songs?"

We both know the setting that waits for us. Honestly, a cruise is not the most ideal place for worshipping God. The theater atmosphere is usually stale and predictable, for a quick turnaround to please the tourist crowd. Jon doesn't hesitate, however, especially since he's already planned on accompanying me on the trip. So there he comes, this man who's performed in front of millions with the most advanced tools and the greatest sound systems set in place. He plugs in his keyboard and sets it up at center stage, without a backdrop or anything else around him. I pray over him, recognizing he is somewhat nervous in this new atmosphere. As I lay hands on Jon, I advise him to simply flow with God, that it's in him, and when he gets to that piano and opens his mouth it will pour out of him for the purposes of God. Sure enough, when he opens his mouth and starts singing and worshipping, something happens.

Suddenly there are 200 women weeping, including me. Half of them are lying on the floor giving praise to God. The Presence of God is profound and powerful. It is a holy moment of awe in which even the workers on the cruise ship who snuck in to see the "Journey guy" are at a standstill with a reverence of divine manifestation. I know Jon has to be wondering what's going on here. Yet I know exactly what is happening. Everything has come together and nothing has been forced. *This* is the organic way God works, the anointing He pours over us. Jon has never played with me before, but, like the first time I met him, it feels like we've been swimming together in these waters for all our lives.

Jon brings his sweet, soft heart to this place and enters a new arena, one that will produce a Christmas and multiple worship albums. He finds a new purpose and destiny, not just to play to millions as he continues to tour and make music as part of the band Journey, but to use his creative abilities in any way to honor God. As he will say in an interview, he feels some kind of supernatural rush come over him. Jon sees the bigger picture, and as he does, he reactivates something inside me. God continues to remind me of my divine purpose and how His plan will prevail.

During our next trip to South Africa, I am scheduled to speak, and they tell me they have a musician who's going to play for me. Jon tells them "that's okay" and decides to get on stage with me. While I'm preaching, I can feel the shift that happens spiritually when Jon starts playing. My assignment to preach the gospel has always brought forth the fruit of salvation, deliverance, and revelation. This time there is a powerful intensity like I have seldom experienced before. It's as if the more Jon plays, the more my spirit is open to the Holy Spirit downloading His power, insight, wisdom, and Word through me. I am in awe as much as the congregation is. Something greater is taking place in the way I minister and the results of that ministry.

As I begin to reflect, I realize after having nineteen life crises, I had started to play it safe. I unconsciously and perhaps cowardly pulled back to my comfort zone of teaching the Word of God. I know there is a mantle on my life for moving in the power of God through His taught Word. I found it easier to settle for less than what God had called me to do in the fullness of His plan. Obedience has a price, and the "oil" of God will cost you something. When Jon and I start walking in purpose together, something is ignited on the inside of me, a passion and renewal for what I know I was born to do, for my purpose. The one God showed an eighteen-year-old tarrying at the altar, the one He revealed to me when I saw myself speaking to millions all over the world, the one He positioned me to fulfill when I first began to preach and when I started Paula White Ministries.

There is a lot to be said about "covering," and God's divine order according to His Word. There are times in the Word that God Himself made exceptions, but that is not the norm for how He operates. Culture has done a great job at bringing confusion and contradiction about what God's plan and perfect will was always intended to be. Two truly are better than one, and when God has joined them together, their life as one in purpose will always glorify Him.

This is what I was born to do, what God's ultimate calling is in my life. I'm meant to go out and to deliver a Word to people all over the world. God weaves two new lives together with Jon and me, and together we find a greater purpose, which was fashioned before the beginning of time.

To everything there is a season, according to Ecclesiastes chapter 3. To everything there is a time and a purpose under Heaven. When we are in the timing of God, we are positioned to release the purpose of God in our lives. The difference between anything here on earth is seasons. When we do not discern the shift of God's season, there will be lack in our life. It is possible to be in a season that we are not cooperating with. The difference between our today and our tomorrow is our decision to agree with our "yes" to God's purpose for our life.

In 2011, Donald Trump calls me and asks if I can bring some people together for their advice and prayers as he considers running in next year's presidential race. He's mentioned this to me before and has asked me to pray about it, and now I can see he's seriously considering it. Around thirty pastors meet with him at Trump Tower to petition God and ask for His guidance on this monumental decision.

With a final decision needing to be made in a manner of days, Trump truly wants to hear from God. We pray for hours. This might seem strange for some of the others, praying so fervently over this businessman they only know in the media and hearing from his heart, but to me this is very normal and natural.

The following day I go back to his office to talk with him.

"What do you think, Paula? What's God saying to you?"

He asks this often. What do I feel, and what do I sense God is telling me? These are the natural conversations we've had when he's shared parts of his life with me, when he's asked me to pray for family members or personal situations. Naturally he's asking the same sort of thing anybody might ask their pastor. As always, I tell him exactly what I'm thinking.

"It would be great to have you as president for our country, sir. But as my friend, I'd hate to see that happen to you."

I can only imagine how things would change dramatically in his life, and how his open-door policy would no longer be there, along with the personal impact it will have on his family and business. Potentially, he has nothing to gain and so much to lose unless this is genuinely a "calling" and part of God's plan for his life. From a logical and selfish position, it seems crazy. He has an ideal life, which seems absurd to give up for the brutal world of politics unless it's a mandate or part of your purpose.

"I don't feel it's the right timing," I tell him.

"I don't, either. But keep it tucked away."

This means for me to keep praying about it, something he knows I will always do for him. Over the next few years, every time I see him, he will remind me about this, to keep praying. I can tell it's something in his spirit, not just his mind.

By 2014, Trump makes up his mind. One day while Jon and I are visiting him in New York, I'm praying over him once again, asking God to show Trump His will. We're the only ones here, and he is holding this idea close to his chest. After we leave, he calls me up with a decision.

"I'm going to go for this," Trump says.

Now I know our prayers need to intensify.

He tells me he would love to meet with pastors and asks if I can be in charge of reaching out to the evangelicals. In many ways, we both pretty much assume this, since back in 2011 he had asked me to gather some pastors together to pray over him. Basically, he wants me to be the bridge between him and the evangelicals in our country.

"I'd be honored, Mr. Trump."

Right away, before making any calls or plans or lists, I go into serious prayer. I seek Godly counsel from those whom I submit myself to and speak into my life. I've met and spoken with previous presidents and those who were running for the highest office in the country and perhaps the world, but I've never done politics on this level. This is not a photo op or a few speaking engagements or a roundtable discussion to hear my opinion. I am being requested to come all the way in by more than Mr. Trump but by God Himself. I suddenly realize this is very real. This is happening.

This is all part of the bigger assignment, Paula.

As soon as Trump asks me to gather together religious leaders for him to talk to, I know I need to implement a plan. I seek God for a strategy. My vision and goals and plan come together in my spirit quickly. I think about Trump and the perception they might have of him. It's very different than the person I know. It makes me think of my own life, and I understand in some respects. People have sound bites and snapshots of Pastor Paula, but some of them are flat-out wrong, and others are only half true. This is what I think about Trump. People know the tough businessman, the New Yorker from Queens, the author of *The Art of the Deal,* the guy always saying, "You're fired." But there's so much more about this man that people need to discover.

If I can bridge people—if I can help with the evangelicals who don't know Trump—and if I can somehow make it as if they're one-on-one having lunch with him, or riding in a golf cart with him as I've had the privilege to see and experience over and over in my life... then maybe they won't put him on the hot seat but instead they'll build a relationship.

Life is all about relationships, as I've said before. It's the people around you; it's the quality of the relationships you have.

This is what I strive to do: to form a bridge between the Christian leaders out there and the Donald Trump I know. To let them hear his heart, versus playing the sound clips from the fake media that's fighting him or the narrative that's trying to be created about him.

"We need an endorsement from the evangelical community," Corey Lewandowski, Trump's campaign manager, tells me as the Minnesota primary approaches. This is something Trump never says or asks for. I have no official position here. I'm here to help those in my world hear what Trump has to say. But very quickly I realize what they need.

"You're not getting an endorsement from someone," I tell Corey. "You're getting a board. I'm going to deliver a group to you. If not, they'll pluck us off one by one."

Over the years, I've developed many friendships with people in ministry. I know within our Christian landscape the left side such as Pentecostals and Charismatics will join in unison with the more evangelical right. So I reach out to some of these friends of mine. Dr. Tim Clinton is one of the first I contact. As the president of the American Association of Christian Counselors, Tim is someone I've known for more than twenty years. As everybody who knows me can attest, I'm a loyal person. I maintain long relationships that are built on trust and integrity. When I talk to these friends and ask them to meet with Trump, to hear what he has to say, they agree, knowing it's not an endorsement for him but it's an opportunity to be involved in the presidential process, to be able to have a say and also make a grounded decision on the candidate they choose.

The initial meetings to introduce key Christian leaders to Trump are instrumental to the campaign. There are usually thirty to forty people who come to meet with him. I send him the bios of everybody who will be there so Trump can study them before greeting them in person. Before each gathering, I meet with him in his office to go over the list of names and the items on the agenda.

Over time, a strong group of faith leaders will be on Trump's evangelical executive advisory team. Along with me and Tim Clinton, here are some of those individuals on the board:

Jerry Falwell Jr., president of Liberty University

Dr. James Dobson of Focus on the Family

Ralph Reed, the founder of the Faith and Freedom Coalition

Greg Laurie, senior pastor of Harvest Christian Fellowship

Eric Metaxas, author and host of *The Eric Metaxas Show*

Sammy Rodriguez, president of the National Hispanic Christian Leadership Conference

Franklin Graham, evangelist and CEO of the Billy Graham Evangelistic Association and of Samaritan's Purse

Johnnie Moore, CEO of Kairos

Jentezen Franklin, senior pastor of Free Chapel, host of *Kingdom Connection*

James Robison, evangelist, president of Life Outreach International

Kenneth and Gloria Copeland, evangelists, Kenneth Copeland Ministries

Harry Jackson, senior pastor of Hope Christian Church

Dr. Jack Graham, senior pastor of Prestonwood Baptist Church

Michelle Bachmann, former congresswoman

Dr. George Wood, general superintendent of the General Council of the Assemblies of God

Darrell Scott, senior pastor of New Spirit Revival Center

Ronnie Floyd, senior pastor of Cross Church

Dr. David Jeremiah, senior pastor of Shadow Mountain Community Church and founder of Turning Point radio and television ministries

Robert Morris, senior pastor of Gateway Church

Dr. Richard Land, president of Southern Evangelical Seminary

Dr. Tom Mullins, senior pastor of Christ Fellowship

Apostle Guillermo Maldonado, senior pastor of El Rey Jesús

Marcus and Joni Lamb, founders of Daystar Television Network

Robert Jeffress, senior pastor of First Baptist Church of Dallas

The core team starts here along with many other notable leaders that expand to Trump's Faith Leadership Team made up of thousands.

There are meetings with Trump and his campaign team, along with calls, much prayer, advice, and activation. I become consumed working on this assignment that I now recognize God has given me from years ago. Like every assignment in fulfilling my purpose, I count the cost, seek Godly counsel, and do a lot of praying with fasting. I ask myself the tough questions facing the very concerns that I have for Trump early on. I realize that I potentially have a lot more to lose from a rational standpoint than to gain. I also recognize that I did not choose this assignment—it chose me. I can turn my back on Trump and play it safe, or I can fulfill what God is asking me to do and step out of the boat into the deep and uncharted waters waiting for me.

I choose to follow what God has for me, fully knowing it will often be misunderstood and controversial. When news first starts getting out about our meetings, things turn ugly quickly. I am in Paris when it feels like every activist group and even many whom I have been longtime friends or colleagues with begin to viciously attack me on social media. While staying up that night, I watch my Twitter account drop by the tens of thousands of followers. My creative director calls me to ask if I want to put out a statement to smooth things over and be "non-political."

"Absolutely not," I respond. "People may not understand now, or ever for that matter. It may cost me relationships, reputation, and resources, but I know when I hear from God, He is the one I will obey."

I know it will be a bumpy road, but I also know God will give His strength to do what He has called me to do.

The first priority of this board, more than anything else, is to pray over Trump. "So today for Donald Trump. We pray for his family. We pray for his associates. We pray that what he has heard today from those who have spoken in his life he will consider."

As Pastor David Jeremiah prays for Trump, forty other evangelicals stand alongside them with heads bowed and eyes closed. It's September 2015, and we're meeting Trump in his New York office. He's already announced he's running, so this is one of the many meetings I help to orchestrate to bring the Trump I know before these Christian leaders.

"Lord, whatever it is You're going to do to bring around him the right people as he moves forward in this campaign, we ask You to give him direction and give him hope," Pastor Jeremiah says. "And, Lord, thank You for allowing us to be here for this special moment. Perhaps we'll look back on this day and remember that we stood together and we prayed over the next president of the United States."

I ask Franklin Graham to pray next. His deep and refined Southern accent has the echoes of his father layered throughout it.

"Father, you said in your Word, any man that lacks wisdom, let him ask of God, that giveth to all men liberally, and upbraideth not..."

I can't help remembering when Trump turned sixty in 2006, giving him something he once told me he wanted the most: a Bible signed by one of his heroes, evangelist Billy Graham. Now Graham's son will continue to lift up Trump before the Lord.

"No man can be successful as president of the United States without Your wisdom. And so we ask You today to give this man Your wisdom. Boldly make sure and certain that he hears. Manifest Yourself to him. And we thank You and praise You for a bold man, a strong man, and an obedient man. We praise You and we thank You. In Jesus's name."

As Trump stands in the center of us holding his Bible, I pray our final prayer. With one hand on his arm and the other on his chest, I reverently seek God as I lift my friend up to Him.

"Father, we just secure him right now by the blood of Jesus," I declare.

"We thank You that no weapon formed against him will be able to prosper. And any tongue that rises against him will be condemned according to the Word of God. Even as we lay hands on him right now, let Your hand be laid upon him. Let him have a greater encounter with You. A greater encounter with the Spirit of God. That according to Ephesians 1:17 and 18, the eyes of your heart may enlighten his, and that he will see the riches of the glory of Your inheritance in the saints. That any veil would be removed and his eyes would be opened to see the glory and the goodness of God. All of his days let him live well. I secure him. I secure his children. I secure his family. I secure his calling and his mantle. In Jesus's name. Amen."

As everyone says, "Amen," Trump thanks me and gives me a warm and gentle hug, the kind I might receive from my father if he were still alive. Trump genuinely appreciates everybody around him. He realizes the gravity of the journey he's embarking on, and he is seeking favor from the only person we need to ask for it.

Jon is by my side and witnesses what everybody else does in the meeting. Afterward, he tells me his initial reaction.

"God is doing something here," he says. "Trump listened to everything they said and could hear their hearts. He laid it out and told them he's a businessman who doesn't always say the right thing."

Jon can see the same thing I see, and he understands now.

"God's doing something in Donald Trump for the country," Jon says.

There's no way I can survive the campaign without Jon by my side. He's my gatekeeper, helping to lead me and stabilize me. In my times of exhaustion when I'm pouring myself into work, he comforts me and encourages me to stand strong. He keeps me on track.

When Jon and I got married, we made a commitment to do life together and to put God at the forefront of everything. When he is on tour, I am by his side where I hub in the city with him, flying back and forth to the church I pastor in Florida or to my preaching engagements. My plate is full, but as with all seasons of serving my purpose and staying faithful to my "yes," God gives me a sustaining grace and Jon will give me his love.

In January 2015, I fly with Trump and his team from West Palm Beach to Virginia, where he will deliver the convocation at Liberty University. Along with Trump are his daughter Ivanka, Jared Kushner, and the current campaign manager, Corey Lewandowski. I've been working closely with Corey, and others who are coming on board. There will be many flights like these in the months to come.

On this flight, I spend time explaining the evangelical landscape to Jared. The Harvard graduate is quite brilliant, a man with a good heart and integrity. He's a very caring and compassionate soul, and a fitting mate for someone like Ivanka. This is one of the reasons I'm here, because of my understanding of the landscape of ministry.

There are evangelicals, as everybody calls us, and we know we're all Christians, but many people in Washington don't understand the difference between Episcopal and Presbyterian and Methodist and Baptist and Southern Baptist and Independent Baptist and Church of God and Church of God in Christ. And on and on.

As I quickly give an overview of this to Jared, I can see his mouth dropping at all the complexities and nuances in the various denominations of Christianity.

This is one of several visits to Liberty that Trump will make. After meeting with Jerry Falwell Jr., the president of the university, Trump speaks to the students. As always, I pray over him for a minute and then sit down as he goes onto the stage. This speech is memorable and makes the rounds in the press simply because of one single word he pronounces.

"Two Corinthians 3:17. That's the whole ballgame," Trump says during his speech. When he gets off stage, Corey points out to him, "It's Second Corinthians." Trump looks at me and asks me if that's correct, and I tell him yes.

"That's not what he said," Trump says, pointing to the person who told him the Bible verse to say before he went out and spoke. I watch this unfold firsthand, and I've been told that this particular person is planning on supporting another candidate in the days to come.

Social media has a field day making jokes about this, while the media machine jumps at this to make some sort of commentary on Trump's faith that is absolutely absurd. In comparison to the daily vitriol he receives a year later, this is nothing. I'm not sure if Trump is set up or not, but I am realizing everything's changed for him now.

By now I've already seen and heard an ongoing narrative. The discussion about whether the candidate will be able to win over evangelicals. The more Trump continues to be open about his faith, the more backlash he receives. One example of this is in August of 2015 at the Family Leadership Summit in Ames, Iowa. When asked, "Have you ever asked God for forgiveness?" a loaded question that elicits laughter from the crowd simply because they know he's asking someone known for his confidence, Trump responds in his authentic manner, referring to communion as "when I drink my little wine...and eat my little cracker."

Trump is very business and politics savvy, and he assumes this question is more about personal behavior. I realize it's a theology question, one of several instances when someone manages to get a "gotcha!" moment from Trump.

Eventually I sit down with Mike Huckabee and Trump and respectfully address this issue of him sharing his faith.

"Sir, I suggest you make a decision whether you go public with your faith or whether you keep it very private and hold it close to your chest," I say.

The media is ruthlessly looking for any opportunity or creating one to categorize Trump as something he's not. He is proud to carry his Bible and talk about growing up in church, his confirmation and faith. I quickly see there is a hypocritical double standard that leaves Trump in a "darned if you do, darned if you don't" state in regard to his faith. Most people don't know "Christianese" (a reference often used for church culture). The fake news reminds me of the Pharisees trying to continually trap Jesus or his disciples. For the most part, it certainly feels like it is more about hype, drama, and ratings rather than respectable journalism.

"If you do go public, you need to know the theological angles they will come after you and be ready for that," I continue to say. "Otherwise I'd hold it close to my chest."

I see it as someone asking me to build a building. I wouldn't know the first thing to tell a builder. That's why you hire an architect, so they will be able to talk specifics and know the language of construction. That is his world, just like mine is being able to expound on the Word of God.

Trump understands I'm recommending holding his faith close to his chest. Those around him and in these meetings hear where he stands, often asking him very straightforward, tough questions, which he answers. Otherwise, he never talks about specifics after that day, not publicly. He won't carry his Bible, either. Even when asked in October 2016 by Raymond Arroyo from Fox News about what he prays for, Trump responds with the following: "I don't want to talk to you about that. I pray. It's very personal to me. I'm a person of belief. I certainly—I pray for my family. I pray for our country. But I don't want to talk to you about that. I think that's very personal."

"Okay. Between you and God."

"It *is* between me and God," Trump says.

When the issue of faith comes up from here on out, he will refer to what Pastor Robert Jeffress says all the time. Jeffress is one of the earliest faith leaders to support Trump's bid for the presidency.

"Look, I might not choose this man to be a Sunday school teacher in my church, but that's not what this election is about," Pastor Jeffress says. "It's about choosing the best leader to reverse the downward spiral of the nation."

"God, please give Mr. Trump Your words and Your mind. Use him, Lord. Let his words be Your words. Let him be sensitive to your Holy Spirit."

In the silence of my hotel room, I pray fervently. With the rest of the world outside, I petition God and I wait. Time stops in this space with the Lord. I've been here for hours, but it doesn't seem that way. I know I'm supposed to be here, praying for Donald Trump as he prepares to give his acceptance speech tonight at the Republican National Convention.

The urgency comes over me this morning at breakfast. Jon and I are downstairs enjoying our time with everyone, and Eric Trump says, "Paula, your prayers worked last night." Eric delivered a powerful and moving speech. Just as he went on the stage, his teleprompter went out, yet he kept going with an unction and passion that came from a deep place. He knocked it out of the ballpark. I say, "God is faithful," then turn to Jon and tell him

I need to go back to the hotel room because I feel a quickening in my spirit to pray for Mr. Trump.

"I need to go fast," I tell him. "God wants to speak to Donald."

Hours pass as I am locked away in the Presence of God interceding. Suddenly, I receive a phone call requesting me to go upstairs and meet with Mr. Trump just moments before he leaves for the convention center. Jon and I go up to Trump's room, where he waits with Melania and his son Barron. As has happened so many times and moments on this campaign and in our lives before it, I'm given the opportunity to pray over Trump. God gives me a very specific order to call out to the Lord for. Trump can feel the power of God in his room as we pray, a strong stirring of the Holy Spirit.

I ask God to anoint Donald and give him strength and clarity when speaking to the American public.

Jon and I have been in Cleveland for the Republican National Convention since the start, where I delivered the benediction for the opening night on Monday. I'm honored to be asked and humbled to be the first woman to do this at the convention. I'm equally honored to be here with the Trump family, to be a part of their lives, to be a part of this journey for America.

We believe in faith that it's time for darkness to be dispelled. This is what I say in my prayer earlier this week. It's time for this nation to live out its holy calling on the earth. We believe in faith and that it's time for us to become the light that this world desperately needs.

Jon remarks how calm and articulate Trump is tonight. There is a different tone with his speech. He does extremely well. He is assertive and speaks to Americans in an authentic manner. I can see his heart open to God.

Near the end of his speech, he addresses the faith community that has helped him get to this place. Trump has always held a respect for men and women of God, starting from the days he attended Billy Graham crusades. He genuinely wanted to hear the heart of a community that's the heart and soul of what this nation was founded upon.

"At this moment, I would like to thank the evangelical community who have been so good to me and so supportive. You have so much to contribute to our politics, yet our laws prevent you from speaking your minds from your own pulpits.

"An amendment, pushed by Lyndon Johnson many years ago, threatens religious institutions with a loss of their tax-exempt status if they openly advocate their political views.

"I am going to work very hard to repeal that language and protect free speech for all Americans. We can accomplish these great things, and so much else—all we need to do is start believing in ourselves and in our country again. Start believing. It is time to show the whole world that America is back—bigger and better and stronger than ever before.

"In this journey, I'm so lucky to have at my side my wife, Melania, and my wonderful children, Don, Ivanka, Eric, Tiffany, and Barron: you will always be my greatest source of pride and joy. My dad, Fred Trump, was the smartest and hardest-working man I ever knew. I wonder sometimes what he'd say if he were here to see this and to see me tonight."

As I watch the Republican Party's nominee for president of the United States, I can't help wondering the same thing.

If only Daddy could see me here tonight.

Later that evening we join Mr. Trump, along with some of his close friends and family. Jon congratulates him on his fine speech and the Republican nomination, and he turns to Jon and says, "I really felt something when Paula prayed over me." I am humbled and grateful once again to fulfill an assignment in the bigger picture of God's purpose and to stay faithful to my "yes."

Mom says, "Life is funny. You can't make it up." This is never more true than in 2016, when one night I'm praying over the Republican nominee for president of the United States, then the next I'm praying for and cheering on the keyboard player for a rock and roll band.

On the road with Journey, I'm reminded of purpose again. It's the last song of the night, and I stand on the side of the stage right behind Jon, who begins to play the timeless chords of "Don't Stop Believin'" on the piano. Directly in front of him is Arnel Pineda, whose voice begins to soar over the souls all gathered together at this stadium. While the audience takes over to sing the song in unison, I continue to take photos of Jon with my camera, something I love to do while I'm sharing life with him like this.

Night after night, I see the same amazing thing. I see my husband and his band mates playing a venue like this with a screen that costs millions, with a massive crew and an assortment of buses and an amazing light show. People pay a lot to see them perform for a couple of hours. The crowd is thrilled as they sing along to songs they grew up listening to, tunes they're now belting out with their children. I love what Jon is doing, and I respect it. I know what it has taken to not only get to this place of massive success but to maintain it.

With more than 100 million albums sold, the number one most downloaded rock and roll song ever, multiple awards, a place in the Rock and Roll Hall of Fame and the Hollywood Walk of Fame, a 2005 *USA Today* opinion poll naming them the fifth best rock band in history, Journey's career spans five decades. Jon has lived at the top of his career after enduring multiple struggles in the music industry in the early days. God has given Jon a gift of music, which he has been responsible to develop and steward. In turn, it has given Jon a tremendous platform where he honors God and uses it for the betterment of humanity.

Night after night, I watch him going into the venue early to play cornhole with fans and auction off guitars from Neal Schon or drumsticks from Steve Smith, all of which have raised millions of dollars for Make-a-Wish and other charities over the span of his career. I'm honored to stand by his side and serve purpose together. In all things, we honor and serve God together. Jon has opportunities to share his faith and stand boldly for God in places that many will never reach. I watch him gratefully and humbly do that constantly.

Six days before the election, I travel with Trump and his team all over the country attending rallies and speaking. By the time we arrive back in Florida, it is early morning. He asks me my thoughts on how the faith community will vote.

"Don't worry," I say. "The evangelicals are going to show up for you."

"What makes you think that, Paula?"

My belief in this starts from the spiritual side of me, a depth I can't fully explain to him. Yet there's also a practical reality as well.

"Mr. Trump. You wear a mantle that perhaps you don't fully understand. God has a purpose and a plan. He will use you for that. But you're also an activator. You have the highest viewership ever, with eighty-six million. You have the highest rallies ever. That has to translate to something. You also have a drive and work ethic like few I have ever seen. You will outwork them."

So many people are watching Trump, from his debates to his speeches to his daily tweets, to the meetings.

"The evangelicals (as they call all of us) will come together," I tell him. "They have gotten to know you and where you stand on the issues as you have given them unprecedented access."

I feel the same way I felt from day one.

Donald Trump is going to be our president.

This isn't arrogance; it's confidence, and it's one that comes from God.

When we have a vision and we start preparing for something bigger than us, then God will say that's the person I'll bring opportunity to. That's a person for whom I'm going to open supernatural doors that no man can shut. That's a person I'm going to favor. That's a person My Spirit will be upon.

"I'll send opportunity to you," God says. "I'll send opportunity to you and no demon can stop it."

I'll send opportunity to you, and there will be no lack to what I'm going to do in your life.

I'll send opportunity, and people will say, how did you become the spiritual advisor for the president of the United States? How did you reach all those places? How did this happen? How did you break down those walls of division? How did you build those bridges? How did you preach the gospel around the world?

It's because of God. It's because God says if you'll prepare, I'll send the opportunity to you.

All preparation needs is opportunity.

For such a time as this...

Many people in my life are saying this. Telling me, texting me, and emailing me. Family and friends and even enemies are all expressing this. I'll let them say it because it's not my place to comment. I personally feel like the same girl who said "yes" to God at eighteen years old and will walk out His purpose for my life.

Just a short time from now, Donald Trump will take the presidential oath and be sworn in as the forty-fifth president of the United States. All I can say is I'm overwhelmed with gratitude today. Overwhelmed by the plans and the details and the things that still need to be done. Overwhelmed from the lack of sleep.

The last few days have been a blur. There's been so much planning and organizing that I've been a part of, that I've been doing to prepare for the five different faith services being held around the fifty-eighth presidential inauguration. There's a private service and a cathedral service and celebrations and events, and I'm keeping track and corresponding and connecting with people who can come and who need to be there and who are bringing two more people...

And in just a few moments I will be the first clergywoman to pray at a presidential inauguration. If I weren't so humbled and grateful to be here, I might feel how exhausted I am. It's been nonstop, pushing so many details forward and putting them all in their place. Even though I'm not directly participating in all of the services, I'm still helping to put them together. I'm working behind the scenes to coordinate from A to Z nonstop, no sleep and a lot of adrenaline. I've been around Trump and Melania long enough to know their taste and style and what is honorable and respectable for them. I know what they'll enjoy and what sort of things they'd cringe at. I realize how best to celebrate God and them during this time.

When we first come into the swearing-in ceremony, they put Jon in a seat up above us. I'm glad to see he's in the circle. I sit down next to Dick and Lynne Cheney. George W. and Laura Bush are in front of us, with the Clintons right next to them and the Obamas right in front of them. Franklin Graham, Sammy Rodriguez, Rabbi Marvin Hier, Wayne Jackson, and Archbishop of New York Timothy Cardinal Dolan are behind me. It's fun watching everybody before the ceremony begins. George W. Bush is cutting up with everybody. At one point as I go to take a picture on my phone, someone says something. Dick Cheney leans over to me.

"You're not supposed to do that," he says with a little wink.

"Oh, I'm so sorry," I say, laughing as I put my phone away. "I'm a newbie. This is my first one."

He grins underneath the Stetson he's wearing. "Just call me Uncle Dick."

Everyone is very kind and talkative to me.

Wow, this is a long way from Tupelo, Mississippi.

Despite all the millions of people I've spoken in front of throughout my life, I'm honestly a little nervous. I've been praying the rain off, my voice is trashed, it's freezing cold outside, and I'm operating on no sleep. I think of my prayer, yet my thoughts resemble the number of spectators facing us. There's my to-do list—the next event and who's speaking at the cathedral and on and on.

I stop the storm and the noise inside of me. I look up at the heavens and I remember the clouds. Then I close my eyes and take a deep breath.

God, I want to be very present in this moment. I want this etched into my memory. I want to understand.

I honor this moment and begin to thank God so much.

There are defining moments in your life, and too many times you keep running through them. Sometimes you don't stop and realize what is truly happening. These are moments when your whole life comes before you, and if you calm your spirit for a moment, you realize what's brought you to this point.

I think about that little girl standing on that hill staring up at the sky, watching with wonder, talking without hesitation. A heart full, bursting over, but believing she's being heard. Believing the sound of the music box can match her soul one day. Believing in this big world and her place in it.

Believing in something greater.

I'm grateful. So incredibly grateful. When you recognize something, you value it, and I recognize this moment. Only God placed me here. There's nothing I did or could ever do to be sitting here surrounded by these people awaiting one of the greatest ceremonies this country has to offer. This is God's goodness, God's purpose. I understand the power of prayer and to declare a thing so that it is established.

Today I'm determined to make famous the name of Jesus. Today I'll be proud that five people pray in the name of Jesus. People are invoking the name of Jesus Christ over our nation. There is a power in that, in His name being uttered.

I memorialize this moment. I stop and put my stone in, thanking God. Then I turn and look over to Jon, thanking the Lord for him, too. God has given him to me to bring me to this place of purpose for something greater.

A peace comes over me as the band begins to play with the trumpets and the drums marching in unison.

"Ladies and gentlemen, the president of the United States."

The crowd begins to chant, "Trump! Trump! Trump!"

With millions of people all over the world watching and listening to this event, I get up and go to pray. I get up and do what I do. What I've always done.

In gymnastics, it's not about the springboard or the vault—it's how you land. To me, it's no different in the big picture. I honor and recognize each assignment. The key is, do I land? Do I finish the course?

As I stand before the world to deliver my prayer, I hear Pastor Paula preaching in my thoughts from a different era and a different pulpit:

Isn't that a miracle that God can take a messed-up Mississippi girl to speak to the world now? Because it doesn't matter where you start in life; it matters where you finish in life.

"We come to You, Heavenly Father, in the name of Jesus with grateful hearts, thanking You for this great country that You have decreed to Your people. We acknowledge we are a blessed nation with a rich history of faith and fortitude, with a future that is filled with promise and purpose.

"We recognize that every good and every perfect gift comes from You and the United States of America is Your gift, for which we proclaim our gratitude.

"As a nation, we now pray for our president, Donald John Trump, vice president, Michael Richard Pence, and their families. We ask that You would bestow upon our president the wisdom necessary to lead this great nation, the grace to unify us, and the strength to stand for what is honorable and right in Your sight.

"In Proverbs 21:1, You instruct us that our leader's heart is in your hands. Gracious God, reveal unto our president the ability to know the will, Your will, the confidence to lead us in justice and righteousness, and the compassion to yield to our better angels.

"While we know there are many challenges before us, in every generation You have provided the strength and power to become that blessed nation. Guide us in discernment, Lord, and give us that strength to persevere and thrive.

"Now bind and heal our wounds and divisions, and join our nation to Your purpose. Thy kingdom come, Thy will be done, the psalmists declared. Let Your favor be upon this one nation under God. Let these United States of America be that beacon of hope to all people and nations under Your dominion, a true hope for humankind.

"Glory to the Father, the Son, and the Holy Spirit. We pray this in the name of Jesus Christ. Amen."

I don't do politics. I do people.

As President Trump delivers the inaugural address, I can't help but think of that. All I ever longed for was to stay faithful to my "yes," the assignment of ministry with Trump. It goes all the way back to asking for God's heart. Perhaps that's why I always find a connection with someone, whether they're the King of Pop or the president of the United States. All I've ever wanted to do was to connect, to see through God's eyes. I really and truly believe God allows me to see people differently, and I say this with humility. This is what drives me and why I do what I do. This is what has always opened doors in my life. It's always been about God's purpose and my decision to stay faithful to that, whether it was popular or not, comfortable or not.

Thy Kingdom come, Thy will be done in earth as it is in Heaven. You said I couldn't have this. You said I couldn't do this. But while I was going through the valley of the shadow of death, He prepared a table—so get ready!

This place and this moment and this calling—none of this is about *me*. About Paula White-Cain. Everything I've planned has failed; everything else God has done. My life has truly been an orchestration of divinity and a surrendering of obedience even when it's been difficult, misunderstood, or painful.

I'm grateful for my brokenness. God broke Joseph enough that He said, "When you get here to a place of power, you're not going to do your brothers wrong." Joseph was fulfilling God's will; that was his purpose.

My usefulness to the Kingdom of God is determined by my commitment to purpose. So the more I'm committed to my purpose, the intention and the decision of God, the more useful I become.

My brokenness has been my greatest blessing in every area, because it forces me to realize the truth God is telling me: *"Remember, Paula. You're nothing without Me."*

It's not like God only created me to use me. What He wants more than anything is an intimacy. This is the other truth I realize God tells me: *"You're really my girl, Paula, the apple of my eye."*

And that I will always know. No matter who comes or goes, what life hands you or doesn't, I know who I am and whose I am, a child of the Most High God.

21.

READINESS

Mom, you have to hang on..."

On the way to the airport with Jon driving, I pray for my mom, who feels so far away from me and doesn't have much time to live. A busy 2018 is coming to an end, but not in the way I imagined it might when I thought about Christmas spent with the family.

Now I hope and pray I can spend just a few more moments with Mom.

Shortly before this, Jon has two end-of-the-year Journey gigs, one a corporate appearance in San Antonio, Texas, and one at a casino in Reno, Nevada. I call my doctor to make sure I can fly with him after unexpected back-to-back foot surgeries. What was supposed to be a pretty simple bunion surgery on October 19 turned out to be much more extensive than originally anticipated. When the front pins came out, my foot had not fused together, and the pin in the middle of my foot migrated out, causing excruciating pain. "We have to get you back in surgery ASAP," the doctor explained. So I flew back to California for a second reconstructive foot surgery on November 29.

Wow, I didn't expect this... It wasn't on my calendar.

Barely being able to walk and still in a boot cast, I take off with Jon the weekend of December 15 to spend a few days after his Reno show in Sonoma, California, with his children for an early Christmas together. This will be great to get my mind off the pain and mental anguish of the foot surgeries. We drive in from Reno to Sonoma on that Monday, looking forward to quality time with the kids and to see my doctor to get the pins removed from the second surgery.

Ahhhhh...A little bit of normalcy and fun finally! This is going to be a great week.

We are all settled in at a quaint little resort to enjoy one of our many Christmas gatherings when I receive the call from Ronnie, my mom's love for the last twenty years of her life.

"Paula, something is wrong with your mom," Ronnie says. "The paramedics came to get her and took her to the hospital."

"What do you mean?" I ask. "Is she going to be okay?"

I can't seem to get the answers or comfort I am looking for. My foot is throbbing but not nearly as much as my pounding heart. As executor of my mom's will and durable power of attorney for her healthcare, I call Methodist Hospital in Memphis, Tennessee, to make sure everything is okay. Even though Mom requires oxygen for breathing, she is relatively healthy. She hasn't had an episode in a few years, and when I talked to her just days ago she was her jovial self with no indications of even a cold.

What in the world could be going on to cause her to go to the hospital?

I get on the line with the ER nurse, who quickly tells me my mom has just arrived at the hospital and is breathing but unresponsive. *Unresponsive? What? Not my mom!* She rushes me off the line to care for my mom and tells me to call back in forty-five minutes. It feels like the longest forty-five minutes of my life. An elephant is back on my chest. Jon is out golfing with his son, Weston, and I feel like I am about to hyperventilate.

Stop getting so worked up, Paula, everything will be okay, I tell myself.

In just a few hours, my pins will be taken out of my foot, and then Jon and I will go to dinner with the kids. I call back promptly forty-five minutes later. Dr. Malcoff gets on the line and politely but very matter-of-factly proceeds to tell me the situation.

"Your mother is in a coma. She has a large bleed in her head at the basal ganglia. This is hyper-acute, and unfortunately it is going to kill her. We recommend you come to say goodbye."

Nooooooooo... This is not happening! Not now. Not to my mom. PLEASE, DEAR GOD—give me a miracle...

I am sobbing, bewildered, stunned, hurting, and confused. I fall on my face and do what I always do, cry out to God! I am hours from an airport, and it is afternoon in California. I call my assistant and travel agent to get me on the first flight I can get to Memphis.

"By the time you get to the airport, all the flights will have left for today," she tells me. "There is nothing until tomorrow."

"Find me something, anything. You have to get me to Memphis right away."

I continue to call the hospital, checking on the condition of my mom. My assistant calls me back, telling me she has found a red-eye out of Sacramento (a few hours' drive from where I am) leaving at ten p.m., and flying into Charlotte, North Carolina, then arriving into Memphis at eight-thirty a.m. the next morning.

"Book me now," I say.

I have been calling my son Brad, who is very close to his "Mamcap." He is praying over me, calming me, and reminding me of God's promises. I finally get Jon, who comes back to the resort just as I am having my pins removed from my foot with a final examination. He quickly drives me to the airport. I just want to be there. I call the nurse every fifteen minutes, checking on Mom.

"Her vitals are very low, but she is hanging in there," the nurse tells me. Brad books a flight and will be arriving about the same time I will. I know the power of prayer, and I continue to ask God to let me be by her side just one more time.

"C'mon, Mom, you can do this! Hang in there, fight, don't leave until I can get to you. Please."

Jon drives as fast as he can. As I look out the car window at the sprawling California countryside, I can't help but think why I'm here in the first place.

It is so far from Tennessee. I question myself, knowing if I had been in Florida I would already be with her. I know better than to do this, but I can't stop my mind from racing with all types of thoughts. I am a person of faith, but that doesn't mean the enemy won't send fiery darts of doubt and discouragement that I know I must fight off. We chose that week to be with the kids because I could get my pins out of my foot, and instead of making two trips to California we would make it one big, easy trip.

My foot. The same foot I stuck in my brother's plate of spaghetti when I was five and got mad at him. The same foot that's been taking me all over the world, the same one that's spent so much time in four-inch heels.

Even this reminds me of my mother. As a little girl, I was obsessed with heels and begged my mom to let me wear them. There's something about them that is genuinely part of my identity. Mom said I had to wait until I was in the seventh grade, and as a fifth grader, this felt like forever. The clock was so slow, and I thought about it all the time. I even created a countdown marking off every month, week, and day before the big moment arrived. Finally on the first day of seventh grade, I held my mom to her word, and sure enough, we went and bought my first pair of high heels. A tan pair of Candies.

Situations and circumstances can come to rob you of your identity and your joy. Just like the moment in Tampa when I told myself to look at these legs of mine and how strong they've been in order to get myself to start running and to get my step back, I'm determined to push through the pain of the surgeries and this setback to get motion back in my foot.

I'm fighting just like I know my mom is fighting right now. We were both born fighters. The only difference is that I watched Mom my entire life to learn what it truly means to have such a backbone and what it looks like to work so hard, to push through barriers and have tenacious fortitude.

Keep pushing, Mom. Be tenacious one more time.

I am pleading with God, continually texting throughout the flights and calling during the layovers to check on Mom. My heart aches with a pain I have not felt before. It is different than other deaths and losses I have experienced in my life.

At two a.m., the nurse calls me.

"How far out are you now? She probably won't make it another hour."

I have six hours to get there.

She has to make it ... PLEASE, MOM!

I talk to her, to God, to myself between the gulf of tears gushing out. I am determined to be with her before she leaves this earth.

On the plane as I continue to pray and break down, with tears and snot flowing down my face while I answer texts asking me when I'm going to be arriving in Memphis, I think about my mom, my best friend while I try to block any thoughts that she will pass before I arrive.

The blessing of looking back on my fifty-two years is to reflect on all the gifts God has given me. Mom is one of the greatest treasures He has given me. In so many ways, I wish I could be writing her story instead of my own; there are more memories than volumes could contain.

The story of my mom is full of ups and downs, love and life, pain and tragedy. It had all those things that all our lives have ... moments. She was a fiery pistol of passion and love. She was one of the most intelligent and resourceful persons I have ever known. She suffered as all of us have in areas. She was a story of recovery and restoration. She was a rare gift to all who knew her.

Keep fighting, Mom. Don't let go. Please wait for me.

I've got to get back to see her, and nothing is going to stop me. As Mom used to say, "The only person that could come down and change your mind is Jesus." And she's right about that. This isn't a stubbornness or rebelliousness but rather an inner drive, one Mom helped to instill inside me. Just like the Jeep I was bound and determined to have when I first started driving.

The memory makes me smile.

After turning sixteen, I wanted to buy a car. I was working at a Wendy's while we lived in Danville, California, but I still didn't have enough to purchase a vehicle. I asked my grandmother for $500, but she didn't have it for me. This didn't stop me from going down to the Jeep dealership and finding a used one for around $5,000 that looked perfect. I told the man at the dealership that was the car I wanted, and at the time I assumed I might be able to have my grandmother release some of my money from my trust fund. When this didn't happen, I had to go back to the dealer the next day to tell him I couldn't get the money.

"Yeah—I didn't think so," the salesman told me. "Don't worry. Maybe one day you'll have one. Or maybe not. I doubt it."

The moment these words came out of this man's mouth, I decided I would get that Jeep in the very same way that I made up in my mind that I would land that aerial in gymnastics. Even as a teenager, I believed people are all basically the same; we just have different opportunities. Therefore, we should never judge anybody, and right then and there, this used car salesman was judging me—the same way people surely used to judge my mom when she was a single mother raising two children and working.

Yes, I'll own a Jeep one day, and not only that, but I'll buy everybody a Jeep if I have the ability to.

Mom awakens that inner drive, and that was always God's plan for me. He was preparing me all the way back to my childhood. Sure enough, I do purchase that Jeep, and I'll continue to drive them all throughout my life. When I turned fifty, since Jon already owned his own, I decided to give my Jeep to my mom.

Mom is a fighter, and she waits for us. I arrive on the morning of December 19, and I'm able to spend precious last moments kissing her and telling her how much I love her. I pray with her while Brad reads Scripture over her. My niece, Lauren, and sister-in-law, Anna, make it up. Ronnie is with us. We anoint her, and at 3:47 p.m. on the Wednesday before Christmas, Mom is released to be in her Savior's arms.

I miss you, Mom. More than I could have ever anticipated. But I know you are with Jesus.

I remember all the times I would crawl up in bed with you, even when I was fifty years old. You would always hold me and let me pour out my worries on you. Even though we bickered and debated about everything from politics to basketball, we always smiled and laughed at the end.

You have always been my rock, trusted friend, wise counselor, and listening ear. You were fierce, funny, and free-spirited! You were a gift from God, Mom. I cry knowing without a doubt that you came to have a truly amazing love of Jesus. And He loved you.

Your story is truly one of God's amazing goodness and restoration power. I know you never did like it when I spoke about the bad times from my childhood, but we both know that this became something that God used to bring thousands if not millions to Jesus Christ. This is what makes me smile about God. He always uses what the enemy means for bad for good. No matter how something looks, nothing is impossible with God. Nothing.

Mom, you are evidence of that. You were amazing. God is amazing.

For now I will simply say what you have said to me all my life: "I love you madly—you're my sweetheart."

I will miss you dearly and will see you again.

Mom dearly loved Jon, and like me, he misses her. Once he came into my life, there was a peace she had. I think for my entire life, she never wanted me to settle for something less. I think she might have always worried, wondering if I'd be safe and okay. This seemed to all go away after Jon arrived. She just adored him. She could see the way he not only loves me but protects me. Maybe this is why she would tell me something over and over again in the recent months: "I'm ready to go now. I know you are okay. Brad is okay. You all have landed."

Mom knew I was truly covered in my marriage, maybe even more than I knew it myself. She knew that Brad had turned the corner, finding and fulfilling his purpose and being an amazing father to his two children, Asher and Nicholas.

I know I wasn't mistakenly given to my mom and my dad. I think I was supposed to have that exact DNA. Those qualities that existed in both of my parents are the same ones that would always push me back to God, starting with that young girl opening up her music box and talking to the heavens. That five-year-old thinking and saying and believing that there's something greater out there.

My son's words about me while discussing this memoir come to mind. Brad is so smart like his grandmother; that's one of the many reasons why they were so close. He looked at the parents he has, Dean and me, and sees the divine purpose in it.

"To me, my biological parents are shoehorns that fit what God has planned for me and future generations. We fit in the bigger context and patchwork for the kingdom of God. In order for me to be who I am on the earth, I had to have the mom she was. She had to have the challenges she had. I have to learn from her positives and her mistakes. What I want to do and what I don't want to do. What I want to do in ministry and what I don't want to do. My understanding of my purpose has been very much influenced implicitly by her actions."

It's amazing to have a son articulate those sentiments. I agree with him and feel the same way about my own parents.

Even amid this incredible hurt inside of me, I can see the truth my life has always shown: there is always something greater that comes even from these times of tragedy. In this pain, there is this overwhelming peace and a sense of joy forming. God is going to do something amazing.

The place I find my refuge and strength is in the Lord. I seek His Word and I meditate on it. It is my nourishment. Even though I am going through a mourning process in this very moment, I am joyful because our God is very real. Our Savior is life even in death. And I am grateful.

James 4:14 (NIV) says, "You do not even know what will happen tomorrow. What is your life? You are a mist that appears for a little while and then vanishes."

If you aren't sure that if you died today, or maybe you have a loved one who needs help or doesn't know if they died today that they would go to Heaven, I cannot pass up this opportunity to make sure you come to know Jesus. To be saved. Christ died on the cross for you. For your family. He rose again on the third day, conquered death, Hell, and the grave to give *you* life and give it more abundantly. You can have eternal life with Jesus. Will you confess Him as your Lord and Savior? Even gather your family together right now and pray this prayer to God PLEASE!

Father, I come to You in the Precious name of Jesus. Please forgive all of my sins. I receive Jesus Christ as my Lord and Savior. I believe He is the only begotten son of God. Holy Spirit, fill me and give me power to serve God until I see Him face-to-face. Amen.

If you prayed this prayer, welcome to the Family of God!

POSTLUDE

Mom! When we have children, I know what they're going to call you."

Brad speaks in an unusually breathless and passionate voice on the phone. I know he's calling me from church since it's a Sunday morning. The fact that he and Rachel have been unsuccessful in their attempts to start a family doesn't deter my son's belief one bit.

"You're not going to be called Mimi," Brad says. "You're going to be Abra."

I chuckle in surprise. "Abra?"

Ever since Kristen, Angie, and Brandon had kids, I've been called Mimi. I was far too young to be referred to as Grandma, so I chose Mimi.

"Yes—Abra."

"That's crazy," I tell him. "I'm not going to be 'Abra.' They're going to go to school and call me that and their classmates are going to laugh at them and say, 'What's that?'"

Brad is serious, and even days later when I bring it up again, he's not going to bend.

"But I like Mimi," I tell him. "It has a cool sound. That's what I've always been called."

"Mom! My children will not call you Mimi. The Lord says you are Abra. Today I make this declaration, and I don't care what you tell them to call you. They're calling you Abra."

You are just like me. Just a younger, male version of me.

There have been many moments in my life when my son's been ferociously defiant with me, but I never could have imagined he would be so stubborn about what his children would call me.

261

"I don't get it. Why?"

It dawns on me even as I say this that I haven't bothered to look up the meaning of the word, something that's crazy because I'm such an etymology person. Brad's steady, dark eyes look at me with the same fierce devotion that captured my heart the moment he was born.

"*Mimi* comes from Mara and means bitter," he says. "And you will *not* die in your old age as a bitter woman! *Abra* means mother of many nations, and God says you will be a mother of many nations."

I am moved with a flood of emotions. As tears roll from my eyes and run down my cheeks, I realize God had my beginning and He has my ending. I literally got a name change from God through my son, and I am forever grateful.

I hold my grandson in my arms and know God has once again given me an incredible gift. Staring up at the stage, at fifty-two years old I feel a wholeness and completeness and hear the melody from the speakers harmonizing with my heart. The ballerina in the pink dress, my granddaughter, twirls in the aisle to the swelling chords of "Why I Breathe" sung by my husband. Sitting on the front pew in the middle of an open sanctuary filling my overflowing soul, I talk to my love and best friend, knowing God has always, always, *always* heard me.

God smothers me with everything I've ever wanted or desired.

The answers about my Heavenly Father pour out of me.

How good is God to me?

This would have only been a dream at one point in my life, but not now. It's a Wednesday night at City of Destiny in Apopka, Florida. The little ballerina is Asher while the little angel in my arms is Nick. Abra and the grandchildren watch G-Pa on stage, ministering one of his worship songs. Brad has preached an incredible message from the Word, and I'm reminded by the anointing on his life about the promises God gave me when he was just a baby in my womb.

As Jon sings, I think back to his life story of how God never, ever gave up on that boy who survived that grade-school fire. I think about Brad and

Rachel and how they tried to start a family for five years, and how God ultimately blessed them with these two precious lives.

Nick's tiny hand tightens over my finger as he looks up at me in wonder. I think about the email my mom sent me after I showed her pictures.

Thanks so much, Paula. He's a beautiful baby boy. I love the pictures of Asher looking at him. She's a proud big sister. Tell Rachel she looks fantastic. She's a wonder. Brad looks so in love with his family.

Paula—you are and will be a leading force in all their lives for many years. A blessing. Let Asher and Nick know who I am. Speak over them like Momma Annie spoke over you. They are our future.

I love all of you so much.

Love you,
Mom

The brevity of her words vehemently pierces my soul. This scene and this moment—this is my something greater. This is God's greatness in my life. His great restoration process. Yes, I've been called to "shake nations" to preach the gospel, yet I've always known my greatest contribution to this gift called "life" will be my legacy—what I leave.

My son is serving the Lord in such a great capacity. We've landed in a good place in ministry, building people of discipleship at City of Destiny while launching Story Life.

Seeing Jon...he is truly the love of my life. I recently told him he makes me cry with happy tears because the goodness God has shown me through him. He inspires me, brings fulfillment, joy, and completeness to my heart.

"I've loved Jesus for thirty-four years," I tell him. "And you're making me fall in love with Jesus even more."

Watching God really work in his life has increased my faith and love. I thought I understood what a relationship looked like, what love in this place looked like, but I'm discovering a wholeness for the first time. I no longer need to be the provider, the protector. I can still be strong and fierce but not for "survival" purposes.

More than anything else in my life, more than my ministry and my role in President Trump's life, I know this is where I'm supposed to be. Right here in this moment. The tendency these days is to look at negatives and what's wrong in life. What's missing in our lives. But there's so much that's *right* in life, so many great blessings. So much to look up and say thank You, God. He's taken me to a greater place, and this is my greatest blessing of all. I thank the Lord through the living waters of his Word.

Have you ever come on anything quite like this extravagant generosity of God, this deep, deep wisdom? It's way over our heads. We'll never figure it out.

    Is there anyone around who can explain God?
    Anyone smart enough to tell him what to do?
    Anyone who has done him such a huge favor that God has to ask his advice?
    Everything comes from him;
    Everything happens through him;
    Everything ends up in him.
    Always glory! Always praise!
      Yes. Yes. Yes.

Romans 11:33–36 MSG

In so many ways, I haven't wanted to tell this story, my story. In the past, I would honestly have no idea what to write about and what parts to share. I always want to be as open and vulnerable as I can be, to be truly authentic and helpful, yet I've never wanted to harm anyone.

Since I'm a preacher and a teacher, I know Bible verses that I can reference without a second of thought. I can write one hundred books on the wisdom and lessons from stories in the Bible. But this particular story about Paula White-Cain is the one that I've struggled to write for many years.

The truth is God still needed to add a few chapters, and He needed me to put some punctuation marks at the ends of the chapters I'd already written.

My other question comes down to the *so what?* I don't want to simply tell my story to sell books and get interviews. I need to help someone; that is my oxygen, something I have to do. All I've ever wanted to do is to inspire and encourage others to fall in love with this amazing God who loves them with an unfathomable love. Uncle Butch showed me how to do this years ago. He simply opened up the Bible and began to show me the answers to all the questions I had.

Those answers are still there, and I discover new ones every day.

Underneath everything is the core truth of the Word of God. That's what's in my heart. Now more than ever before, I think every believer struggles with our culture and with what's become acceptable.

At the end of the day, it's not about Paula White-Cain's story, and it's not about being a Democrat or Republican, and it's not whether we're black or white. The question is only, *DO I BELONG TO GOD? IS HIS WORD TRUTH AND INERRANT? DO I SURRENDER MY LIFE TO HIM UNCONDITIONALLY IN EVERY WAY, EVERY DAY?*

Throughout my whole childhood and everything that happened, there was this longing. I just didn't know who I was looking for until Uncle Butch told me. There was always this pull to something greater, this longing in my heart. And when I discovered Jesus, I prayed for God to do something with my life, to let God do this through me. I desired to have those AWE moments with God.

A great big AWE came when Trump became president. But the awe wasn't in the surprise of his victory but rather in the amazement of my place in it to be positioned to serve all humanity and write history by acts of faith. As I've said, over and over I'd hear, "You were raised up for such a time as this." But that's not the first thing I think of.

God used Donald Trump in my life as much as I was used in his life.

When it comes to my assignment to the president of the United States, I have come to understand that vindication is in the womb of time. I will stay faithful to what God has called me to do all the days of my life, and I don't try to figure it out.

Deep in my heart, I stand in awe of God that He would allow me to be used in this way and in this time. He didn't use any brilliant thing about myself; God used my brokenness. And like Joseph, whom God broke enough to not do his brothers wrong later in his life, God made one thing very clear:

"Paula, you are nothing without Me."

Something greater means something different to every single person.

Can you see that little girl hearing her father has died? Can you see her abuse, her pain, her lost soul, her longing?

Can you identify with a passion so bright it eclipses all around it? Can you relate to a faulty and fractured relationship that turns fatal in the end? Can you wonder if you will ever love again?

Can you feel the pinging pains of desperation?

Can you ever imagine that there's something bigger for you, something better for you, something greater for you?

Can you see that whatever tragedies and trials you face in life, God will bring you through to triumph?

We all have a purpose in this life. It is your supreme reason for being. Your "yes" to the intention, decision, and choice God made about you before you were ever formed in your mother's womb. Maybe you've been called to raise two children and send them off to college. I don't look at what I've done on earth as being any greater than what Momma Annie did.

It certainly matters who you are. It does matter where you are.

But what really matters is *why*.

Every day, God reminds me of my why. He has put eternity in my heart.

Through my brokenness I found and continue to find His wholeness. Every time life, the enemy, circumstances, haters, and difficulties determined it was over for me, God determined to not only bring me through but to bring me to *something greater*.

God has that same determination for you. His love for you is everlasting and immeasurable. His plan for you is to prosper you and not to harm you. Plans to give you hope and a future (Jer. 29:11). Your latter will be greater than your former; it's the way God does when you decide not to quit, give up, or become bitter over the difficult seasons or injustices. The Bible reminds us all to cling continually to our unchanging God who is no respecter of persons: "David became greater and greater, for the LORD of hosts was with him" (1 Chron. 11:9 AMP). Now, replace David's name with yours and know God has something greater for you!

ACKNOWLEDGMENTS

There are so many people who I am grateful to beyond words. I thank God for everyone who has profoundly impacted my life in a myriad of ways. Many of you are in *Something Greater*. From the depths of my heart... Thank you!

To my husband Jon:

You are an amazing gift from God who has filled my heart with a love and completeness I have never known. You are the love of my life and more than I could have ever imagined. I adore you and thank God for the strength you are to me every day.

To my son Brad:

I fell in love with you the moment they laid you on me. You have continued to take my breath away with an indescribable love. You are a powerful voice that carries great purpose. I am so proud of you.

To Rachel:

God brought His best into our life and family when you married Brad. Your joy, love, perseverance, and compassion are rare and unique. You are a valuable gift that I cherish and love dearly.

To Asher:

You are my sunshine. I never knew so much love could be contained in the bundle of joy you are to me. You bring passion to my pursuit of purpose to reach generations. I love you, "mini me."

To Nicholas:

You were born for greatness. You already shine as a beacon of light for God. You are my little man who has Abra's heart.

To my extended family:

Your love and support have been pillars to uphold me.

To my friends:

You have been a wellspring of life and laughter for me. A friend loves at all times but a brother is born in adversity. Thank you for standing with me in my life.

To every person who stands with me to fulfill the call of God and serve His purpose:

There is no way to fully express my appreciation. Great will be your reward. Your labor of love will be capped with: "Well done, thou good and faithful servant." You have transformed millions of lives…only eternity can tell of your magnitude.

To Hachette Book Group:

Thank you for believing in me and laboring to bring God's message to the masses. I am grateful.

To Hank:

Your steadfast belief, creativity, and faith to fuel the vision have carried the call with excellence. You are rare and exceptional. Thank you for all you do.

To Sheila:

You have been invaluable in my life and call. Your friendship is priceless. Your servant's heart and wisdom have impacted multitudes untold. I love you.

ABOUT THE AUTHOR

Paula White-Cain is the president of Paula White Ministries, headquartered in Apopka, Florida, and the spiritual adviser to President Donald Trump. She hosts *Paula Today* and is a renowned life coach, bestselling author, and highly sought-after motivational speaker. Paula's commitment to humanity is felt worldwide as she reaches out through numerous charities and compassion ministries, fulfilling her mission and call to transform lives, heal hearts, and win souls. She lives in the Orlando area with her husband, Jonathan Cain.